Veterinary Clinical Parasitology

Eighth Edition

Veterinary Clinical Parasitology

Eighth Edition

Anne M. Zajac

Gary A. Conboy

Under the auspices of the **AAVP**
American Association of Veterinary Parasitologists

WILEY-BLACKWELL

A John Wiley & Sons, Inc., Publication

This edition first published 2012 © 2012 by John Wiley & Sons, Inc.
First, Second editions, 1948, 1955 ©Iowa State College Press
Third, Fourth, Fifth, Sixth editions, 1961, 1970, 1978, 1994 ©Iowa State University Press
Seventh edition, 2006 ©Blackwell Publishing

Wiley-Blackwell is an imprint of John Wiley & Sons, formed by the merger of Wiley's global Scientific, Technical and Medical business with Blackwell Publishing.

Registered office: John Wiley & Sons Ltd, The Atrium, Southern Gate, Chichester, West Sussex, PO19 8SQ, UK

Editorial offices: 2121 State Avenue, Ames, Iowa 50014-8300, USA
The Atrium, Southern Gate, Chichester, West Sussex, PO19 8SQ, UK
9600 Garsington Road, Oxford, OX4 2DQ, UK

For details of our global editorial offices, for customer services and for information about how to apply for permission to reuse the copyright material in this book please see our website at www.wiley.com/wiley-blackwell.

Library of Congress Cataloging-in-Publication Data
Zajac, A.
    Veterinary clinical parasitology / Anne M. Zajac, Gary A. Conboy. – 8th ed.
        p. ; cm.
    Includes bibliographical references and index.
    ISBN-13: 978-1-1186-3749-4 (pbk. : alk. paper)
    ISBN-13: 978-0-8138-2053-8 (pbk. : alk. paper)
    ISBN-10: 0-8138-2053-7 (pbk. : alk. paper)   1. Veterinary clinical parasitology.   I. Conboy, Gary A. II. Title.
    [DNLM: 1. Parasitic Diseases, Animal–Laboratory Manuals.   2. Parasitology–Laboratory Manuals. SF 810.A3]
    SF810.A3S58 2011
    636.089'696–dc23
                                                                          2011021939
A catalogue record for this book is available from the British Library.

Set in 10/12 pt Times New Roman by Toppan Best-set Premedia Limited
Printed and bound in Singapore by Markono Print Media Pte Ltd

Disclaimer
The publisher and the author make no representations or warranties with respect to the accuracy or completeness of the contents of this work and specifically disclaim all warranties, including without limitation warranties of fitness for a particular purpose. No warranty may be created or extended by sales or promotional materials. The advice and strategies contained herein may not be suitable for every situation. This work is sold with the understanding that the publisher is not engaged in rendering legal, accounting, or other professional services. If professional assistance is required, the services of a competent professional person should be sought. Neither the publisher nor the author shall be liable for damages arising herefrom. The fact that an organization or Website is referred to in this work as a citation and/or a potential source of further information does not mean that the author or the publisher endorses the information the organization or Website may provide or recommendations it may make. Further, readers should be aware that Internet Websites listed in this work may have changed or disappeared between when this work was written and when it is read.

1   2013

CONTENTS

Companion website

This book is accompanied by a companion website:

www.wiley.com/go/zajac

The website includes powerpoints of all figures from the book for downloading.

PREFACE

Since the publication of the 6th edition of *Veterinary Clinical Parasitology* in 1994, the proceeds of this book have gone to support graduate student travel to the annual meeting of the American Association of Veterinary Parasitologists and thus encourage the development of new scientists in the field of veterinary parasitology. In this 8th edition, we have attempted to expand coverage of areas of increasing concern in veterinary parasitology. Although the focus of the book continues to be on the morphologic identification of parasites, we have also added a chapter by Dr. Karen F. Snowden of Texas A&M University describing immunologic and molecular techniques of diagnosis and provided a list of tests currently available commercially in the United States. These tests are growing in number and use in the diagnosis of parasitic infection and disease.

As always, our goal is to provide a practical, useful book for those learning the techniques required for diagnosis of parasite infection and for the practicing diagnostician, and we hope that this 8th edition of the book will continue to be helpful to all those involved in diagnosis of veterinary parasites.

Anne M. Zajac
Gary A. Conboy

ACKNOWLEDGMENTS

We are very grateful to the members of the American Association of Veterinary Parasitologists (AAVP) and others who provided material for *Veterinary Clinical Parasitology*. Appeals for photographs distributed through the AAVP listserv brought responses from as far away as Germany, Brazil, and Australia. Although the source of each figure is credited in the figure legend (with the exception of photos provided by chapter authors), we would also like to list all the contributors here with our deepest thanks:

Mr. Gary Averbeck, College of Veterinary Medicine, University of Minnesota, Minneapolis, MN

Dr. David Baker, School of Veterinary Medicine, Louisiana State University, Baton Rouge, LA

Dr. Byron Blagburn, College of Veterinary Medicine, Auburn University, Auburn, AL

Dr. Dwight Bowman, College of Veterinary Medicine, Cornell University, Ithaca, NY

Dr. George Conder, Pfizer Corporation, Kalamazoo, MI

Dr. Hany M. Elsheikha, School of Veterinary Medicine and Science, University of Nottingham, Loughborough, UK

Dr. James Flowers, College of Veterinary Medicine, North Carolina State University, Raleigh, NC

Dr. Alvin Gajadhar, Centre for Animal Parasitology, CFIA, Saskatoon, Saskatchewan, Canada

Mr. James Gathany, Centers for Disease Control and Prevention, Atlanta, GA

Dr. Ellis C. Greiner, College of Veterinary Medicine, University of Florida, Gainesville, FL

Dr. Larry Hammell, Atlantic Veterinary College, University of Prince Edward Island, Charlottetown, PE, Canada.

Dr. Bruce Hammerberg, College of Veterinary Medicine, North Carolina State University, Raleigh, NC

Dr. Patricia Holman, College of Veterinary Medicine and Biomedical Sciences, Texas A&M University, College Station, TX

Dr. David Lindsay, Virginia-Maryland Regional College of Veterinary Medicine, Virginia Tech, Blacksburg, VA

Dr. Susan Little, College of Veterinary Medicine, Oklahoma State University, Stillwater, OK

Dr. Aaron Lucas, Luray Clinic of Veterinary Medicine, Luray, VA

Dr. Eugene Lyons, Department of Veterinary Science, University of Kentucky, Lexington, KY

Dr. Charles Mackenzie, College of Veterinary Medicine, Michigan State University, East Lansing, MI

Dr. Gil Myers, Myers Parasitological Service, Magnolia, TN

Dr. Thomas Nolan, School of Veterinary Medicine, University of Pennsylvania, Philadelphia, PA

Dr. Christopher Paddock, Centers for Disease Control and Prevention, Atlanta, GA

Dr. Fernando Paiva, Universidade Federal de Mato Grosso do Sul, Campo Grande, MS, Brazil

Dr. Andrew Peregrine, Ontario Veterinary College, University of Guelph, Guelph, Ontario, Canada

Dr. Sally Pope, Faculty of Veterinary Science, University of Sydney, Sydney, New South Wales, Australia

Dr. Steffan Rehbein, Merial GmBH, Rohrdorf, Germany

Dr. Robert Ridley, College of Veterinary Medicine, Kansas State University, Manhattan, KS

Dr. Nick Sangster, Faculty of Veterinary Science, University of Sydney, Sydney, New South Wales, Australia

Dr. Philip Scholl, Porto Alegre, RS, Brazil

Dr. Stephen Smith, Virginia Maryland Regional College of Veterinary Medicine, Virginia Tech, Blacksburg, VA

Dr. Karen F. Snowden, College of Veterinary Medicine and Biomedical Sciences, Texas A&M University, College Station, TX

Dr. T. Bonner Stewart, School of Veterinary Medicine, Louisiana State University, Baton Rouge, LA

Dr. Bert Stromberg, College of Veterinary Medicine, University of Minnesota, Minneapolis, MN

Dr. Donald B. Thomas, U.S. Department of Agriculture Subtropical Agriculture Research Laboratory, Weslaco, TX

Dr. Donato Traversa, Department of Comparative Biomedical Sciences, Faculty of Veterinary Medicine, Teramo, Italy

Mr. Chris Tucker, Department of Animal Science, University of Arkansas, Fayetteville, AK

Dr. Isabelle Verzberger-Epshtein, NRC Institute of Nutrisciences and Health, Charlottetown, PEI, Canada

Mr. Martin Visser, Merial GmBH, Rohrdorf, Germany

Dr. Jerry Weintraub, Agriculture Canada, Lethbridge, Alberta, Canada

Dr. Jeffrey F. Williams, Vanson HaloSource Inc., Redmond, WA

Dr. Roy P. E. Yanong, Tropical Aquaculture Laboratory, University of Florida, Ruskin, FL

Dr. Tom Yazwinski, Department of Animal Science, University of Arkansas, Fayetteville, AK

Dr. Gary Zimmerman, Zimmerman Research, West Montana, Livingston, MT

Dr. Kurt Zimmerman, Virginia-Maryland Regional College of Veterinary Medicine, Virginia Tech, Blacksburg, VA

AUTHORS

Anne M. Zajac, DVM, PhD
Department of Biomedical Sciences and Pathobiology
Virginia-Maryland Regional College of Veterinary Medicine
Virginia Tech
Blacksburg, VA 24061

Gary A. Conboy, DVM, PhD
Department of Pathobiology and Microbiology
Atlantic Veterinary College
University of Prince Edward Island
Charlottetown, Prince Edward Island C1A 4P3
Canada

Ellis C. Greiner, PhD
Department of Infectious Diseases
College of Veterinary Medicine
University of Florida
Box J-137
Gainesville, FL 32610

Stephen A. Smith, DVM, PhD
Department of Biomedical Sciences and Pathobiology
Virginia-Maryland Regional College of Veterinary Medicine
Virginia Tech
Blacksburg, VA 24061

Karen F. Snowden, DVM, PhD
Department of Veterinary Pathobiology
College of Veterinary Medicine and Biosciences
Texas A&M University
College Station, TX 77843-4467

Veterinary Clinical Parasitology

Eighth Edition

CHAPTER 1

Fecal Examination for the Diagnosis of Parasitism

The fecal examination for diagnosis of parasitic infections is probably the most common laboratory procedure performed in veterinary practice. Relatively inexpensive and noninvasive, fecal examination can reveal the presence of parasites in several body systems. Parasites inhabiting the digestive system produce eggs, larvae, or cysts that leave the body of the host by way of the feces. Occasionally, even adult helminth parasites may be seen in feces, especially when the host has enteritis. Parasitic worm eggs or larvae from the respiratory system are usually coughed into the pharynx and swallowed, and they too appear in feces. Mange or scab mites may be licked or nibbled from the skin, thus accounting for their appearance in the feces. Many parasitic forms seen in feces have characteristic morphologic features that, when combined with knowledge of the host, are diagnostic for a particular species of parasite. On the other hand, certain parasites produce similar eggs, oocysts, and so on, and cannot be identified to the species level (e.g., many of the strongylid-type eggs from livestock). Fecal examination may also reveal to a limited extent the status of digestion, as shown by the presence of undigested muscle, starch, or fat droplets.

COLLECTION OF FECAL SAMPLES

Fecal exams should be conducted on fresh fecal material. If fecal samples are submitted to the laboratory after being in the environment for hours or days, fragile protozoan trophozoites will have died and disappeared. The eggs of some nematodes can hatch within a few days in warm weather, and identification of nematode larvae is far more difficult than recognizing the familiar eggs of common species. Also, free-living nematodes rapidly invade a fecal sample on the ground, and differentiation of hatched parasite larvae from these free-living species can be time-consuming and difficult.

Owners of small animals should be instructed to collect at least several grams of feces immediately after observing defecation. This will ensure the proper identification of the sample with the client's pet (i.e., a sample from a stray animal will not be collected) and that feces rather than vomitus or other material is collected. The limited amount of feces recovered from the rectum on a thermometer or fecal loop should not be relied on for routine parasitologic examination, since many infections that produce only small numbers of eggs will be missed. Owners should be instructed to store fecal samples in the refrigerator if the sample will not be submitted for examination for more than an hour or two after collection.

Feces should be collected directly from the rectum of large animals. This is particularly important if the sample is to be examined for lungworm larvae or cultured for identification of third-stage larvae, since contaminating free-living nematodes and hatched first-stage larvae of gastrointestinal nematodes may be confused with lungworm larvae. If rectal samples are unavailable, owners should be asked to collect feces immediately after observing defecation. The process of development and hatching of common strongylid eggs can be slowed by refrigeration. Development is also reduced when air is excluded from the sample by placing the collected feces in a plastic bag and pressing out the air before sealing the bag.

STORAGE AND SHIPMENT OF FECAL SAMPLES

If collected feces cannot be examined within a few hours, the sample should be refrigerated until it can be tested. Feces should not be frozen, because freezing can distort parasite eggs. If a sample needs to be evaluated for the presence of protozoan trophozoites like *Giardia* and trichomonads, it should be examined within 30 minutes after collection. The trophozoite is the active, feeding form of the parasite and is not adapted to environmental survival; it dies soon after being passed in the feces.

If fresh fecal material is submitted to another laboratory for examination, it should be packaged with cold packs. Helminth eggs may also be preserved with an equal volume of 5%–10% buffered formalin. The use of formalin for fixation of samples has the additional benefit of inactivating many other infectious organisms that may be present. Special fixatives, such as polyvinyl alcohol (PVA), are required to preserve protozoan trophozoites and are not routinely used in veterinary practices.

Slides prepared from flotation tests do not travel well, even if the coverslip is ringed with nail polish, since hyperosmotic flotation solutions will usually make parasite eggs or larvae unrecognizable within hours of preparing the slide. However, slides from flotation tests can be preserved for several hours to several days by placing them in a refrigerator in a covered container containing moist paper towels to maintain high humidity. It is best to place applicator sticks under the slide to prevent it from becoming too wet.

FECAL EXAM PROCEDURES

Before performing specific tests on the fecal sample, its general appearance should be noted; consistency, color, and the presence of blood or mucus may all be indicative of specific parasitic infections. Hookworm disease in dogs, for example, commonly produces dark, tarry feces, whereas diarrheic feces caused by whipworms may contain excess mucus and frank blood. The presence of adult parasites or tapeworm segments should also be noted.

Fecal Flotation

The technique most commonly used in veterinary medicine for examination of feces is the fecal flotation test. This procedure concentrates parasite eggs and cysts and removes debris. Fecal flotation is based on the principle that parasite material present in the feces is less dense than the fluid flotation medium and thus will float to the top of the container, where it can be collected for microscopic evaluation. Flotation tests are easy and inexpensive to perform, but in busy practices the choice of flotation solution and test procedure often does not receive much consideration, despite the substantial effect these choices can have on the sensitivity of flotation exams.

Choice and Preparation of Flotation Solutions

Many different substances can be used to make flotation solutions. The higher the specific gravity (SPG) of the flotation solution, the greater the variety of parasite eggs that will float. However, as the SPG increases, more debris will also float, and the risk of damage to eggs from the hyperosmotic solution also increases. These factors limit the range of useful flotation solutions to SPG ranging from approximately 1.18 to 1.3. The flotation solutions widely used in veterinary parasitology include sugar solution and various salt solutions. No fecal solution is perfect for all parasites, and advantages and disadvantages of each should be considered when selecting a solution for general use.

Salt solutions are widely used in flotation procedures. Saturated solutions of sodium chloride (SPG 1.20) and magnesium sulfate (Epsom salts, SPG 1.32) are inexpensive, easy to purchase and prepare, and are effective in floating common helminth eggs and protozoan cysts.

A common flotation solution used in the United States is a commercially available sodium nitrate solution (Fecasol®, Vétoquinol USA, Inc., Fort Worth, TX), with SPG 1.2. This solution will also float common helminth eggs and protozoan cysts. The commercial solution is not a saturated solution of sodium nitrate (SPG 1.33). Slides prepared with any salt solution need to be examined relatively quickly after they are prepared because crystals form as slides dry, making them more difficult to read. In particular, cysts of *Giardia* collapse rapidly in most flotation solutions. If detection of *Giardia* is required, a better flotation solution is a 33% zinc sulfate solution (SPG 1.18), which does not cause rapid destruction of *Giardia* cysts and allows them to be more easily recognized in flotation preparations. Zinc sulfate solution can be made in veterinary practices or purchased commercially. None of these flotation solutions (commercial sodium nitrate, saturated sodium chloride, saturated magnesium sulfate, and 33% zinc sulfate) will reliably float most trematode eggs and some tapeworm and very dense nematode eggs.

Another common solution used in routine flotation exams is Sheather's sugar solution (SPG 1.2–1.25). Sheather's solution is also more effective than some of the salt solutions for flotation of tapeworm and nematode eggs of higher density. In addition, it does not distort eggs as rapidly as the salt solutions. Sheather's solution is recommended for recovery of *Cryptosporidium* oocysts in fecal samples, but it does not appear to be as effective as 33% $ZnSO_4$ solution for detection of *Giardia*. Sheather's solution is inexpensive and easy to prepare and is commercially available in the United States, but it is very viscous and sticky. The advantages and disadvantages of these solutions are shown in Table 1.1 and instructions for preparing them are given below.

Although the SPG of flotation solutions is not often measured in practices, it can be easily determined with an inexpensive hydrometer from a scientific supply company. A hydrometer will last indefinitely and should be considered part of quality control for the veterinary practice laboratory.

33% ZINC SULFATE SOLUTION (SPG 1.18)

1. Combine 330 g zinc sulfate with water to reach a volume of 1000 mL.
2. Additional water or zinc sulfate can be added to produce an SPG of 1.18 (if zinc sulfate solution is used with formalinized feces, the SPG should be increased to 1.20).
3. Check the SPG with a hydrometer.

SATURATED SODIUM CHLORIDE (NaCl, SPG 1.2) OR MAGNESIUM SULFATE SOLUTION (MgSO₄, SPG 1.32)

1. Add salt to warm tap water until no more salt goes into solution and the excess settles at the bottom of the container.

Table 1.1.   **Comparison of commonly used flotation solutions**

Flotation Solution	Specific Gravity	Advantages	Disadvantages
Sodium nitrate (NaNO₃) Fecasol Saturated NaNO₃	1.2 1.33	Floats common helminth and protozoa eggs and cysts	Distorts *Giardia* cysts rapidly; does not float most fluke and some unusual tapeworm and nematode eggs
33% Zinc sulfate (ZnSO₄)	1.18	Floats common helminth and protozoa eggs and cysts; preferred for *Giardia* and some lungworm larvae	Less effective for flotation of common tapeworm eggs than others; does not float most fluke and some unusual tapeworm and nematode eggs
Saturated sodium chloride (NaCl)	1.2	Floats common helminth and protozoa eggs and cysts	Distorts *Giardia* cysts rapidly; does not float most fluke and some unusual tapeworm and nematode eggs
Saturated magnesium sulfate (Epsom salts)	1.32	Floats common helminth and protozoa eggs and cysts	Distorts *Giardia* cysts rapidly; does not float most fluke and some unusual tapeworm and nematode eggs
Sheather's sugar solution	1.25	Floats common helminth and protozoa eggs and cysts; preferred for *Cryptosporidium* oocysts; in general, causes less damage to parasite eggs and cysts than salt solutions	Does not float most fluke and some unusual tapeworm and nematode eggs; less sensitive than ZnSO₄ for *Giardia*; creates sticky surfaces

2. To ensure that the solution is fully saturated, it should be allowed to stand overnight at room temperature. If remaining salt crystals dissolve overnight, more can be added to ensure that the solution is saturated.
3. Check the SPG with a hydrometer, recognizing that the SPG of saturated solutions will vary slightly with environmental temperature.

SHEATHER'S SUGAR SOLUTION (SPG 1.2–1.25)

1. Combine 355 mL (12 fl oz) of water and 454 g (1 lb) of granulated sugar (sucrose). Corn syrup and dextrose are not suitable substitutes.
2. Dissolve the sugar in the water by stirring over low or indirect heat (e.g., the top half of a double boiler). If the container is placed on a high direct heat source, the sugar may caramelize instead of dissolving in the water.
3. After the sugar is dissolved and the solution has cooled to room temperature, add 6 mL formaldehyde USP to prevent microbial growth (30 mL of 10% formalin can also be used, with the volume of water reduced to 330 mL).
4. Check the SPG with a hydrometer.

Flotation Procedures

No matter how the flotation procedure is performed, the principle is the same. After mixing the flotation solution and the fecal sample together, the less dense material eventually floats to the top. This process can occur either by letting the mixture sit on the benchtop for a specified time or by centrifuging the mixture. Regardless of the flotation solution used, centrifugation makes the flotation occur more rapidly and efficiently. Many practitioners like to use convenient commercial flotation kits that provide a container for collection of the sample and performing the test. However, the convenience of the kits is offset by the loss of sensitivity in the fecal exam procedure. A smaller amount of feces is used and the test cannot be centrifuged.

The increased sensitivity of the centrifugation procedure is particularly important in infections where the diagnostic form of the parasite is present in low numbers (e.g., *Trichuris* and *Giardia* infections in dogs and cats). Centrifugation is also necessary when using 33% $ZnSO_4$ or sugar solution because of the slightly lower SPG of $ZnSO_4$ solution and the high viscosity of sugar solution, both of which retard the flotation process. A veterinary practice that does not centrifuge flotation tests and relies on the traditional benchtop incubation technique, substantially reduces the sensitivity of its fecal exams.

CENTRIFUGAL FECAL FLOTATION PROCEDURE

This is the preferred technique for the standard fecal flotation test regardless of the flotation solution used. It is particularly important to use this procedure with Sheather's sugar and 33% $ZnSO_4$ flotation solutions to ensure that the flotation is effective:

1. Mix 3–5 g (about 1 teaspoonful) of feces with a small amount of flotation solution in a paper or plastic cup. Cat feces and small ruminant pellets, which are sometimes too hard to break up easily, can be ground with a mortar and pestle or allowed to soak in water until they become softer.

    If the sample appears to contain a large amount of fat or mucus, an initial water wash is performed, and water should be used in Step 1. The water wash can be eliminated for most fecal samples of normal appearance.
2. Strain the mixture of feces and flotation solution (or feces and water if a water wash is performed) through a double layer of cheesecloth or gauze. A tea strainer can also be used.
3. Pour the mixture into a 15-mL centrifuge tube. If the rotor on the centrifuge is not angled (i.e., if the tubes hang straight when not spinning), the centrifuge tube can be filled with flotation solution until a reverse meniscus is formed and a coverslip is added (Fig. 1.1). The tube is spun with the coverslip. The centrifugal force generated by the centrifuge will hold the coverslip in place. If the centrifuge has an angled rotor, fill the tube as full as possible and place in the centrifuge.
4. Spin the mixture in a benchtop centrifuge for about 5 minutes at approximately 500–$650 \times g$ ($650 \times g$ is 2500 rpm on a 4-in. rotor), regardless of whether the feces have been mixed with water or with the flotation solution. If a specific g force and speed setting cannot be determined, spinning the tube at the same speed used to separate serum from blood cells is sufficient.

    If the initial spin is a water wash, the supernatant should be discarded, the sediment resuspended with flotation solution, and Steps 3 and 4 repeated.
5. Allow the centrifuge to stop without using the brake. The slight jerking that results from the use of the brake may dislodge parasites from the surface layer.
6. Following centrifugation, there are several ways to harvest the surface layer of fluid containing parasite eggs. If the tube has been spun with the coverslip in place, lift the coverslip off the tube and quickly place it on a microscope slide. When the tube is spun without the coverslip, remove the tube from the centrifuge after spinning and place in a test tube rack. Fill the tube with additional flotation solution to form a reverse meniscus. Place a coverslip on the tube and allow it to sit for an additional 5–10 minutes before removing the coverslip and placing it on a slide.

    Alternatively, after the centrifuge comes to a stop, gently touch the surface of the fluid in the tube with a glass rod, microbiologic loop, or base of a small glass tube and then quickly touch the rod to a microscope slide to transfer the drop or two of adhering fluid. This procedure will be less efficient than allowing the tube to stand with a coverslip in place.

Fig. 1.1. Centrifuge tube filled with flotation solution to the top and coverslip placed in contact with the fluid column.

BENCHTOP (SIMPLE OR PASSIVE) FLOTATION PROCEDURE

When a centrifugal flotation procedure cannot be performed, sodium nitrate and saturated salt solutions can be used in a benchtop flotation test, although the sensitivity of the test will be reduced. This technique is not recommended for 33% $ZnSO_4$ or sugar flotation tests:

1. Mix several grams (a teaspoonful) of feces with the flotation solution in a cup.
2. Strain the mixture through cheesecloth or a tea strainer.
3. Pour into a test tube, pill vial, or container provided in a commercial kit. Add enough mixture or additional flotation fluid until there is a reverse meniscus on the top of the container. Place a coverslip on the fluid drop at the top.
4. Allow the flotation to stand for at least 10 minutes, remove the coverslip, place it on a slide, and examine. If the test is allowed to stand for too long, the salt may crystallize on the edges of the coverslip so that it will not lie flat on the slide.

FLOTATION SLIDES

Fecal flotation slides should be scanned using the 10× objective lens of the microscope (since most microscopes also have an eyepiece magnification of 10×, using the 10× objective gives a total magnification of 100×). Although most helminth eggs can be detected with the 4× objective, protozoan parasites are easily missed and this low power should not be used for scanning. The 40× lens should be used when there is uncertainty about the identity of structures on the slide and for scanning slides for *Cryptosporidium* oocysts. In some practices, to save expense, coverslips are not used. However, slides without coverslips dry out faster, do not have a flat plane of focus, and cannot be examined with the 40× lens, with the result that some parasites will be identified incorrectly or missed entirely.

EGG-COUNTING PROCEDURES (QUANTITATIVE FECAL EXAMS)

Egg-counting techniques are also flotation tests and are recommended primarily to estimate the extent of parasite egg contamination on pastures grazed by infected animals or to determine the efficacy of drug treatment (discussed in a later section in this chapter). Egg counts are of limited value in making judgments about the clinical condition of individual animals because many factors affect egg production, including parasite species, individual host immunity, and stage of infection. Also, counts performed on combined samples from a number of animals may not accurately reflect parasitism within that herd.

The easiest quantitative test to perform is the modified McMaster test. This test requires the use of special reusable slides (Fig 1.2), which can be purchased from several suppliers (including Chalex Corporation, Wallowa, OR [www.vetslides.com]; Focal Point, www.mcmaster.co.za; JA Whitlock & Co., Eastwood, New South Wales, Australia [www.whitlock.com.au]). The capacity of the counting chamber and the number of chambers counted per sample affect the sensitivity of the test. Several different sizes are available, usually ranging from 0.15 to 0.5 mL. Saturated salt solutions are usually used as the flotation solution in this test.

As it is most commonly used, the modified McMaster test has a sensitivity of 25 or 50 eggs per gram (epg) of feces. This level of sensitivity is acceptable in most situations since parasite control programs do not usually require detection of lower egg numbers. However, the accuracy of the McMaster test is reduced when egg counts are at the lower limits of detection. When egg counts of less than 200 epg are typical in a group of animals being evaluated (e.g., in adult cattle or camelids) or when it is important to detect low numbers of eggs more accurately (e.g., in fecal egg count reduction tests [FECRTs]), a modification of the test is appropriate. The sensitivity and accuracy of the test can be improved by using slides that allow examination of larger quantities of the egg/flotation solution mixture, or by counting additional aliquots of the sample. Alternatively, the Wisconsin sugar flotation test (double centrifugation procedure) or a modified Stoll egg-counting test can be used for quantitative exams. These procedures permit detection of fewer than 10 epg of fecal material but are more time-consuming to perform.

Regardless of the procedure used to count parasites, the most important element is consistency. Each step of the procedure should be performed in the same way for every sample.

Modified McMaster test.

1. For ruminants, combine 4 g of fecal material with 56 mL of flotation solution to yield a total volume of 60 mL. The test can also be performed with 2 g of feces and 28 mL of flotation solution when only small amounts of feces are available. For horses, it is becoming standard in the United States to use 4 g of feces and 26 mL of flotation solution. See Note 1 below for modified

Fig. 1.2. McMaster slide used in the modified McMaster procedure for quantitative egg counts.

calculations. Portable electronic scales that weigh in 0.1-g increments are now widely available and inexpensive.

2. Mix well and strain through cheesecloth or a tea strainer if desired. The mixture does not have to be strained, but it will be much easier to read the slide if large pieces of debris are removed. An alternative to straining is to use a filter pipette to transfer material to the counting chamber (a pipette with 12 mesh/cm wire mesh at the end is available from JA Whitlock & Co. [www.whitlock.com.au]).

3. Immediately fill each chamber of the McMaster slide with the mixture using a pipette or syringe. The entire chamber must be filled, not just the area under the grid. If large air bubbles are present, remove the fluid and refill.

4. Allow the slide to sit for at least 5 minutes before examining to allow the flotation process to occur.

5. Look at the slide with the 10× lens, focusing on the top layer, which contains the air bubbles. At this level, the lines of the grid will also be in focus. Count eggs, oocysts, and any other parasite stages, in each lane of both chambers. Each type of parasite should be counted separately. In some cases, eggs can be identified to genus or perhaps to species (e.g., *Strongyloides*, *Trichuris*, and *Nematodirus*), whereas others must be counted as a category of parasites (coccidia, strongylid eggs).

To determine the number of parasite epg of feces, add the counts for both chambers for each parasite. The most commonly used McMaster slides in the United States are calibrated so that the number of eggs counted in a single chamber represents the number present in 0.15 mL of fecal mixture. If both chambers are counted and the results are added, the total represents the number of eggs present in 0.3 mL, which is 1/200th of the total volume of 60 mL; therefore, the number of eggs must be multiplied by 200. However, since a total of 4 g of feces was used in the test, the result must be divided by 4 to yield epg of feces. Multiplying by 200 and dividing by 4 is equivalent to multiplying the number of eggs counted by 50. Therefore, each egg observed represents 50 epg in the final count. The same level of sensitivity can be achieved by using 2 g of fecal material and 28 mL of flotation solution. The smaller amount of feces may be preferred when evaluating small lambs or kids.

Additional Notes

1. If a sensitivity of 25 epg is desired, the McMaster test should be performed with 4 g of feces and 26 mL of flotation solution (results are then multiplied by 100 and divided by 4 as described above). Other combinations of manure and flotation solution can also be used with appropriate calculations using the formula

    $$\text{eggs}/\text{g} = [\text{no. eggs counted} \times (T/V)]/F$$

    where T = total volume of feces/flotation solution mixture, V = volume of aliquot examined in slide, and F = grams of feces used.

2. If pelleted feces are very hard, 2–5 mL of water can be added first and left to soften manure for at least an hour. The flotation solution is then added to the softened manure (flotation solution volume reduced by the amount of water used to soften feces).

3. A variety of methods can be used to homogenize feces and liquid. As alternatives to mixing with a tongue blade or other utensil, some laboratories use a mechanical or handheld kitchen mixer to homogenize feces and water/flotation solution. Shaking manure and fluid in a jar with

glass beads has also been used, but as previously stated, whatever method is used, it should be consistent across samples.

4. In another procedure for the McMasters test, feces is mixed initially with water, strained, and centrifuged, and the supernatant is discarded. Flotation solution is added to resuspend the sediment and mixed, and the mixture is used to fill the counting chambers. For example, 3 g of feces is mixed with 42 mL of water, strained and the fluid used to fill a 15-mL centrifuge tube, which is then centrifuged at 300–650 × g for 2 minutes. The supernatant is then discarded and flotation solution is added to partially fill the tube, which is either shaken or stirred to resuspend the sediment. Additional flotation solution is added to fill the tube, and the counting chamber is filled. If the eggs in a volume of 0.3 mL are counted, the number of eggs seen is multiplied by 50 to give the number of eggs per g. The number of epg can also be calculated using the formula described in Note 1. This procedure is the most effective for reducing debris but increases the time required to perform each test.

Modified Stoll test.

Like the McMaster test, the modified Stoll egg-counting procedure is based on determining the number of eggs present in an aliquot of the prepared feces/flotation solution mixture. Any of the fecal flotation solutions can be used in this procedure.

1. Combine 5 g of feces and 20 mL of water in a cup.
2. Mix into a slurry and transfer 1 mL of the mixture to a centrifuge tube. If the mixture is not strained, a widemouthed or mesh-covered filter pipette is needed to transfer the mixture.
3. Fill the tube with flotation solution.
4. Place the tube in the centrifuge and add flotation solution until a slight inverse meniscus is formed.
5. Place a coverslip on top of the tube. It should contact the mixture without causing any to overflow.
6. Centrifuge (properly balanced) at 300–650 × g for 10 minutes.
7. Remove the coverslip and place on a glass slide.
8. Examine with the 10× objective lens.
9. Count and record the number of each type of parasite egg/cyst seen, systematically scanning the slide and counting eggs or cysts of each parasite species or group separately. Care must be taken to ensure that each microscope field on the coverslip is examined once but only once so that no eggs are missed or counted twice.

In this test, all the eggs present in 1 mL of the feces/flotation solution mixture were counted following centrifugation. This represents 1/25 of the volume of the mixture so the number of eggs counted multiplied by 25 represents the total number of eggs present, but this must be divided by 5 (grams of feces used) to yield epg. In this situation, the multiplication factor is 5 and the minimum sensitivity of the test is 5 epg. If the volume of fluid added to feces in the first step is 45 mL, the final multiplying factor would be 10.

Wisconsin, Cornell-Wisconsin egg-counting test (double centrifugation procedure).

The Wisconsin egg-counting test or double centrifugation flotation test is the most sensitive procedure because all the eggs in the fecal sample are counted. This procedure should only be used to quantitate eggs when low counts are expected. More than 100 epg are difficult to count accurately on a slide with no grid. Any flotation solution can be used in this test:

1. Combine 1–5 g feces and 12–15 mL of water in a cup. Mix and strain into another cup, rinsing first cup with 2–3 mL of water and straining, pressing the liquid through. Pour into a 15 mL centrifuge tube.
2. Centrifuge (properly balanced) at 300–650 × g for 5–10 minutes.
3. After spinning, discard the supernatant and resuspend the pellet in flotation solution.
4. Either spin the tube with a coverslip in place or allow additional incubation after spinning as described for the centrifugal flotation procedure.
5. Remove the coverslip and place on a glass slide.
6. Examine with the 10× objective lens.
7. Count and record the number of each type of parasite egg/cyst seen, systematically scanning the slide and counting eggs or cysts of each parasite species or group separately. Care must be taken to ensure that each microscope field on the coverslip is examined once but only once so that no eggs are missed or counted twice.

This technique allows the quantification of less than 1 epg of feces.

Additional Notes

1. If desired, the initial water wash can be omitted and the sample can be mixed directly with flotation solution and then centrifuged.
2. Alternatively, 22 mL of flotation solution is mixed with 5 g of feces, and the resulting mixture is divided between two tubes. This modification increases the accuracy of the procedure.

For additional information on quantitative egg-counting procedures, see references by Ballweber (2006), Taylor et al. (2007), Coles et al. (2006), Egwang et al. (1982), and the Ministry of Agriculture, Fisheries and Foods (1986).

Additional Procedures for Fecal Examination

The following procedures are used for identification of specific parasitic infections.

Direct Smear and Stained Fecal Smears

The direct smear is used to identify protozoan trophozoites (*Giardia*, trichomonads, amoebae, etc.) or other structures that float poorly or are readily distorted by flotation solutions. Because very little fecal material is used, the sensitivity of this test is low. It is not recommended for routine fecal examinations:

1. Mix a very small amount of feces with a drop of saline on a microscope slide to produce a layer through which newsprint can be read. Saline should be used because water will destroy protozoan trophozoites.
2. Use a coverslip to push large particles of debris to the side and place the coverslip on the slide. Examine with 10× and 40× magnification. The 100× lens (oil immersion) cannot be used effectively with fecal smears.

3. If the fecal layer is too thick, it will be impossible to see small, colorless protozoa moving in the field. Movement is the principal characteristic that allows recognition of trophozoites in fresh fecal smears. A drop of Lugol's iodine will enhance the internal structures of protozoan cysts but will also kill trophozoites present. To maximize the use of this test, it is best to look at an unstained smear before adding iodine.

Fecal smears can also be stained for identification of intestinal protozoa. Several stains can be used for identification of *Cryptosporidium*, including Ziehl–Neelsen, Kinyoun, carbol-fuchsin, and Giemsa stains. Trichrome stain is widely used in human medicine for detection of *Giardia* cysts. In general, however, stains are not used extensively in veterinary practices and are not required for the identification of parasitic organisms. For details on performing these stains, a standard text on human parasitologic diagnosis should be consulted.

Fecal Sedimentation

A sedimentation procedure is used to isolate eggs of flukes, acanthocephalans, and some other tapeworms and nematodes whose eggs do not float readily in common flotation solutions. In the simple sedimentation test, tap water is combined with feces and allowed to settle briefly before the supernatant is removed. This allows the removal of fine particulate material, but unlike the flotation exam, sedimentation tests have only limited concentrating ability. Fat and mucus can be removed from the fecal sample if a centrifugal sedimentation exam is performed using ethyl acetate. Unfortunately, ethyl acetate is toxic and very flammable. It should be stored in a flameproof cabinet and used only in well-ventilated areas. An alternative to ethyl acetate is Hemo-De, available through Fischer Scientific (www.fischerscientific.com), which is generally regarded as a safe compound and appears to give equivalent results in a centrifugal sedimentation procedure (see Neimester et al. 1987).

The Flukefinder® is a commercially available apparatus for performing sedimentation tests in the laboratory. It utilizes several screens to rapidly remove fecal debris. This device is very useful in practices conducting routine fecal examinations for flukes. Information on the Flukefinder can be obtained at www.flukefinder.com.

SIMPLE SEDIMENTATION TEST

1. Mix about 100 mL of water with about 10 g of feces, strain, and place in a beaker or other container.
2. Allow mixture to sit for 1 hour and then decant the supernatant.
3. Add more water, mix, and repeat the sedimentation procedure.
4. Stir remaining mixture and place a few drops on a microscope slide. If desired, add one drop of 0.1% methylene blue. The methylene blue will stain the background debris blue but will not stain fluke eggs, which will stand out with a yellowish brown color.
5. Coverslip and scan the slide using the 10× objective lens.

A smaller amount of feces and water can be used, placed in a test tube, and left to sit for 3–5 minutes between decantation steps. Addition of a drop of dishwashing soap to the water used in the test helps to free eggs from surrounding debris.

CENTRIFUGAL SEDIMENTATION TEST

1. Mix 1 g of feces with about 10 mL of 10% buffered formalin or water. Pour mixture into a 15-mL centrifuge tube (with cap) until it is one-half to three-quarters full.
2. Add ethyl acetate (see above discussion on safety) or Hemo-De until the tube is almost full. Because organic solvents may dissolve some plastic centrifuge tubes, it is recommended that glass or polypropylene tubes be used for performing this test.
3. Cap and shake the tube approximately 50 times.
4. Centrifuge for 3–5 minutes at about $500 \times g$ (as for centrifugal flotation procedure).
5. When the tube is removed from the centrifuge, it will have three layers: (1) an upper layer containing ethyl acetate, fat, and debris; (2) a middle layer containing formalin or water and fine particulate matter; and (3) a bottom layer of sediment. Using an applicator stick, loosen the top debris plug that sticks to the sides of the tube, then decant the supernatant, leaving only the bottom sediment.
6. Resuspend the sediment in a few drops of water or formalin, place one or two drops of the sediment on a slide, coverslip, and examine with the 10× microscope objective.

Baermann Test

The Baermann test is used to isolate larvae from fecal samples and is employed most often to diagnose lungworm infections. *It is very important that the fecal sample be fresh.* If feces of a grazing animal are being examined and an old sample is used, strongylid or *Strongyloides* eggs may have hatched, or free-living nematodes may have invaded the sample, making nematode identification much more difficult. In small-animal samples, hookworm eggs may hatch very quickly and can be confused with lungworm or *Strongyloides* larvae.

A Baermann test requires equipment to hold the fecal sample in water so that larvae can migrate out and be collected. This can now be most easily accomplished with the use of a plastic wine glass with a hollow stem. In the absence of disposable wine glasses, the original Baermann apparatus can be used. This consists of a funnel clamped to a metal stand. A short piece of tubing with a clamp is attached to the end of the funnel. Larvae in feces placed either in the bowl of the wine glass or in the funnel migrate out of the sample and fall down into the hollow stem or the tubing above the clamp, where they can be easily collected (Fig. 1.3):

1. Place at least 10 g of feces in a piece of double-layer cheesecloth. Gather the cheesecloth around the sample so that it is fully enclosed. Use a rubber band to fasten the cheesecloth, and pass through the rubber band two applicator sticks, a pencil or other object that will rest on the edges of the glass or funnel and suspend the sample. Alternatively, place the sample on a suspended piece of wire mesh or sieve.
2. Fill the funnel or wine glass with lukewarm water. Make sure that the corners of the cheesecloth do not hang over the edge of the funnel or glass, because they will act as wicks for the water.
3. Allow the sample to sit for at least 8 hours, preferably overnight.
4. If using the disposable plastic glass, remove the fecal sample and collect the material at the bottom of the hollow stem using a Pasteur pipette or syringe. Transfer some of the fluid to a microscope slide, coverslip, and examine with the 4× or 10× objective lens.
5. If using the funnel, release the clamp and collect the first 10 mL of fluid into a centrifuge tube. Spin as for a flotation exam, discard the supernatant, and examine the sediment. Alternatively, the very steady handed can carefully loosen the clamp and collect the first three or four drops onto a microscope slide.

Fig. 1.3. (A) The traditional Baermann apparatus consisting of a suspended funnel with clamped tubing attached. For diagnostic testing of fecal samples, it is much more convenient to perform the Baermann exam with a disposable plastic wine glass (B).

Immunologic and Molecular Methods of Parasite Diagnosis

Immunologic methods have been important in the diagnosis of blood and tissue parasites for many years, and they are now being used increasingly for identification of specific parasites in fecal samples. Molecular diagnostic methods are also now being applied to detection of parasites in fecal samples. Although these techniques cannot currently replace morphologic exam of feces as a routine screening procedure for multiple infections, they are useful for specific diagnosis of some protozoan parasites that are detected in feces. For the discussion of these procedures and a list of commercially available tests in the United States, see Chapter 4.

QUALITY CONTROL FOR FECAL EXAM PROCEDURES

Although the concept of quality control is not often applied to fecal exams, attention to both equipment and training will help ensure that fecal exams are consistently done correctly:

1. Keep microscopes in good repair. Objective lenses and eyepieces should be routinely cleaned with lens cleaner and lens paper. Have microscopes professionally cleaned and checked every few years.
2. Check the SPG of flotation solutions with a hydrometer to ensure that they will recover parasites effectively.
3. Use an ocular micrometer (see section on microscope calibration later in this chapter) to measure structures seen on fecal exams. If possible, recalibrate the microscope when it is cleaned.

4. Make sure that personnel performing the fecal exams are adequately trained. It is not unusual for untrained assistants to be given rudimentary instruction on performing flotation tests and then be assigned to do them. Under these circumstances, it is hardly surprising that air bubbles are identified as coccidia and that smaller parasites are missed entirely.

5. As a check on the diagnostic accuracy of in-clinic fecal exams, periodically submit duplicate portions of fecal samples to a diagnostic laboratory. Both negative and positive samples should be submitted.

USE OF THE MICROSCOPE

There are several points to remember in using the compound microscope to examine preparations for parasites:

1. Use the 10× objective lens of the microscope for scanning slides. This will provide a total magnification of 100× since most microscope eyepieces contain an additional 10× lens. Start in one corner and systematically scan the entire slide. The 40× objective lens (400× total magnification with eyepiece) is useful for closer examination or for looking for very small organisms such as *Giardia* or *Cryptosporidium*. The 100× (oil immersion) lens should not be used for flotation preparations. Not only is it likely that flotation solution will contact the lens and possibly damage it, but the pressure of the lens on the coverslip will create currents in the fluid on the slide, keeping everything in motion and making examination of structures difficult.

2. Most parasite eggs and larvae have little or no color and do not stand out well, so it is important to maximize the contrast between the parasites and their backgrounds. Using a microscope with a substage condenser kept in the low position while scanning slides is the best way to increase contrast. Even when a substage condenser is not available, reducing the intensity of light projected on the slide is generally advisable, either by decreasing the microscope rheostat setting or by reducing the aperture of the iris diaphragm. A higher power used for close examination will, of course, require an increased amount of light.

3. When reading a slide, it is helpful to focus up and down with the fine focus to change somewhat the plane of focus. Frequently, worm eggs will be at a slightly different level than protozoan cysts or oocysts, and a small manipulation of the fine focus may make structures more readily visible (Figs. 1.4–1.6).

Microscope Calibration

The ability to measure the size of parasitic organisms and structures is very helpful when identifying unusual parasites or where different organisms are similar in appearance but differ in size. For measurements, a micrometer disc, also known as a reticle (Fig. 1.7), is inserted into the ocular tube of the microscope and calibrated against a known reference in the form of a stage micrometer (Fig. 1.8). Each objective lens of the microscope must be individually calibrated with the ocular lens/ micrometer combination to be used, and the calibrations should be posted close to the microscope for easy reference. The calibration will be accurate only for that particular microscope ocular and objective combination. Even if each lens is not calibrated with the stage micrometer, the ocular

36 µm

Fig. 1.4–1.6. The importance of small changes in the microscope focus can be seen in these three photos of the same field in a canine fecal flotation test. In each case, a slight manipulation of the fine focus brings a different parasite into clearer view (first *Isospora* oocysts, then *Ancylostoma* eggs, and finally *Toxocara* eggs) since each egg or oocyst type may be present on a slightly different level.

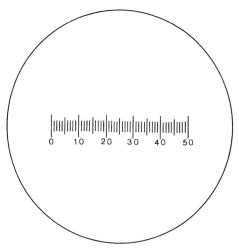

Fig. 1.7. A typical ocular micrometer of 50 divisions. The divisions have no meaning until calibrated against a stage micrometer.

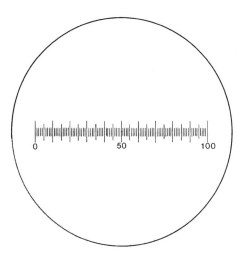

Fig. 1.8. A typical stage micrometer of 1 mm total length. Each division represents 10 μm.

grid will provide a consistent reference against which to compare objects seen in fecal samples. These ocular micrometer discs and stage micrometers are not expensive and can be purchased from scientific catalogs that include microscope equipment.

Calibration of the 40× objective illustrates the procedure for calibration of the micrometer:

1. To calibrate the 40× objective, place the stage micrometer on the stage of the microscope and focus until the lines are sharp. In the example (Fig. 1.9), the stage micrometer is 1 mm (1000 μm) long and is divided into 100 parts; thus, each small division of the stage micrometer represents 10 μm.

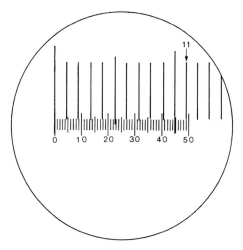

Fig. 1.9. Appearance at 40× of an ocular micrometer being calibrated with a 10 µm/division stage micrometer. Note the conjunction of line 11 of the stage micrometer with line 49 of the ocular micrometer.

2. Superimpose any convenient numbered line of the ocular micrometer (usually the 0 mark) on a convenient line of the stage micrometer (the first large line in the example). The field should now resemble Figure 1.9.

3. Find the two lines that are exactly superimposed. In the example, line 49 of the ocular micrometer falls exactly on line 11 of the stage micrometer. Thus, 49 divisions of the unknown ocular micrometer represent 11 divisions, each 10 µm in length, for a total of 110 µm. To complete the calibration, divide 110 µm by 49 divisions, resulting in a calibration factor of 2.24 µm per division for the ocular micrometer in the example.

4. Repeat this procedure for each objective lens to be calibrated on the microscope.

To use the calibrated microscope, superimpose the ocular micrometer scale on an egg or cyst and count the number of divisions subtended by the specimen, for example, 12. Multiply 12 by the calibration factor (2.24 for the 400 lens in the example; $12 \times 2.24 = 26.88 \mu m$, the size of the object measured).

PSEUDOPARASITES AND SPURIOUS PARASITES

Fecal samples may contain deceptive "pseudoparasites" and "spurious parasites." Pseudoparasites are ingested objects that resemble parasite forms; these include pollen grains, plant hairs, grain mites, mold spores, and a variety of harmless plant and animal debris (Figs. 1.10–1.14). "Spurious parasites" are parasite eggs or cysts from one species of host that may be found in the feces of a scavenger or predator host as the result of coprophagy or predation (Figs. 1.15 and 1.16). One of the best ways to avoid misidentifying these pseudo- and spurious parasites is to appreciate the variety of parasites that normally infect a host species. If a fecal sample contains a possible pseudoparasite or spurious parasite, it is best to repeat the examination with another sample collected at a later time.

Fig. 1.10. Examples of pseudoparasites. (A) Pine pollen is a common pseudoparasite found in fecal samples of many animals (400×). (B) Adult free-living nematodes are also commonly found in fecal samples collected from the ground. These nematodes can rapidly invade fecal material. The presence of adults and variation in size and morphology (indicating different stages of the life cycle) are helpful in distinguishing these worms from parasitic larvae.

Fig. 1.11. Examples of pseudoparasites. (A) In this ovine fecal sample, both a strongylid egg and a pseudoparasite (*arrow*) are present. Characteristics helpful in the recognition of pseudoparasites are lack of clear internal structure and discontinuities in the outer layer. (B) Pseudoparasite, probably a pollen grain (400×).

Fig. 1.12. Examples of pseudoparasites. (A) Insect hair from the feces of an insectivorous bird. Insect and plant hairs may be confused with worms but have no internal structure. (B) This artifact in ruminant feces appears to have structures resembling the hooks of a tapeworm embryo, but there is no distinct embryo and the outer layer is poorly defined with projections that are variable in size and shape (40×).

Fig. 1.13. Examples of pseudoparasites. (A) Plant hairs and other fibrous material can resemble nematode larvae. They can be present in a variety of shapes and colors, but can usually be easily differentiated from nematodes because they lack clear internal structures like a digestive tract. Also, while one end is tapered, the other end often looks as though it has been broken off another structure. (B) This photo shows *Saccharomycopsis guttulatus*, a nonpathogenic yeast common in rabbits and seen occasionally in dogs (400×).

Fig. 1.14. Examples of pseudoparasites. (A) Free-living mites that contaminate animal feed can be found in fecal flotation procedures. Unlike many parasitic mites, free-living species lack specialized structures on their legs (suckers, combs, etc.) for adhering to the host. (B) Eggs from free-living mites will also float in flotation solution. They are usually very large (>100 μm). Developing legs of the mite can sometimes be seen inside the egg (*arrow*).

Fig. 1.15. Spurious parasites are parasite eggs or cysts from another host that are acquired through predation or coprophagy and have merely passed through the digestive tract of the animal being tested. (A) Tapeworm egg found in a fecal sample from a calf. Although the configuration of hooks inside this egg clearly identifies it as a tapeworm, it is most likely a rodent or bird tapeworm egg. (B) Spurious parasites are common in samples from dogs that ingest fecal material. Eggs of livestock strongylid species can be found in feces of manure-eating dogs. Ruminant and equine strongylid eggs look like canine hookworm eggs but are larger.

Fig. 1.16. Examples of spurious parasites. (A) Large cyst of *Monocystis*, a protozoan parasite of earthworms found in the feces of a snake that feeds on earthworms (100×). (B) *Eimeria* oocysts (*arrow*) are a typical spurious parasite in dog feces. This photograph also contains an individual *Monocystis* oocyst (M) that had been freed from a large cyst like the one shown in Figure 1.15A. These individual *Monocystis* oocysts are common pseudoparasites (400×).

IDENTIFICATION OF NEMATODE LARVAE RECOVERED WITH FECAL FLOTATION OR BAERMANN PROCEDURES

Nematode larvae are passed in the feces of animals infected with various species of lungworms (*Aelurostrongylus abstrusus*, *Angiostrongylus vasorum*, *Crenosoma vulpis*, *Dictyocaulus* spp., *Filaroides hirthi*, *Muellerius capillaris*, *Oslerus osleri*, *Protostrongylus* spp., and others) or the intestinal threadworm, *Strongyloides stercoralis*. Accurate identification of nematode larvae detected on fecal flotation or Baermann tests tends to be a challenge for the veterinary laboratory diagnostician. In many cases where larvae are detected on fecal flotation, the damage due to the effects of high SPG flotation media obscures the larval morphology to the point that identification is not possible (Fig. 1.17). Therefore, the Baermann technique is the preferred method to recover first-stage nematode larvae from feces except in the case of *O. osleri* or *F. hirthi* infection in dogs. The Baermann technique is effective in recovering larvae that are vigorous and able to move out of the fecal matter. The larvae present in feces of dogs infected with *Oslerus* and *Filaroides* are sluggish and unable to migrate out of the feces. Therefore, zinc sulfate centrifugal flotation is the recommended method for the detection of larvae in the feces of dogs infected with these lungworms.

A further complication in larval identification may occur when there is a loss of sample integrity due to improper collection. Fecal samples that are not collected immediately after deposit on the ground may be invaded by free-living soil or plant parasitic nematodes. The challenge of sorting out these nematodes from the true parasitic ones is beyond the training and experience of most veterinary laboratory diagnosticians. In addition, hookworm, strongyle, or trichostrongyle eggs, if present in feces, can develop and hatch in a short time under warm conditions, resulting in the detection of larvae that will be difficult to distinguish from those parasites normally passed as larvae in the feces. In small-animal practice where pet owners collect the fecal sample, the clients must be given guidance as to the requirements for a proper fecal sample. In the case of dogs, clients should be instructed to collect the fecal sample immediately after deposit and place it in an airtight, leakproof container. If submission to the veterinarian cannot occur within several hours of collection, the sample should be refrigerated at 4°C. In the case of cats, the litter pan should be cleaned and the next fecal sample observed in the pan should be collected and handled as above. Ruminant or horse samples should be collected from the rectum. If clients are collecting samples from the ground, they should be instructed to avoid collection of the portion of manure in direct contact with

Fig. 1.17. Larva detected on fecal flotation from a dog infected with lungworm. The larva is damaged due to the osmotic pressure of the high specific gravity flotation fluid. Loss of morphologic detail to this degree prevents specific identification.

Fig. 1.18. Vaginal opening (*arrow*) of a free-living adult female nematode recovered from the feces of a dog. The feces were left on the ground long enough prior to collection to allow free-living soil nematodes to invade the sample.

the soil. Lastly, a further complication in test evaluation can be the presence of spurious parasites acquired through predation or coprophagia.

The first question in the decision tree when evaluating nematode larvae is: parasite or free-living? Parasite larvae range in size from 150 to 400 μm in size and their simple anatomy consists of a mouth opening leading to a buccal tube, esophagus, intestine, and anus. There may also be a discernable genital primordium. Free-living/soil/plant nematodes often occur in multiple life stages (from egg to adult), and size measurements are highly variable. The presence of adult female (eggs in the uterus, vaginal opening—Fig. 1.18) and/or adult male (spicules—Fig. 1.19) worms or the presence of an oral stylet in the buccal tube (Fig. 1.20) indicates that the sample may have been invaded by free-living nematodes. Unfortunately, *Strongyloides* spp. have a free-living generation that will develop if the sample is incubated and therefore are also a possibility when adult stages

Fig. 1.19. Tail of an adult male free-living nematode recovered from an improperly collected fecal sample of a dog. Note the chitinized spicules (*arrow*) at the cloacal opening.

Fig. 1.20. Anterior end of a plant parasitic nematode recovered from an improperly collected fecal sample of a dog. Note the oral stylet (*arrow*) in the buccal chamber. The stylet is a daggerlike structure used in the feeding process to pierce plant roots. No parasitic first-stage larvae have this structure.

are recovered in a fecal sample. Detection of adult worms in the sample is an indication that the animal should be resampled and a fresh fecal sample should be submitted.

Detection of larvae on microscopic examination of a slide prepared from a Baermann test is facilitated by the eye-catching vigorous motion of the larvae. However, once detected, a careful evaluation of the morphologic features is not possible in actively motile larvae. Therefore, it is necessary to kill them in a way that does not damage the morphology. Larvae are best killed by adding a drop of dilute Lugol's iodine (the color of weak tea) to the edge of the coverslip. The iodine will be slowly drawn across the coverslip resulting in the death of the larvae. Alternatively, the larvae can be heat killed by passing the coverslip over the flame of a Bunsen burner to effect (several to many times). Larvae recovered on fecal flotation may or may not be already dead. Fecal flotation slides should be viewed as quickly as possible since the larval damage due to osmotic

Fig. 1.21. (A) Anterior end of a first-stage larva of *Strongyloides stercoralis* recovered from the feces of a dog. This larva has been killed and stained with dilute iodine. The rhabditiform esophagus is well defined and obvious. Note the short buccal tube (*arrow*) and the rhabditiform esophagus made up of the corpus (C), isthmus (I), and muscular bulb (MB). Also note the distinct border demarcating the end of the esophagus and the start of the intestine (GI). (B) Anterior end of an iodine-stained first-stage larva of *Crenosoma vulpis* recovered from the feces of a dog. Note the poorly defined esophagus (E). It is difficult to discern the demarcation between the end of the esophagus and the start of the intestine (GI).

pressure will progressively worsen over time. Differentiation of the various parasitic nematode first-stage larvae is based on overall size and the morphology of the esophagus and tail. First-stage larvae of intestinal parasites (i.e., *S. stercoralis* or hookworm–strongyle–trichostrongyle eggs that have hatched) can be differentiated from the numerous lungworm larvae based on the presence of a distinct rhabditiform esophagus (Figs. 1.21A, 1.22, and 1.24). The rhabditiform esophagus consists of an anterior corpus that narrows to an isthmus and then ends in a muscular bulb. The rhabditiform esophagus is sharply delineated and well defined with an obvious sharp demarcation between the end of the esophagus and the beginning of the intestine. The overall length of the rhabditiform esophagus is less than 25% of the total length of the larvae (Fig. 1.22). In contrast, the esophagus of the lungworm larvae tends to be less well defined and longer, making up about 33%–50% of the total length of the larvae (Figs. 1.21B and 1.23). The relatively short buccal tube differentiates the larvae of *Strongyloides* (Fig. 1.21A) from those of hookworms–strongyles– trichostrongyles, which have a long buccal tube (Fig. 1.24).

Differentiation of the various lungworm larvae is based on tail morphology. In dogs, larvae with a straight tail and lacking a rhabditiform esophagus are *C. vulpis* (see Figs. 1.23 and 1.85). Larvae that have a kinked S-shaped tail but lack a dorsal spine are either *O. osleri* or *F. hirthi* (see Fig. 1.88). Larvae with a kinked tail and a dorsal spine are *A. vasorum* (see Figs. 1.86 and 1.87). In cats, larvae with a kinked tail and a dorsal spine are *A. abstrusus* (see Figs. 1.83 and 1.84).

There should be only a single nematode lungworm larva, *Dictyocaulus viviparus* (see Fig. 1.143), recovered in properly collected fresh feces of cattle. The larvae have an abundance of visible

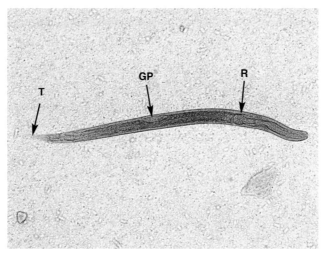

Fig. 1.22. *Strongyloides stercoralis* first-stage larvae recovered from the feces of a dog (Lugol's iodine stained and killed). Note the rhabditiform esophagus (R), prominent genital primordium (GP), and the straight tail (T). The rhabditiform esophagus makes up about 25% of the total length of the larvae.

Fig. 1.23. *Crenosoma vulpis* first-stage larva recovered from the feces of a dog. Note the indistinct poorly defined non-rhabditiform esophagus (E). The esophagus makes up about 33%–50% of the total length of the larvae in metastrongyloid lungworms.

food granules and a straight tail. The same situation occurs with the horse, although infection with *Dictyocaulus arnfieldi* (see Fig. 1.168) is patent in donkeys, but only rarely in the horse. In small ruminants, there are two larvae with straight tails, one with an abundance of visible food granules (*Dictyocaulus filaria*) (see Fig. 1.143) and the other without (*Protostrongylus rufescens*) (see Figs. 1.141 and 1.142). Another lungworm, *Muellerius capillaris*, produces larvae with a kinked tail and dorsal spine (see Figs. 1.139 and 1.140). *Cystocaulus* and *Neostrongylus* are small ruminant lungworms that are found in parts of Europe, the Middle East, and Asia. The tails of their larvae have additional spines that can be used to differentiate them from *Muellerius* larvae.

Fig. 1.24. Anterior end of a first-stage larva of a hookworm, *Uncinaria stenocephala*, recovered from an improperly collected fecal sample of a dog. This larva has been killed and stained with dilute iodine. As with *Strongyloides*, note the corpus (C), isthmus (I), and muscular bulb (B) of the rhabditiform esophagus and the intestine (GI). In contrast to *Strongyloides*, note the long buccal tube (BT).

TECHNIQUES FOR EVALUATION OF STRONGYLID NEMATODES IN GRAZING ANIMALS

Grazing animals are infected with a variety of species of strongylid nematodes, which produce eggs that are not easily differentiated. In veterinary practices, it is usually unnecessary to identify individual species because treatment and control are generally directed to the entire group of nematodes rather than to a single species. If identification of the strongylid genera present in an animal or group of animals is needed, the most convenient method for identification is culture of eggs to the third larval stage. In ruminants, these larvae can then be identified to parasite genus. In horses, this technique can be used to differentiate large and small strongyle larvae and identify some genera specifically. Currently, researchers are developing protocols for identification of parasite genera using molecular techniques (polymerase chain reaction [PCR]), but these procedures are not yet commercially available.

Fecal Culture

1. Fresh feces from cattle or horses should be thoroughly mixed and moistened with water if dry. Feces should not be wet, only moist. Larvae do not survive well in very wet fecal material. If feces are very soft or liquid, peat moss or vermiculite can be added to create a more suitable consistency. Sheep and goat pellets can be cultured as they are, without breaking them up. Rectal fecal samples are preferred for culture to prevent contamination with free-living nematodes.

2. Place feces in a cup or jar in a layer several centimeters deep. The container should have a loose cover that does not prevent air circulation but will deter flies and reduce desiccation. The culture can be kept at room temperature for 10–20 days or at 27°C for 7 days. Daily stirring of the culture will inhibit mold growth and circulate oxygen for the developing larvae. Additional water can be added if feces begin to dry out.

3. Following the culture period, harvest larvae with the Baermann test described previously.

Identification of Ruminant and Camelid Third-Stage Larvae

To identify larvae, place a drop or two of liquid containing larvae from the Baermann procedure on a microscope slide. Add an equal amount of Lugol's iodine. The iodine will kill and stain the larvae so that they can be examined closely.

Larvae recovered from ruminant fecal material can be most easily identified by a combination of morphology and size. The shape of the head and the shape of the tail and of the sheath extending beyond the tail at the posterior end of the larva are important characteristics, and both should be evaluated on each larva before an identification is made. The sheath is the retained cuticle of the second larval stage and provides larvae with increased protection from environmental conditions. Measurements of total larval and sheath length are helpful as well (Table 1.2), but sizes often overlap between genera and size characteristics can be affected by culture conditions and age of larvae. Consequently, measurements alone should not be used to identify larvae.

Relative proportions of parasite genera in larval cultures cannot be used to predict numbers of adult worms in the gastrointestinal tract. For example, *Haemonchus contortus* is highly prolific and may dominate in small ruminant fecal cultures, even when adult parasites of other genera are present in substantial numbers. Figures 1.25–1.35 show morphologic characteristics of common third-stage larvae of small ruminants and cattle.

Table 1.2. Morphologic characteristics of infective third-stage strongylid larvae of domestic ruminants

Genus	Overall Length (μm)	Anus to Tip of Sheath (μm)	End of Tail to Tip of Sheath (μm)	Other Characteristics
Trichostrongylus				Head rounded; tail of sheath short; tail may have one or two tuberosities
Sheep	622–796	76–118	21–40	
Cattle	619–762	83–107	25–39	
Ostertagia				Head squared; tail of sheath shorter in sheep
Sheep	797–910	92–130	30–60	
Cattle	784–928	126–170	55–75	
Haemonchus				Head rounded; sheath tail medium length, offset
Sheep	650–751	119–146	65–78	
Cattle	749–866	158–193	87–119	
Cooperia				Head squared with two refractile oval bodies at anterior end of the esophagus; medium-length sheath tail tapering to fine point
Sheep	711–924	97–150	35–82	
Cattle	666–976	109–190	47–111	
Nematodirus				Broad, rounded head; intestine with eight cells; tail notched and lobed; long thin sheath tail
Sheep	922–1118	310–350	250–290	
Cattle	1095–1142	296–347	207–266	
Bunostomum				Small larva with rounded head; long thin sheath tail
Sheep	514–678	153–183	85–115	
Cattle	500–583	129–158	59–83	
Oesophagostomum				Rounded head; long thin sheath tail; 16–24 triangular intestinal cells
Sheep	771–923	193–235	125–160	
Cattle	726–857	209–257	134–182	
Chabertia				Rounded head; long thin sheath tail; 24–32 rectangular intestinal cells
Sheep	710–789	175–220	110–150	

Sources: Bowman (2009) and Ministry of Agriculture, Fisheries and Food (1986).

Fig. 1.25. Third-stage larvae of common small ruminant strongylid genera collected from fecal culture. This photo shows the relative size relationships among the larvae. The following photographs show the details and the anterior and posterior ends of the individual larvae. *Nematodirus* spp. larvae are usually not encountered in cultures and are not illustrated here. They are bigger in total length and have a longer tail sheath than other larvae. (*A*) *Trichostrongylus*, (*B*) *Teladorsagia*, (*C*) *Oesophagostomum/Chabertia*, (*D*) *Haemonchus*, and (*E*) *Cooperia*. Photo courtesy of Dr. Tom Yazwinski and Mr. Chris Tucker, Department of Animal Science, University of Arkansas, Fayetteville, AK.

Additional photographs and a key to ruminant third-stage larvae can be found at the website of the RVC/FAO Guide to Veterinary Diagnostic Parasitology: www.rvc.ac.uk/review/Parasitology/Index/Index.htm.

Identification of Horse Third-Stage Larvae

Horses are infected with over 30 species of strongylid parasites, but only a few can be identified on the basis of the third-stage larva. Most of the small strongyle species can only be identified as cyathostome parasites from the infective larval stage (Fig. 1.36 and Table 1.3). The posterior portion of the sheath of horse strongyle larvae is very long and filamentous, making these larvae easily recognizable as infective parasite larvae. The number of intestinal cells in these larvae is variable and is useful in identification.

Fecal Egg Count Reduction Test (FECRT)

One of the principal uses of quantitative egg counts is the evaluation of drug efficacy. Anthelmintic resistance in strongylid nematodes of horses and small ruminants is rapidly increasing worldwide, and drug-resistant strongylid nematodes of cattle have also been identified in a number of countries. While there are several techniques for evaluating anthelmintic efficacy, the only one currently practical for field use in all host species is the FECRT. In this procedure, the percentage reduction in strongylid fecal egg counts following treatment is calculated to evaluate the efficacy of the product. This test has also been used to evaluate resistance to anthelmintics in equine *Parascaris equorum* infections.

Although there is some variation in protocols for conducting FECRT, the following general principles are presented followed by comments specific to host species.

Test Groups and Selection of Animals

An accurate FECRT requires adequate animal numbers. In cases where owners wish to test very small flocks or herds, it is important to be cautious in interpretation of results. Ideally, 10–15 animals will be used for each drug to be tested. For horses, where herd sizes are often low, at least five horses per group have been recommended. In very large herds, 10% of the total population is adequate.

The World Association of the Advancement of Veterinary Parasitology (WAAVP) also recommends that an additional group of untreated animals be included. An untreated group controls for either increases or decreases in herd egg counts unrelated to drug treatment (e.g., because of seasonal changes in parasite populations). If inclusion of another group is impractical, however, the FECRT can be performed without a control group.

Animals used in the FECRT should have >150 epg (>100 epg for cattle) if a standard McMaster procedure is used to quantify egg counts. If at all possible, fecal egg counts should be determined before group allocation to ensure that all animals meet the minimum fecal egg count and to create reasonably balanced groups so that individual animals with very high egg counts do not distort results. It will be helpful to perform the FECRT at the time of year when fecal egg counts are expected to be the highest, based on epidemiology of the parasites in any region. If fecal egg counts cannot be determined in advance, younger animals (postweaning and before sexual maturity) may be used for the test because their egg counts will usually be higher and less dramatically skewed in distribution than those of adult animals. The use of young animals is less desirable with horses because a shorter egg reappearance period may follow treatment in immature animals, which may cause an underestimation of drug efficacy. If it is not possible to identify enough animals with the minimum fecal egg count, an alternative test for quantifying parasite eggs must be used to provide an accurate picture of drug efficacy. Alternatives include increasing the sensitivity of a McMaster test by using larger sample aliquots (e.g., using larger counting chambers available from several companies) or using other tests based on centrifugal flotation procedures (Stoll or Wisconsin egg-counting procedure; see section on "Egg-Counting Procedures [Quantitative Fecal Exams]").

Test Drugs and Collection of Posttreatment Samples

Once the test groups of animals have been established, each animal should be individually weighed and treated with an oral formulation of the test drug at the manufacturer's recommended dose. Use of injectable or topical drug formulations may complicate the evaluation of drug efficacy because of persistent activity.

Fig. 1.26. *Teladorsagia* larva from sheep, head (A) and tail sheath (B). The head of *Trichostrongylus* larvae is tapered and the tail sheath is short. The tail may end in one or two tuberosities. Photo courtesy of Dr. Tom Yazwinski and Mr. Chris Tucker, Department of Animal Science, University of Arkansas, Fayetteville, AK.

Fig. 1.27. Ovine *Teladorsagia* head (A) and tail sheath (B). *Teladorsagia* can be confused with *Trichostrongylus*, but *Teladorsagia* is generally larger and the head is squared, not tapered. The sheath of the tail of *Teladorsagia* is short. Photo courtesy of Dr. Tom Yazwinski and Mr. Chris Tucker, Department of Animal Science, University of Arkansas, Fayetteville, AK.

On farms where individual animals cannot be weighed, the fecal egg count reduction (FECR) can be approximated by treating all animals with the drug dose for the estimated heaviest animal in the group. The results, however, will not be entirely accurate because some animals will be receiving more than the recommended dosage, which may be temporarily effective against worms resistant to the recommended dosage. This will lead to an overestimation of drug efficacy.

Fig. 1.28. *Oesophagostomum/Chabertia* head (A) and tail sheath (B). The larvae of these two genera are not easily distinguishable, but they are not difficult to differentiate from other genera. The tail sheath is long and filamentous, and the head is broad and rounded. Photo courtesy of Dr. Tom Yazwinski and Mr. Chris Tucker, Department of Animal Science, University of Arkansas, Fayetteville, AK.

Fig. 1.29. *Haemonchus* head (A) and tail sheath (B). The larvae of *Haemonchus* have the most narrowly rounded head of the common larvae. The tail sheath is medium in length and often has a slight kink at the end of the tail. Photo courtesy of Dr. Tom Yazwinski and Mr. Chris Tucker, Department of Animal Science, University of Arkansas, Fayetteville, AK.

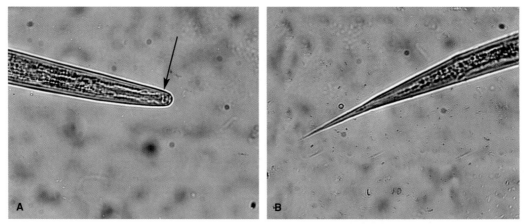

Fig. 1.30. *Cooperia* from a sheep, head (A) and tail sheath (B). *Cooperia* third-stage larvae are distinguished by a pair of refractile bodies (*arrow*) present in a squared head. These bodies are difficult to photograph but easy to appreciate under the microscope. The sheath of the tail is medium in length and tapering or finely pointed. Photo courtesy of Dr. Tom Yazwinski and Mr. Chris Tucker, Department of Animal Science, University of Arkansas, Fayetteville, AK.

Fig. 1.31. *Strongyloides papillosus* is a nematode of ruminants that is unrelated to the important strongylid nematodes. Infective third-stage larvae of *Strongyloides* may be present in larval cultures. They do not have a sheath and the esophagus is very long (E). Additionally, free-living nematodes may be numerous in cultures contaminated with soil. For information on identifying free-living nematodes, see the section on identifying larval nematodes in fecal samples. Photo courtesy of Dr. Tom Yazwinski and Mr. Chris Tucker, Department of Animal Science, University of Arkansas, Fayetteville, AK.

Fig. 1.32. Third-stage *Cooperia* larvae from cattle. Several species of *Cooperia* infect ruminants, and the length of the tail sheath is variable. *Cooperia oncophora* (A) produces larvae with a longer tail sheath than other species of the genus (B). Photo courtesy of Dr. Tom Yazwinski and Mr. Chris Tucker, Department of Animal Science, University of Arkansas, Fayetteville, AK.

Fig. 1.33. Tail sheath of *Ostertagia* (A) and *Trichostrongylus* (B). Both genera have a short tail sheath, but *Osertagia* has a blunter head. Photo courtesy of Dr. Tom Yazwinski and Mr. Chris Tucker, Department of Animal Science, University of Arkansas, Fayetteville, AK.

Fig. 1.34. Tail sheath of *Haemonchus* (A) and *Oesophagostomum* (B) from cattle. The tail sheaths of the parasites occurring in cattle are similar to those in sheep. Photo courtesy of Dr. Tom Yazwinski and Mr. Chris Tucker, Department of Animal Science, University of Arkansas, Fayetteville, AK.

Fig. 1.35. Tail sheath of *Bunostomum*. Species of this ruminant hookworm infect both cattle and sheep. The third-stage larva is smaller than those of other genera and has a thin tail sheath. Photo courtesy of Dr. Tom Yazwinski and Mr. Chris Tucker, Department of Animal Science, University of Arkansas, Fayetteville, AK.

The optimum time following treatment for collection of posttreatment samples varies with the test drug because of variable effects on larval stages and temporary sterilizing effects on adult parasites. For ruminants, the following intervals are recommended:

- levamisole 3–7 days,
- benzimidazoles 8–10 days,
- macrolides 14–17 days.

Fig. 1.36. Infective third-stage larvae of both large and small equine strongyles have a very long filamentous extension of the sheath. (A) The larvae of small strongyles (cyathostomes) have eight intestinal cells, which can be easily counted in the larva shown here. (B) Larvae of large strongyle species have more than eight intestinal cells, like this *Strongylus vulgaris* larva with at least 28 cells.

Table 1.3. Morphologic characteristics of infective third-stage strongylid larvae of horses

Genus	Characteristics
Strongyloides	Sheath absent; esophagus almost half the length of the body
Trichostrongylus axei	Tail of sheath short, not filamentous
Most small strongyles (Cyathostominae)	Long filamentous sheath; eight triangular intestinal cells
Gyalocephalus (small strongyle)	Long filamentous sheath; 12 rectangular intestinal cells
Oesophagodontus (small strongyle)	Large larva; long filamentous sheath; 16 triangular intestinal cells
Posteriostomum (small strongyle)	Long filamentous sheath; 16 roughly rectangular intestinal cells
Strongylus equinus (large strongyle)	Long, thin larva with filamentous sheath; 16 poorly defined rectangular intestinal cells
Triodontophorus (large strongyle)	Medium-length and broad larva with filamentous sheath; 18–20 well-defined rectangular intestinal cells
Strongylus edentatus (large strongyle)	Smaller larvae with filamentous sheath; 18–20 poorly defined and elongated intestinal cells
Strongylus vulgaris (large strongyle)	Large larvae with filamentous sheath; short esophagus; 28–32 well-defined, rectangular intestinal cells

Note: Adapted from Ministry of Agriculture, Fisheries and Food (1986).

For convenience in both ruminants and horses, a standard period of 14 days before collection of the posttreatment samples is often recommended.

Interpretation of Results

When using a control and treated group, the % FECR is calculated using arithmetic group means in the following formula:

$$\%FECR = ([\text{control FEC} - \text{treatment FEC}]/\text{control FEC}) \times 100$$

If pre- and posttreatment results for each animal are used instead of a control group, the formula is altered accordingly, using pretreatment and posttreatment arithmetic means:

$$\%FECR = ([\text{pretreatment FEC} - \text{posttreatment FEC}]/\text{pretreatment FEC}) \times 100$$

When small groups of animals are used, individuals with particularly high fecal egg counts can dramatically skew the FECR when group means are used. In these cases (e.g., in small groups of horses), it is best to calculate individual FECR using the above formula and then average the individual FECR to obtain a group average.

Fully effective modern anthelmintics in ruminants can reliably decrease fecal egg counts by >95%. However, under typical field conditions, it may be more practical to suspect that some portion of the worm population is resistant if the percentage reduction is less than 90%. For example, if the percentage reduction is 10%, a large proportion of worms in the animals are probably resistant. If the reduction is 80%, the proportion of resistant worms is much smaller, but still significant. For horses, minimum cutoff values for drug efficacy in FECRT have been suggested as 95% for macrolides and 90% for benzimidazoles and pyrantel.

To further evaluate which worm genera are resistant in ruminants, feces from both control and treatment groups can be cultured, and the larvae can be identified (see above). In horses, drug resistance is present in small strongyles (cyathostomes), which cannot be differentiated to species by larval indentification.

IDENTIFICATION OF ADULT WORMS

Tapeworm segments and adult gastrointestinal nematodes may occasionally be passed in feces and presented for identification by concerned owners. Segments of common tapeworms can usually be readily identified to the level of genus by shape and identification of eggs in the segments (see Figs. 1.97, 1.98, and 1.147 for photographs of common tapeworm segments), but nematode parasites may be more difficult to identify. When preserving nematodes for further identification, it is helpful to place them first in tap water and refrigerate the container for several hours. This will relax the worms and make them easier to examine. After relaxation, the worms can be placed in 10% buffered formalin. This is not the optimum preservative for all helminths but is readily available for most veterinarians.

The most common nematodes presented by pet owners are the ascarids (roundworms; see Fig. 1.64). These large, stout-bodied worms are common in feces and vomitus of kittens and puppies. Equine owners might also see equine ascarids that are up to 50 cm (about 20 in.) in length. Smaller nematode worms present in equine manure may be the large and small strongyles or pinworms (*Oxyuris*). Larval or adult horse strongyles are usually red and no more than about 2–4 cm in length (see Fig. 1.160). *Oxyuris*, the equine pinworm, can reach 15 cm, and the females have distinctive long, thin tails (see Fig. 1.166). Nematodes are most likely to be seen in diarrheic feces or following treatment.

Specific identification of adult nematodes is usually based on morphologic variations of the outer layer, or cuticle, of the worms. Microscopic examination of the mouthparts and accessory sexual structures may be required. To enhance visualization of these structures, the worm can be mounted in a clearing solution, which dissolves the soft tissue, leaving only the cuticle. If the worm is large, the areas of diagnostic importance (usually the anterior and posterior ends) can be cut off and mounted in a few drops of the clearing solution. Unfortunately, these solutions require either controlled or hazardous substances. Recipes for Hoyer's and Lactophenol solutions are given below, but they are not usually prepared in veterinary practices. Depending on the parasite species, accurate worm identification may require the evaluation of subtle morphologic characteristics that will be unfamiliar to most practicing veterinarians. When specific parasite identification is needed, worms should be submitted to a parasitologist for examination.

Hoyer's Solution

Hoyer's solution can be used indefinitely and a single recipe will last for many years. It also provides a permanent mounting medium for specimens, although the clearing process will continue until eventually internal structures will no longer be visible:

- 30 g gum arabic,
- 16 mL glycerol,
- 200 g chloral hydrate,
- 50 mL distilled water.

Dissolve the gum arabic in water with gentle heat. Add the chloral hydrate, then the glycerol.

Lactophenol

- 20 mL glycerin, pure;
- 10 mL lactic acid;
- 10 mL phenol crystals, melted;
- 10 mL distilled water.

Combine all ingredients.

PARASITES OF DOMESTIC ANIMALS

The following photographs in this chapter illustrate the diagnostic stages found in feces of a wide variety of both common and some uncommon parasites of major domestic species. Because an appreciation of relative sizes of parasite eggs, cysts and oocysts, is very helpful in identification, a line drawing precedes sections showing parasites of common mammalian hosts (Figs. 1.37, 1.38, 1.111, 1.112, 1.154, 1.172). Generally, photographs of eggs and cysts were taken using the high-dry (40×) objective, although some photographs using the 10× objective are included to show relative sizes of eggs and cysts.

The figures in which each parasite appears are listed after the name. They may include figures in other sections where more than one parasite is illustrated.

An effort has been made to minimize taxonomic information while still permitting an appreciation of the larger groups to which each individual species belongs. For more specific taxonomic information, a textbook of veterinary parasitology should be consulted.

Helminth Ova and Protozoan Cysts
as found in freshly voided feces of the
Dog, Wolf, Coyote and Fox

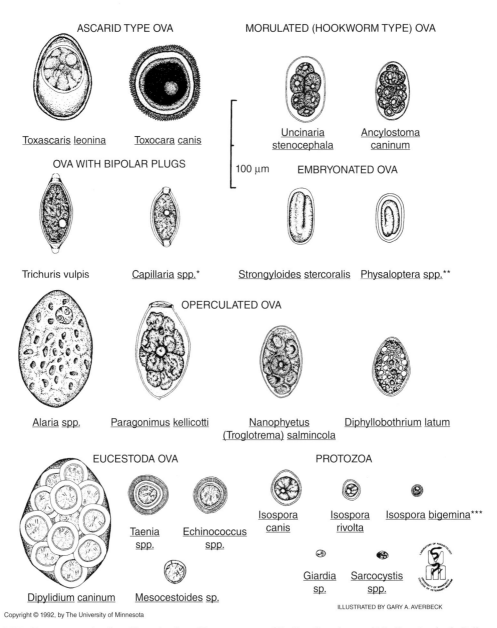

ASCARID TYPE OVA

Toxascaris leonina   Toxocara canis

OVA WITH BIPOLAR PLUGS

Trichuris vulpis   Capillaria spp.*

MORULATED (HOOKWORM TYPE) OVA

Uncinaria stenocephala   Ancylostoma caninum

100 μm   EMBRYONATED OVA

Strongyloides stercoralis   Physaloptera spp.**

OPERCULATED OVA

Alaria spp.   Paragonimus kellicotti   Nanophyetus (Troglotrema) salmincola   Diphyllobothrium latum

EUCESTODA OVA

Taenia spp.   Echinococcus spp.

Dipylidium caninum   Mesocestoides sp.

PROTOZOA

Isospora canis   Isospora rivolta   Isospora bigemina***

Giardia sp.   Sarcocystis spp.

ILLUSTRATED BY GARY A. AVERBECK

Fig. 1.37. Common parasites found in canine feces. Figure courtesy of Dr. Bert Stromberg and Mr. Gary Averbeck, College of Veterinary Medicine, University of Minnesota, Minneapolis, MN. *Capillaria* spp. of small animals have been reclassified as *Pearsonema*, *Aoncotheca*, and *Eucoleus*. **Spirocerca lupi*, which is common in many parts of the world, has a larvated egg similar in appearance to *Physaloptera*, but more elongated. ***Species names *bigemina* and *rivolta* are no longer used for small canine *Isospora* oocysts.

Helminth Ova, Larva, and Protozoan Cysts
as found in freshly voided feces of
Cats

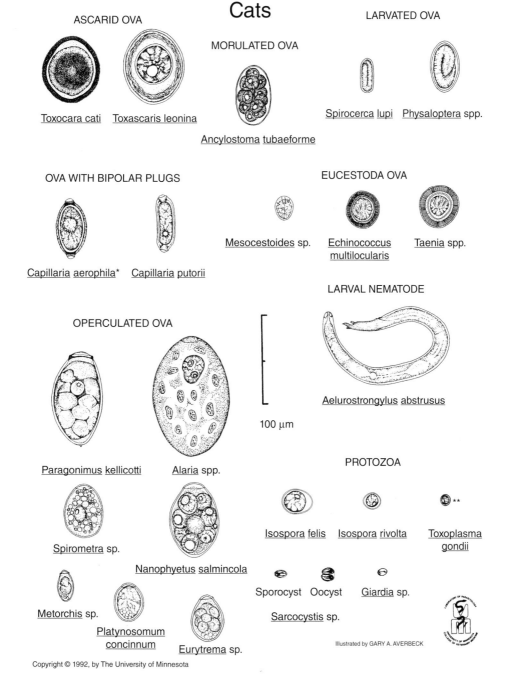

ASCARID OVA

Toxocara cati   Toxascaris leonina

MORULATED OVA

Ancylostoma tubaeforme

LARVATED OVA

Spirocerca lupi   Physaloptera spp.

OVA WITH BIPOLAR PLUGS

Capillaria aerophila*   Capillaria putorii

EUCESTODA OVA

Mesocestoides sp.   Echinococcus multilocularis   Taenia spp.

LARVAL NEMATODE

Aelurostrongylus abstrusus

OPERCULATED OVA

100 μm

Paragonimus kellicotti   Alaria spp.

PROTOZOA

Isospora felis   Isospora rivolta   Toxoplasma gondii

Spirometra sp.

Nanophyetus salmincola

Sporocyst   Oocyst   Giardia sp.

Sarcocystis sp.

Metorchis sp.

Platynosomum concinnum   Eurytrema sp.

Illustrated by GARY A. AVERBECK

Copyright © 1992, by The University of Minnesota

Fig. 1.38. Common parasites found in feline feces. Figure courtesy of Dr. Bert Stromberg and Mr. Gary Averbeck, College of Veterinary Medicine, University of Minnesota, Minneapolis, MN. *Capillaria spp. of small animals have been reclassified as *Pearsonema*, *Aoncotheca*, and *Eucoleus*. **Oocysts of *Hammondia hammondi* and *Besnoitia* spp. are similar in appearance to *Toxoplasma* oocysts.

41

Protozoan Parasites

PARASITE: *Isospora* **spp.** (Figs. 1.39–1.43, 1.46, 1.65, 1.73, 1.93)
    Common name: Coccidia.

Taxonomy: Protozoa (coccidia). Several host-specific species are found in the dog (*I. canis*, *I. ohioensis*, *I. neorivolta*, *I. burrowsi*) and cat (*I. felis*, *I. rivolta*).

Geographic Distribution: Worldwide.

Location in Host: Small intestine, cecum, and colon.

Life Cycle: Cats and dogs are infected by ingestion of sporulated oocysts or transport hosts (often rodents, but also including rabbits, ruminants, birds, and other prey animals). Following development in the final host, oocysts are passed in feces and undergo sporulation in the environment.

Laboratory Diagnosis: Oocysts are detected by centrifugal or simple fecal flotation examination. Oocysts have smooth, clear cyst walls, are elliptical in shape, and contain a single, round cell (sporoblast) when freshly passed.

Size:	*I. canis*, *I. felis*	38–51 × 27–39 μm
	Other *Isospora* spp.	17–27 × 15–24 μm

Clinical Importance: These are the organisms typically referred to as "coccidia" of dogs and cats, although other parasites also fall into this taxonomic group. Oocysts can be found in the feces of many clinically normal young dogs and cats. Clinical coccidiosis most often occurs in puppies and kittens, often in association with weaning, change of owner, or other stress factors. Signs include diarrhea, abdominal pain, anorexia, and weight loss. In severe cases, bloody diarrhea and anemia may occur. Respiratory and neurologic signs have also been reported in some animals. Clinical disease has been difficult to reproduce in experimental infections.

Fig. 1.39. Dog and cat coccidia species produce oocysts of different sizes. This figure shows *I. canis* (larger oocysts) and an oocyst of the *I. ohioensis* complex (smaller oocyst). Photo courtesy of Dr. David Lindsay, Virginia-Maryland Regional College of Veterinary Medicine, Virginia Tech, Blacksburg, VA.

Fig. 1.40. *Isospora* oocyst and two iodine-stained *Giardia* cysts (*arrows*) in a canine fecal sample. Photo courtesy of Dr. Robert Ridley, College of Veterinary Medicine, Kansas State University, Manhattan, KS.

Fig. 1.41. Following passage in the feces, *Isospora* spp. oocysts undergo sporulation. The sporulated oocyst contains two sporocysts, each containing four sporozoites. Two sporozoites can be seen in each sporocyst of this oocyst, as well as the large, round residual body that is present in each sporocyst.

PARASITE: ***Toxoplasma gondii, Neospora caninum*** (Fig. 1.44)

Taxonomy: Protozoa (coccidia).

Geographic Distribution: Worldwide.

Location in Host: Intestine and other tissues of cats and other felids (*Toxoplasma*) and dogs and other canids (*Neospora*).

Life Cycle: *Toxoplasma* is transmitted to cats by ingestion of cysts containing bradyzoites in tissues of intermediate hosts. Prenatal and transmammary transmission as well as direct transmission through ingestion of sporulated oocysts can also occur. Transmission of *Neospora* in dogs appears to be similar to *Toxoplasma* transmission.

Laboratory Diagnosis: Oocysts are detected in feces by centrifugal or simple flotation techniques. However, very few oocysts of *Neospora* appear to be produced in infected dogs. Immunodiagnostic tests are available to identify current and past exposure to *Toxoplasma* in cats but are usually not positive until after fecal passage of oocysts has ceased. Dogs can also be tested for antibody to *Neospora*. The small, spherical-shaped oocysts of the two genera are morphologically identical, have a clear smooth cyst wall, and contain a single round sporoblast.

Size: $11-14 \times 9-11\,\mu m$

Clinical Importance: *Toxoplasma* infections in cats are generally well tolerated. Clinical disease (ocular, respiratory, etc.) can occur in cats, especially young or immunosuppressed animals. Toxoplasmosis is an important zoonotic disease with especially serious consequences in pregnant women and the immunosuppressed. Congenital *Neospora* infection can result in severe central nervous system disease in dogs. *Neospora* infection is also an important cause of abortion in the bovine intermediate host.

Fig. 1.42. *Isospora* oocysts usually require a minimum of 1–2 days to become infective for the next host (sporulated). In warm conditions, oocysts undergo the first cell division soon after being passed in the feces. In the two-cell stage, they may be mistaken for sporulated oocysts. In this fecal sample, a sporulated oocyst (*arrow*) is adjacent to one in the two-cell stage.

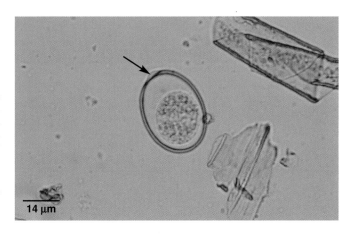

Fig. 1.43. *Eimeria* spp. oocysts are sometimes seen in dog and cat feces. *Eimeria* does not infect these hosts, but oocysts consumed as a result of predation or coprophagy will pass unharmed through the gastrointestinal (GI) tract and may be misidentified as *Isospora*. Many (but not all) *Eimeria* oocysts have a knob at one end called the micropyle cap (*arrow*), whereas *Isospora* spp. lack a cap. If this cap is present, an oocyst in dog or cat feces can be identified as a "spurious parasite."

Fig. 1.44. *Neospora* and *Toxoplasma* oocysts are similar to common *Isospora* spp., but they are smaller. The oocysts of these two coccidia genera are similar in appearance and also cannot be distinguished from oocysts of *Hammondia*, another coccidian genus of small animals. This photo of a feline fecal sample also shows an oocyst of *Isospora rivolta* (*arrow*).

PARASITE: *Sarcocystis* **spp.** (Figs. 1.45 and 1.46)

Taxonomy: Protozoa (coccidia). A number of species infect dogs or cats, each with a specific intermediate host.

Geographic Distribution: Worldwide.

Location in Host: Small intestine of dogs and cats.

Life Cycle: Cat and dog definitive hosts are infected by ingesting intermediate host tissue containing sarcocysts. Sexual reproduction in dogs or cats leads to formation of oocysts that sporulate while still in the intestinal tract.

Laboratory Diagnosis: Oocysts form within the gastrointestinal tract of dogs and cats. The oocyst wall breaks down in the gut, and small, ellipsoidal sporulated sporocysts are released in the feces. They are detected by centrifugal or simple flotation techniques.

Size: $7–22 \times 3–15 \, \mu m$

Clinical Importance: *Sarcocystis* is generally nonpathogenic in the definitive host, although some species can cause severe disease in the intermediate host (cattle, sheep, pigs, horses).

PARASITE: *Cryptosporidium* **spp.** (Fig. 1.47)

Taxonomy: Protozoa (coccidia). *Cryptosporidium felis* and *C. canis* appear to be the primary species infecting cats and dogs, respectively.

Geographic Distribution: Worldwide.

Location in Host: Small intestine.

Life Cycle: These parasites have a direct life cycle. Cats and dogs are infected following ingestion of oocysts, which are infective as soon as they are passed in the feces. Following asexual and sexual multiplication of the organism in the intestine, oocysts are produced and exit the host in the feces.

Laboratory Diagnosis: Small oocysts in the feces are detected by use of acid-fast or other stains of fecal smears, Sheather's sugar flotation test, fecal antigen tests, or molecular diagnostic procedures. Oocysts of *C. parvum* and *C. canis* are morphologically indistinguishable, while *C. felis* oocysts are smaller than those of the other two species.

Size: *C. felis* $3.5–5 \, \mu m$ in diameter
             C. parvum, C. canis $7 \times 5 \, \mu m$

Clinical Importance: Cryptosporidiosis has been reported as an uncommon cause of chronic diarrhea in cats. Affected cats are often immunosuppressed by other causes. Although implicated in rare instances, *Cryptosporidium* infections in dogs and cats do not appear to be a significant source of zoonotic exposure for humans.

Fig. 1.45. *Sarcocystis* sporocysts are smaller than typical coccidia oocysts and have a smooth, clear cyst wall. Each sporocyst contains four banana-shaped sporozoites. Photo courtesy of Dr. Robert Ridley, College of Veterinary Medicine, Kansas State University, Manhattan, KS.

Fig. 1.46. *Sarcocystis* sporulates in the intestines and the oocyst wall usually ruptures before exiting the body so that only sporocysts are seen. Rarely, intact *Sarcocystis* oocysts are present (*arrow*). Large, round residual bodies can be seen in the sporocysts. This flotation preparation also contains an *Isospora* oocyst.

Fig. 1.47. *Cryptosporidium* sp. in a sugar flotation preparation. The oocysts of *C. canis* and *C. felis* are difficult to distinguish by microscopic techniques; *C. felis* oocysts are slightly smaller in size. *Cryptosporidum* oocysts can also be detected with acid-fast stains and immunodiagnostic tests.

PARASITE: **Trichomonads** (Figs. 1.48 and 1.49)

Taxonomy: Protozoa (flagellate). The species identification of these organisms in dogs and cats is currently under investigation. Recently, trichomonad organisms associated with chronic diarrhea in cats were identified as genetically identical to *Tritrichomonas foetus*, the cause of bovine venereal trichomoniasis.

Geographic Distribution: Probably worldwide.

Location in Host: Large intestine of cats and dogs.

Life Cycle: Very little is known about transmission. Infection is probably by direct contact since no environmentally resistant cyst stage is known to occur.

Laboratory Diagnosis: The presence of trophozoites can be detected in direct saline smears of fresh feces. Flotation solutions will destroy trophozoites. Trichomonad organisms can be confused with *Giardia* but have a rippling, undulating membrane and lack the facelike appearance of *Giardia* trophozoites. For detection of *Tritrichomonas foetus*, a more reliable method of detection in the United States is through use of the InPouch™ TF-Feline culture system, similar to the method used for culturing *T. foetus* infections in cattle (see Chapter 2). Feline feces (0.1 g or less) is added to the system and cultured at 25°C for up to 11 days. A commercial PCR test is also available.

Size: 6–11 × 3–4 μm

Clinical Importance: Cases of chronic diarrhea in cats have been associated with feline *T. foetus* infection; however, most trichomonad infections are generally considered to be of limited pathogenicity.

PARASITE: ***Giardia intestinalis* (=*G. duodenalis*), *G. lamblia*, *G. canis*, *G. cati*, etc.** (Figs. 1.40, 1.50–1.56, 1.58)

Taxonomy: Protozoa (flagellate). The number and correct nomenclature of species are currently under investigation. Molecular analysis is now used to allocate isolates into assemblages. Most isolates from dogs belong to Assemblages C and D, and cat isolates fall into Assemblage F.

Geographic Distribution: Worldwide.

Location in Host: Small intestine of dogs, cats, many other animals, and humans.

Life Cycle: Dogs and cats are infected by ingesting cysts in the environment. Trophozoites are stimulated under certain conditions to encyst and are passed from the host in feces.

Laboratory Diagnosis: Examination of feces for cysts is the most sensitive microscopic technique. Cysts are best detected by 33% $ZnSO_4$ centrifugal flotation; other flotation solutions often cause rapid distortion. Motile trophozoites are occasionally seen in a direct saline smear of fresh diarrheic feces or may be in duodenoscopic aspirates (aspirates should be centrifuged and the sediment examined for trophozoites). Trophozoites are likely to be dead and unrecognizable if fecal examination occurs longer than 30 minutes after sample collection or if the sample has been refrigerated. Multiple fecal examinations (i.e., three exams done on samples collected over a 5- to 7-day period) may be necessary to rule out infection. A point of use fecal antigen test is available in the United States. Fecal enzyme-linked immunosorbent assay (ELISA) and indirect fluorescent antibody (IFA) tests are also available.

Size:　　　Cyst　　　　　9–13 × 7–9 μm
　　　　　　Trophozoite　　12–17 × 7–10 μm

Clinical Importance: *Giardia* is a common parasite of small animals. Many infections are asymptomatic, but *Giardia* may cause acute, chronic, or intermittent diarrhea, particularly in young dogs and cats. Since the role of pets in human *Giardia* infection is controversial, infections should be regarded as potentially zoonotic.

Fig. 1.48. Trichomonad parasites in dogs and cats have a distinctive undulating membrane. In fresh saline smears, they are most easily confused with *Giardia* trophozoites, but trichomonads lack the facelike appearance and the concave ventral surface of *Giardia*.

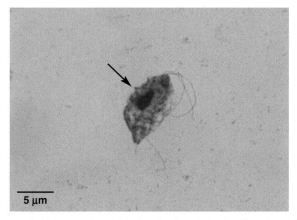

Fig. 1.49. Stained fecal smear of a trichomonad organism showing the anterior flagella and part of the undulating membrane (*arrow*).

Fig. 1.50. *Giardia* cysts recovered with 33% $ZnSO_4$ centrifugal flotation. Cysts are elliptical with a thin, smooth cyst wall and contain two to four nuclei, two slender, linear intracytoplasmic flagella, and two thick, comma-shaped median bodies.

49

Fig. 1.51. A drop of Lugol's iodine may be added to a flotation preparation to stain *Giardia* cysts and make internal structures more prominent. Two nuclei (N), intracytoplasmic flagella (F), and median bodies (M) can be seen in the cyst shown here.

Fig. 1.52. *Giardia* cysts undergo osmotic damage when exposed to the high specific gravity of salt solutions. With time, increasing numbers of cysts appear vacuolated, with a characteristic half-moon shape. Plant pollen and yeast cells that mimic *Giardia* cysts do not undergo this same artifact change.

Fig. 1.53. The structures most often confused with *Giardia* cysts are yeast (*arrows*), which may be found in diarrheic feces in large numbers. Yeast are commonly slightly smaller than *Giardia* cysts and lack the complex internal structure seen in *Giardia* cysts.

Fig. 1.54. Stained *Giardia* trophozoites in a direct smear. Trophozoites are bilaterally symmetrical and pyriform shaped with two nuclei, eight flagella, two rodlike median bodies, and a ventral, concave, adhesive disk that gives them a clown face.

Fig. 1.55. Unstained *Giardia* trophozoite in a fecal smear. Live trophozoites have a characteristic wobbling motion when swimming (often described as looking like a falling leaf) and are easily kept in the microscopic field of view.

Fig. 1.56. *Giardia* trophozoite (*arrow*) associated with a portion of mucosa in a duodenal aspirate. Aspirates should be examined within 30 minutes of collection, before the fragile trophozoites die.

Helminth Parasites

PARASITE: *Ancylostoma* **spp.,** *Uncinaria stenocephala* (Figs. 1.57–1.59, 1.65, 1.70–1.71, 1.103)
Common name: Hookworm.

Taxonomy: Nematodes (order Strongylida).

Geographic Distribution:
Ancylostoma caninum (dogs): worldwide; range in North America extends to southern Canada.
A. brasiliense (dogs and cats): tropical and subtropical distribution; in the United States found in the Gulf Coast region.
A. tubaeformae (cats): worldwide.
A. ceylanicum (dogs and cats): various parts of Asia.
Uncinaria stenocephala (dogs, rarely cats): occurs in the cooler northern temperate regions, including the northern United States, Canada, and Europe.

Location in Host: Small intestine of dogs and cats and wild canids and felids.

Life Cycle: Transmission of *A. caninum* to dogs occurs by transmammary transmission and direct skin penetration by infective larvae (most important), ingestion of infective third-stage larvae from the environment or in paratenic hosts, and transplacental transmission (least important). Transmission of *U. stenocephala* occurs by ingestion of infective third-stage larvae or paratenic hosts, and rarely by direct skin penetration of infective larvae. Cats can be infected with hookworms either by skin penetration by infective larvae or by ingestion of larvae in the environment or in paratenic hosts (rodents). Adult hookworms in the host small intestine produce eggs that exit the host in the feces.

Laboratory Diagnosis: Hookworm eggs are detected using centrifugal or simple flotation fecal examination techniques. *Ancylostoma* and *Uncinaria* eggs are morphologically identical, with an elliptical shape and smooth shell wall containing a grapelike cluster of cells (morula). However, they differ in size.

Size:	*Ancylostoma* spp.	52–79×28–$58\,\mu m$
	U. stenocephala	71–92×35–$58\,\mu m$

Clinical Importance: *Ancylostoma caninum* is common in North America. In heavy infections, particularly in puppies, hookworms can cause severe anemia and death due to their voracious bloodsucking habits. Peracute, acute, and chronic disease syndromes may occur. *Ancylostoma brasiliense* and, to a lesser extent, *A. caninum* pose a zoonotic risk (eosinophilic enteritis and cutaneous larva migrans) to humans. *Ancylostoma* spp. infections in cats are less common than in dogs. Many feline infections are subclinical, but heavy infections causing anemia and weight loss can be fatal. *Uncinaria stenocephala* is less pathogenic than *A. caninum*; infection may result in chronic disease with diarrhea and hypoproteinemia.

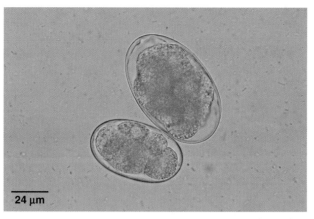

Fig. 1.57. Although *Ancylostoma* is the most common genus of hookworm in the United States, slightly larger *Uncinaria* eggs may also be seen in canine feces, and mixed infections can occur, as shown here.

Fig. 1.58. *Ancylostoma tubaeforme* larvated and undeveloped eggs from a cat. The egg on the right contains a developed first-stage larva; the egg on the left is undifferentiated. Hookworm eggs exposed to warm temperatures for several hours rapidly develop to the larvated stage and hatch.

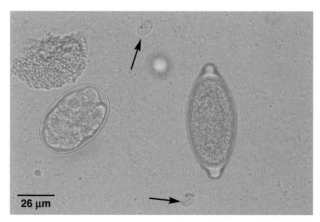

Fig. 1.59. Canine fecal sample containing *Ancylostoma caninum* (hookworm) and *Trichuris vulpis* (whipworm) eggs and two *Giardia* sp. cysts (*arrows*).

PARASITE: *Toxocara* **spp.** (Figs. 1.60–1.66, 1.68, 1.69, 1.71, 1.93, 1.95, 1.103)
Common name: Roundworm.

Taxonomy: Nematode (order Ascaridida).

Geographic Distribution: Worldwide.

Location in Host: Small intestine of dogs (*T. canis*) and cats (*T. cati*).

Life Cycle: Single-celled eggs pass from the host in the feces and develop to the infective stage in the environment. Dogs acquire infections of *T. canis* by transplacental (most important) and transmammary transmission or by the ingestion of larvated eggs or paratenic hosts (rodents). Cats acquire *T. cati* infection by ingestion of larvated eggs or paratenic hosts. Transmammary transmission may also occur in some circumstances.

Laboratory Diagnosis: Eggs are detected using centrifugal or simple flotation examination techniques. *Toxocara* eggs have a dark, round, single-celled embryo contained in a thick shell wall. Eggs of the two species are difficult to differentiate. *Toxocara canis* tends to be subspherical, and *T. cati* tends to be elliptical in shape.

Size:	*T. canis*	85–90 × 75 μm
	T. cati	65 × 75 μm

Clinical Importance: *Toxocara* is an important pathogen in puppies and kittens. Stillbirths, neonatal deaths (*T. canis*), or chronic ill-thrift (*T. canis, T. cati*) can occur in infected animals. Adult dogs and cats are much less likely to have symptomatic infections. Additionally, both species (especially *T. canis*) have zoonotic importance as causes of visceral and ocular larva migrans, particularly in children.

Fig. 1.60. *Toxocara* eggs are typical ascarid eggs with a thick shell. They contain a single cell when first passed in host feces.

Fig. 1.61. When the microscope is focused on the surface of a *Toxocara* egg, the rough, pitted shell wall surface has a golf-ball-like appearance.

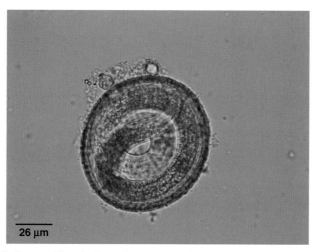

Fig. 1.62. *Toxocara* and other ascarids typically require several weeks of development in the environment before an infective larva forms, although initial larval development can occur in a few days in hot weather.

PARASITE: ***Toxascaris leonina*** (Fig. 1.63)
Common name: Roundworm.

Taxonomy: Nematode (order Ascaridida).

Geographic Distribution: Worldwide.

Location in Host: Small intestine of dogs, cats, wild canids and felids

Life Cycle: The life cycle is similar to that of *Toxocara* spp., although there is no transmammary or transplacental infection. Dogs and cats are infected following ingestion of larvated eggs or paratenic hosts (rodents, rabbits).

Laboratory Diagnosis: Eggs are detected using centrifugal or simple flotation fecal examination techniques. *Toxascaris* eggs are elliptical with a thick, smooth outer shell wall containing a light-colored, single-celled embryo. The internal surface of the shell wall appears rough or wavy due to the vitelline membrane.

Size: 75–85 × 60–75 μm

Clinical Importance: *Toxascaris* is much less common in dogs and cats than *Toxocara* and is considered to be of minor clinical significance.

Fig. 1.63. *Toxascaris leonina* egg and *Toxocara cati* egg. Note the dark single-cell embryo and rough mammillated (pitted) outer shell wall surface of the *Toxocara* egg contrasted to the lighter appearance of the embryo and to the smooth outer shell wall surface of the *Toxascaris* egg.

Fig. 1.64. Ascarids are often passed in the feces or vomitus of dogs and cats, particularly in young or recently dewormed animals. They are the only large, thick-bodied nematodes commonly seen by owners. Rarely, the stomach worm *Physaloptera* is present in vomitus. It usually assumes a C shape when passed out of the host. Two specimens each of *Toxocara* (T) and *Physaloptera* (P) are shown here.

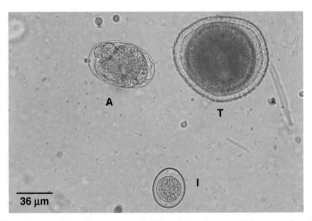

Fig. 1.65. Canine fecal sample containing *Toxocara canis* (T) and *Ancylostoma* (A) eggs and an *Isospora* oocyst (I).

58   VETERINARY CLINICAL PARASITOLOGY

PARASITE: ***Baylisascaris procyonis*** (Figs. 1.66 and 1.67)
Common name: Raccoon roundworm.

Taxonomy: Nematode (order Ascaridida).

Geographic Distribution: Parts of North America and Europe.

Location in Host: Small intestine of raccoons and occasionally dogs.

Life Cycle: Raccoons are infected by ingestion of infective eggs or paratenic hosts (rodents, rabbits, birds). Routes of infection in dogs are presumed to be the same.

Laboratory Diagnosis: Eggs are detected by simple or centrifugal fecal flotation examination. Eggs are thick walled, elliptical in shape, and contain a single, large, round-celled embryo. The eggs are often covered with a brown proteinaceous substance and have a fine granular shell wall surface.

Size: 63–75 × 53–60 μm

Clinical Importance: Infection is well tolerated in the raccoon definitive host. Severe central nervous system or ocular disease can result from exposure of birds, rabbits, rodents, marsupials, and humans to infective *B. procyonis* eggs. Infections in dogs may result in either patent adult worms in the small intestine or larval tissue migration causing central nervous system disease.

Fig. 1.66. *Toxocara canis* egg and *Baylisascaris procyonis* egg (*arrow*). Eggs of *B. procyonis* appear in the feces of dogs due to either patent infections or coprophagy. The larger *Toxocara* egg (85–90 × 75 μm) has a rough, pitted, outer shell wall surface. The *B. procyonis* egg is smaller, has a finely granular shell wall surface, and may be brown in color. *Baylisacaris* eggs are easily misidentified as *Toxocara* in canine fecal exams. Mistakes can be minimized with the use of an ocular micrometer.

Fig. 1.67. *Baylisascaris procyonis* egg from the feces of a naturally infected dog. Usually, *Baylisascaris* eggs are brown in color due to the presence of a protein coat (see Fig. 1.66). When lacking the protein coat, *Baylisascaris* eggs are easily misidentified as *Toxocara canis*. *Baylisascaris* eggs can be differentiated from those of *Toxocara* based on their smaller size and the absence of outer shell wall pitting.

28 µm

Fig. 1.68. The morphology of the anterior end of small animal ascarids can be used to differentiate species. The anterior end of adult *Toxocara cati* has an "arrowhead" appearance due to the cervical alae (winglike expansions of the cuticle). Adult specimens of *Toxocara cati* (A) recovered from the feces or vomitus of cats can be differentiated from *Toxascaris leonina* (B), which has less prominent cervical alae.

Fig. 1.69. The cervical alae of adult *Toxocara canis* (A) are similar in appearance to those of *Toxascaris leonina*. In contrast to the other ascarids infecting dogs (*Toxocara, Toxascaris*), adult *Baylisascaris* (B) lack visible cervical alae.

PARASITE: ***Trichuris vulpis*** (Figs. 1.59, 1.70–1.74)
Common name: Whipworm.

Taxonomy: Nematode (order Enoplida).

Geographic Distribution: Worldwide.

Location in Host: Cecum and large intestine of dogs and wild canids. *Trichuris felis* infection has been reported rarely in cats in Latin America and Australia.

Life Cycle: Dogs are infected by ingesting infective eggs in the environment. Eggs are produced by adult worms in the large bowel and, after leaving the host in the feces, develop to the infective stage in the environment.

Laboratory Diagnosis: Eggs are best detected by centrifugal flotation and less effectively by simple flotation examination of feces. Eggs are typically symmetrical about the bipolar plugs, barrel shaped, and brown. The shell wall surface is smooth.

Size: 72–90 × 32–40 μm

Clinical Importance: Heavy infection in dogs can cause weight loss, unthriftiness, and profuse diarrhea that may be bloody. Infection in humans occurs rarely.

Fig. 1.70. The egg of *Trichuris vulpis* is one of the most common found in canine feces. The bipolar plugs are prominent. Capillarid species also produce eggs with similar polar plugs. In this fecal flotation preparation, an *Ancylostoma caninum* egg is also present (A).

Fig. 1.71. *Toxocara*, *Ancylostoma*, and *Trichuris* eggs in a canine fecal sample. These are the most common intestinal helminths encountered in dogs. Photo courtesy of Dr. Robert Ridley, College of Veterinary Medicine, Kansas State University, Manhattan, KS.

Fig. 1.72. Capillarid egg (C), *Ancylostoma* egg (A), and *Monocystis* cysts (M). The protozoan *Monocystis* cysts seem to have the bipolar appearance of whipworm and capillarid eggs, but they are much too small to be helminth eggs.

DOGS AND CATS

PARASITE: *Eucoleus (=Capillaria) aerophilus, E. boehmi* (Figs. 1.72–1.76, 1.93)
Common name: Fox lungworm (*E. aerophilus*).

Taxonomy: Nematode (order Enoplida). These parasites were formerly in the genus *Capillaria* and are still frequently referred to by that name.

Geographic Distribution: *Eucoleus aerophilus* is found worldwide; *E. boehmi* has been reported from North and South America and Europe.

Location in Host: Trachea, bronchi, and bronchioles of dogs, cats, and foxes (*E. aerophilus*). Epithelium of the nasal turbinates and sinuses of dogs and wild canids (*E. boehmi*).

Life Cycle: The definitive host is probably infected by ingestion of eggs containing infective larvae, although an earthworm intermediate host may be involved.

Laboratory Diagnosis: Eggs are detected by fecal flotation examination or in tracheal or nasal mucus samples. The eggs are clear to golden (*E. boehmi*) or brownish green (*E. aerophilus*), are bipolar plugged, tend to be asymmetrical in shape, and contain a multicelled embryo.

Size: *E. aerophilus*   58–79 × 29–40 μm
             E. boehmi   54–60 × 30–35 μm

Clinical Importance: *Eucoleus aerophilus* is an important pathogen in farmed foxes and causes bronchopneumonia. Infections in dogs and cats are usually subclinical; however, in some cases, chronic cough occurs. *Eucoleus boehmi* infections are usually subclinical. Reported clinical signs include sneezing and a mucopurulent nasal discharge that may contain blood.

Fig. 1.73. The only canine parasite eggs that could be mistaken for whipworm eggs belong to the capillarid parasites *Eucoleus* and *Aonchotheca*. *Trichuris* eggs (T) are larger, have a smooth-walled shell, and are usually browner than the smaller *Eucoleus* egg (E) shown here. *Isospora* oocysts are also present in this sample.

Fig. 1.74. Portion of a *Trichuris vulpis* egg (A) demonstrating the ridges seen in the bipolar plug (*arrow*). Capillarid eggs (B) lack ridges on the plugs. Capillarid eggs are also smaller than whipworm eggs and their bipolar plugs often appear asymmetrical.

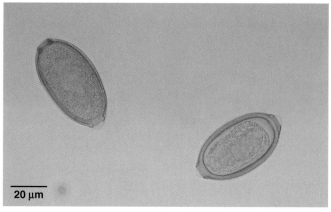

Fig. 1.75. *Eucoleus* eggs are passed in the undifferentiated one- or two-celled stage. *Eucoleus boehmi* (*right*) and *E. aerophilus* (*left*) eggs are similar in appearance, although in fresh feces, eggs of *E. boehmi* already contain a morula (cluster of cells) that does not completely fill the interior of the egg. Differences in the eggshell can also be used to differentiate the species (see Figs. 1.76 and 1.77). Photo courtesy of Dr. Robert Ridley, College of Veterinary Medicine, Kansas State University, Manhattan, KS.

Fig. 1.76. Examination of the surface of the shell wall of small-animal capillarid eggs can be used in making a specific identification. With the high-dry objective (40×) of the microscope, the surface of the *Eucoleus aerophilus* egg has a network of interconnecting ridges. The surface of the shell wall of *E. boehmi* (not pictured) is pitted, giving a stippled appearance.

PARASITE: *Aonchotheca* (=*Capillaria*) *putorii* (Fig. 1.77)

Taxonomy: Nematode (order Enoplida).

Geographic Distribution: North America, Europe, and New Zealand,

Location in Host: Small intestine and stomach of the cat, raccoon, and various wild felids and mustelids.

Life Cycle: Definitive hosts are infected following ingestion of larvated eggs. Adults develop in the gastrointestinal tract and produce eggs that are passed in the feces.

Laboratory Diagnosis: Eggs are detected by centrifugal or simple fecal flotation examination. The yellow-gray eggs are asymmetrical about the bipolar plugs. The sides of the eggs tend to be parallel. The shell wall surface has a network of deep longitudinal ridges.

   Size: 56–72 × 23–32 μm

Clinical Importance: Infections in cats are usually subclinical and are uncommon in North America. Gastritis with vomiting can occur. Hemorrhagic enteritis can occur in mink.

PARASITE: *Physaloptera* spp. (Figs. 1.78 and 1.79)

Taxonomy: Nematode (order Spirurida). Several species have been described (*P. praeputialis, P. felidis, P. pseudopraeputialis, P. rara, P. canis*).

Geographic Distribution: Worldwide.

Location in Host: Stomach of dogs, cats, and various wild animals.

Life Cycle: Cockroach, beetle, or cricket intermediate hosts ingest eggs shed in dog or cat feces. The definitive host is infected by ingesting the insect intermediate host or a paratenic host (reptiles and possibly other animals).

Laboratory Diagnosis: Eggs of this group of nematodes are not reliably detected by fecal flotation due to their density. *Physaloptera* eggs are best detected by fecal sedimentation. The eggs are clear and elliptical, have a smooth shell wall, and contain a larva coiled inside.

   Size: 42–53 × 29–35 μm

Clinical Importance: This common parasite of several wild animal species is considered of minor clinical significance in dogs and cats. Infections may result in clinical signs of vomiting and anorexia.

Fig. 1.77. Eggs of *Aonchotheca putorii* are similar to those of other capillarids (A), but in contrast to the ridges of the *Eucoleus aerophilus* egg, the shell surface of *A. putorii* consists of a network of deep longitudinal ridges (B).

Fig. 1.78. *Physaloptera* eggs do not float consistently in routine flotation exams. The eggs are larger and less elongated than those of *Spirocerca* (Fig. 1.80). *Physaloptera* eggs are smaller and have a thicker shell than larvated hookworm eggs, with which they might be confused. Photo courtesy of Dr. Robert Ridley, College of Veterinary Medicine, Kansas State University, Manhattan, KS.

Fig. 1.79. Adult *Physaloptera* may be seen with gastroscopy in cases where routine fecal flotation does not detect the parasite eggs. Several worms can be seen on the surface of this canine stomach. Photo courtesy of Dr. Michael Leib, Virginia-Maryland Regional College of Veterinary Medicine, Virginia Tech, Blacksburg, VA.

PARASITE: *Spirocerca lupi* (Fig. 1.80)
Common name: Esophageal worm.

Taxonomy: Nematode (order Spirurida).

Geographic Distribution: Worldwide but primarily in warmer regions.

Location in Host: Adults are found in the wall of the esophagus, stomach, and, rarely, aorta of dogs, wild canids, and various other wild animals.

Life Cycle: Dung beetle intermediate hosts ingest eggs in feces. The definitive host is infected by ingesting the insect intermediate host or a paratenic host (rodents, other mammals, birds, reptiles).

Laboratory Diagnosis: Eggs are best detected by fecal sedimentation or (less reliably) by fecal flotation. The eggs are narrow, ellipsoidal, and cylindrical; have a smooth, clear shell wall; and contain a fully developed larva coiled inside.

Size: 30–38 × 11–15 μm

Clinical Importance: Infections are often subclinical. The most common clinical signs are dysphagia and regurgitation, but aortic stenosis, aneurysm, esophageal rupture, or obstruction, cachexia, and esophageal sarcomas may occur. *Spirocerca* infection is uncommon in the United States.

PARASITE: *Strongyloides stercoralis* (Figs. 1.21, 1.22, 1.81, 1.82)
Common name: Intestinal threadworm

Taxonomy: Nematode (order Rhabditida).

Geographic Distribution: Worldwide.

Location in Host: Adult females live in the canine small intestine.

Life Cycle: *Strongyloides* parthenogenetic females in the small intestine release larvae that may develop into infective parasitic larvae or, alternatively, may undergo a single free-living cycle of maturation and reproduction before infective parasitic larvae are formed. Infection of the host from the environment is primarily through skin penetration. Transmammary transmission may also occur if the dog is newly infected during lactation.

Laboratory Diagnosis: First-stage larvae may be identified in fresh feces using a Baermann test. *Strongyloides* larvae do not have the modifications of the tail seen in most lungworm larvae. They closely resemble hatched hookworm larvae or free-living nematodes that may be present in fecal samples that have been allowed to sit for a period of time prior to collection (see section on identification of nematode larvae collected by Baermann exam, which is at the beginning of this chapter). If identification of the first-stage larvae is uncertain, larvae in the feces can be cultured for a few days, and the third-stage larvae can be identified.

Size: 150–390 μm in fresh feces. *Strongyloides* larvae can grow quickly in the environment and their size increases before the molt to the second larval stage. This results in a large size range for the larvae. In addition, the size range may be increased by the mistaken identification and measurement of larger second-stage larvae.

Clinical Importance: Infections may be subclinical, but heavy infection can produce respiratory signs from migrating larvae as well as enteritis associated with adults. *Strongyloides stercoralis* also infects humans and may produce severe and even fatal infections in immunocompromised humans. The degree to which canine strains infect humans is unclear, but because of the seriousness of some human cases, infection in dogs should be considered a zoonosis.

Fig. 1.80. *Spirocerca* eggs do not float consistently in common flotation solutions. These larvated eggs are more elongated than *Physaloptera* eggs. Photo courtesy of Dr. Isabelle Verzberger-Epshtein, NRC Institute for Nutrisciences and Health, Charlottetown, PEI, Canada.

Fig. 1.81. *Strongyloides* first-stage larva. In a fresh fecal sample *Strongyloides* larvae need to be differentiated from larvae of lungworm species. A prominent genital rudiment (*inset*) and a straight tail lacking accessory spines are helpful in identifying first-stage *Strongyloides* larvae.

Fig. 1.82. To confirm identification of *S. stercoralis*, the fecal sample can be cultured for 2–4 days and examined for third-stage larvae, which have a distinctively long esophagus (*arrow indicates junction of esophagus and intestine*) that is not seen in lungworm or hookworm larvae.

PARASITE: *Aelurostrongylus abstrusus* (Figs. 1.83 and 1.84)

Taxonomy: Nematode (order Strongylida).

Geographic Distribution: Worldwide.

Location in Host: Lung parenchyma (terminal respiratory bronchioles, alveolar ducts) of cats and rarely dogs.

Life Cycle: First-stage larvae are released in the airways, coughed up, swallowed, and passed out in the feces. Cats are infected by ingesting a snail or slug intermediate host or paratenic hosts (rodents, birds).

Laboratory Diagnosis: First-stage larvae are detected in feces using the Baermann technique (most reliable) or by $ZnSO_4$ centrifugal flotation. The first-stage larval tail has a severe kink (S-shaped curve) and a dorsal spine.

Size: 360–400 × 15–20 µm

Clinical Importance: Infrequently diagnosed; infected animals may suffer signs of chronic cough and anorexia. Heavy infection may be fatal.

PARASITE: *Crenosoma vulpis* (Figs. 1.21, 1.23, 1.85)

Taxonomy: Nematode (order Strongylida).

Geographic Distribution: Northeastern North America and Europe.

Location in Host: Bronchioles, bronchi, and trachea of dogs, foxes, and various wild carnivores.

Life Cycle: Canid definitive hosts are infected by ingestion of slug/terrestrial snail intermediate hosts containing third-stage larvae. Larvae produced in the respiratory system by adult worms are coughed up, swallowed, and passed from the host in feces.

Laboratory Diagnosis: Detection of first-stage larvae in feces using the Baermann technique (most reliable) or by $ZnSO_4$ centrifugal fecal flotation. First-stage larvae tend to assume a C shape when they are killed by gentle heat or iodine. The terminus of the tail has a slight deflection but does not show the kink and spine seen in other nematode lungworms.

Size: 264–340 × 16–22 µm

Clinical Importance: *Crenosoma vulpis* infection in dogs produces a nonfatal chronic cough. Canine infection is generally rare in North America, except in the Atlantic Canadian provinces, where crenosomosis is a frequent cause of chronic respiratory disease.

Fig. 1.83. *Aelurostrongylus* larva in a feline fecal sample. Larvae have the distinctive S-shaped kink at the end of the tail that is typical of many members of this group of lungworms. These larvae also show a subterminal spine (Fig. 1.84).

Fig. 1.84. Detail of the tail of *Aelurotrongylus abstrusus* larva showing its characteristic subterminal spine that would be absent in other larvae found in feline feces. For further information on identification of lungworm larvae, see the section in this chapter "Identification of Nematode Larvae Recovered with Fecal Flotation or Baermann Procedures."

Fig. 1.85. The tail of *Crenosoma* larvae has a slight deflection but lacks a definite kink or dorsal spine, allowing it to be differentiated from *Aleurostrongylus*, *Angiostrongylus*, and *Filaroides* and *Oslerus*. Larvae of *Crenosoma* can be differentiated from those of *Strongyloides* based on the morphology of the esophagus (Fig. 1.23).

PARASITE: ***Angiostrongylus vasorum*** (Figs. 1.86 and 1.87)
Common name: French heartworm.

Taxonomy: Nematode (order Strongylida).

Geographic Distribution: Canada (Newfoundland), Europe, South America, Africa.

Location in Host: Pulmonary arteries, right ventricle of dogs and foxes.

Life Cycle: First-stage larvae are passed in canine feces, and slugs, snails, and frogs act as inter-mediate hosts of the parasite. Frogs also serve as paratenic hosts. Dogs and foxes are infected when they ingest intermediate hosts or paratenic hosts.

Laboratory Diagnosis: First-stage larvae in fresh feces are detected using the Baermann technique (most reliable) or fecal flotation. The larvae have a cephalic button on the anterior end, and there is a severe kink (S-shaped curve) in the tail, which has a dorsal spine.

Size: 340–399 × 13–17 μm

Clinical Importance: The parasite is a serious pathogen of dogs, causing potentially fatal cardio-pulmonary disease. Ocular and central nervous system disease and bleeding disorders have also been reported.

PARASITE: ***Oslerus (=Filaroides) osleri*** (Fig. 1.88)

Taxonomy: Nematode (order Strongylida). Two other closely related species (*Filaroides hirthi, F. milksi*) occur in the respiratory system of dogs but are rare and even more rarely cause disease.

Geographic Distribution: Worldwide.

Location in Host: Lumenal nodules in the tracheal bifurcation in dogs, coyotes, wolves, dingoes, and foxes.

Life Cycle: Infection follows ingestion of first-stage larvae from sputum or vomitus of an infected dog or other canid. This life cycle varies from that of other strongylid lungworms because the first larval stage is infective for the definitive host. Typically, the third larval stage is the infective form.

Laboratory Diagnosis: Diagnosis is best achieved by visual observation of the nodules on tracheal endoscopic examination. First-stage larvae may be detected in feces by $ZnSO_4$ centrifugal flotation or in transtracheal wash samples. The Baermann technique is *not* the method of choice because larvae passed in the feces are usually moribund or dead. The tail of the first-stage larva has an S-shaped sinus wave curve but lacks a dorsal spine. The first-stage larvae of *O. osleri* are indistin-guishable from those of *F. hirthi*.

Size:	Larvae recovered from feces	232–266 μm
	Larvae recovered from trachea	325–378 μm

Clinical Importance: This is an uncommon infection in dogs in North America. Younger animals tend to be more severely affected than older ones. Respiratory distress, chronic cough, and weight loss can occur. Heavily infected animals may die.

Fig. 1.86. *Angiostrongylus vasorum* first-stage larva. This species is uncommon in North America. Larvae can be differentiated from those of and *Oslerus* in canine feces by the presence of the subterminal dorsal spine.

Fig. 1.87. High-magnification view of *Angiostrongylus vasorum* first-stage larva tail showing the S-shaped curve and the dorsal spine. The tail of *Aelurostrongylus abstrusus* (Fig. 1.84) is similar in appearance.

Fig. 1.88. First-stage *Oslerus* larva in dog feces. The larvae have a kinked tail, but the accessory spine seen in *Aleurostrongylus* and *Angiostrongylus* larvae is not present. Photo courtesy of Dr. Jeffrey F. Williams, Vanson HaloSource, Inc., Redmond, WA.

71

PARASITE: ***Ollulanus tricuspis*** (Fig. 1.89)

Taxonomy: Nematode (order Strongylida).

Geographic Distribution: Europe, North America, parts of South America, Australia.

Location in Host: Adult worms are found in the stomach of cats and other felids.

Life Cycle: Adult female worms in the stomach produce third-stage larvae that primarily leave the host in vomitus. Infection of cats occurs through ingestion of these larvae in vomitus.

Laboratory Diagnosis: Infection is diagnosed by identification of larvae or the small adults in vomitus, using the Baermann test. Rarely, stages of the parasite may be seen in feces, but they are usually digested before reaching the environment.

Size:	Third-stage larvae	500 µm
	Adults	700–1000 µm

Clinical Importance: Infection can cause chronic gastritis and vomiting in cats. Colony and feral cats are most often infected.

PARASITE: ***Dipylidium caninum*** (Figs. 1.90, 1.91, 1.94, 1.97, 1.98)
         Common name: Double-pored or cucumber seed or flea tapeworm.

Taxonomy: Cestode.

Geographic Distribution: Worldwide.

Location in Host: Small intestine of dogs and cats.

Life Cycle: Animals acquire infection through the ingestion of larval cysticercoids contained in fleas or, less frequently, in chewing lice (*Trichodectes, Felicola*). Arthropod intermediate hosts become infected by the ingestion of egg packets/segments.

Laboratory Diagnosis: Tapeworm segments in the perianal area or in feces are often observed by owners. Specific diagnosis is made by identification of egg packets recovered from segments. Occasionally, eggs and/or egg packets are detected on fecal flotation examinations. Egg packets contain 2–63 eggs (average of 25–30 eggs).

Size:	Egg packets	120–200 µm
	Eggs	35–60 µm

Clinical Importance: Infections of this common tapeworm are generally subclinical; however, the passage of segments from the rectum may induce anal pruritis. *Dipylidium caninum* is zoonotic, with young children at greatest risk of acquiring infections from ingesting the infected flea or louse intermediate host.

Fig. 1.89. Adult male *Ollulanus tricuspis* in a fecal sample. Larvae and adult worms are only rarely present in feces. Vomitus should be examined to diagnose infection. These worms can easily be differentiated from ascarids that may be vomited up by cats. The ascarid worms are several inches in length, while *Ollulanus* adults only reach a maximum length of 1 mm. Photo courtesy of Dr. Robert Ridley, College of Veterinary Medicine, Kansas State University, Manhattan, KS.

Fig. 1.90. *Dipylidium caninum* eggs containing a hexacanth embryo occur in packets of about 25–30 eggs. The hooks are readily visible inside the eggs shown here. (Conboy, Gary. Cestodes of Dogs and Cats in North America. Veterinary Clinics of North America: Small Animal Practice. Elsevier, 2009.).

Fig. 1.91. Occasionally, *Dipylidium* eggs are released from the packets and may be detected individually on fecal flotation. Note the clear, thin shell wall of the egg and the refractile hooks (*arrow*) of the embryo.

PARASITE: *Taenia* **spp.** (Figs. 1.92–1.95, 1.97, 1.98)

Taxonomy: Cestode. Numerous species infect small animals, including *T. taeniaeformis* in cats and *T. pisiformis*, *T. multiceps*, *T. hydatigena*, *T. ovis* in dogs.

Geographic Distribution: Worldwide.

Location in Host: Small intestine of dogs, cats, and various wild carnivores.

Life Cycle: Carnivores acquire infections through the ingestion of the immature metacestode stage (morphologic forms include cysticerci, coenuri, and strobilocerci) in the tissues of prey animals. Prey animals become infected with the metacestode through the ingestion of food contaminated with eggs passed in carnivore feces.

Laboratory Diagnosis: Eggs are detected when free in the feces by flotation techniques. Generally, however, eggs are passed from the host contained in tapeworm segments. Therefore, fecal flotation tends to be a poor indicator of infection status.

   Size: 25–40 µm in diameter

Clinical Importance: Infections in the definitive host are generally subclinical; however, the passage of segments from the rectum may induce anal pruritis. *Taenia taeniaeformis* (small-rodent intermediate host) and *T. pisiformis* (rabbit intermediate host) are common species infecting pet cats and dogs, respectively. Metacestode infection in the intermediate hosts can cause disease (*T. multiceps*) or meat condemnation (*T. ovis*).

Fig. 1.92. *Taenia* eggs are brown with a thick shell wall (embryophore) and contain a hexacanth embryo (six hooks). Note the radial striations in the wall of the egg.

Fig. 1.93. Eggs of *Eucoleus* (E), *Toxocara* (To), and *Taenia* (Ta) and oocysts of *Isospora* (I) in a feline fecal sample. Photo courtesy of Dr. Robert Ridley, College of Veterinary Medicine, Kansas State University, Manhattan, KS.

Fig. 1.94. Tapeworm segments from an animal can usually be easily identified as such by squashing the segment between two slides and identifying the eggs. Sometimes, however, segments are passed that contain no eggs. These can still be identified as segments by squashing them and observing the numerous small, round, transparent bodies, called "calcareous corpuscles."

PARASITE: ***Echinococcus* spp.** (Figs. 1.92–1.95, 1.97, 1.98)
Common name: Dwarf dog or fox tapeworm.

Taxonomy: Cestode. *Echinococcus granulosus* and *E. multilocularis* infect dogs and wild canids. Cats are infrequently infected with *E. multilocularis*.

Geographic Distribution: *Echinococcus granulosus* is found worldwide; *E. multilocularis* occurs in the United States, Canada, and in parts of Europe and Asia.

Location in Host: Small intestine.

Life Cycle: Carnivores acquire infections through the ingestion of metacestodes (hydatids) in the tissues of prey animals. Prey animals become infected with the metacestode through the ingestion of eggs passed in carnivore feces.

Laboratory Diagnosis: Like the eggs of *Taenia*, *Echinococcus* eggs have a thick shell wall with radial striations (embryophore). The six hooks of the hexacanth embryo allow it to be distinguished from pollen grains or other debris. The eggs of *Taenia* and *Echinococcus* are morphologically identical.

Size: 25–40 µm in diameter

Clinical Importance: Infections in the definitive host are subclinical. *Echinococcus* spp. are important due to their zoonotic potential. Human infection with hydatid cysts can cause serious disease and death. In some countries, particularly in rural areas, hydatid disease can be an important public health problem. In most areas of North America, canine infection and human hydatid disease are rare.

PARASITE: ***Mesocestoides* spp.** (Figs. 1.96–1.98)

Taxonomy: Cestode. Species include *M. corti*, *M. lineatus*, *M. variabilis*.

Geographic Distribution: Worldwide.

Location in Host: Small intestine of dogs, cats, various wild mammals, and birds.

Life Cycle: The life cycle is not completely known. Dogs and cats acquire infections through ingestion of tetrathyridia contained in the tissues of various reptiles, amphibia, birds, and mammal intermediate hosts. Eggs are passed in motile segments in the feces of infected dogs and cats. The first intermediate host and the form of the first larval stage of *Mesocestoides* are unknown.

Laboratory Diagnosis: Club-shaped segments are passed in the feces. Eggs are contained in a round parauterine organ at the broad end of the segment. Eggs are rarely found free in the feces of definitive hosts but would, presumably, be detected by fecal flotation.

Size: Eggs 30–40 µm in diameter

Clinical Importance: Infection of the definitive host with the adult tapeworm is usually subclinical. Fatal peritonitis due to large numbers of tetrathyridia or acephalic metacestodes has been reported in dogs acting as hosts to the larval stages.

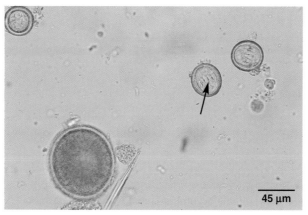

Fig. 1.95. Embryonic hooks are visible in the two *Taenia* or *Echinococcus* eggs in this photo (*arrow*). Hooks can be used to differentiate tapeworm eggs from similar artifacts like pollen grains. The eggs of *Taenia* and *Echinococcus* are morphologically identical. A *Toxocara* egg is also present.

Fig. 1.96. *Mesocestoides* eggs have a thin, clear, smooth shell wall and contain a hexacanth embryo. The hooks of the embryo are readily visible.

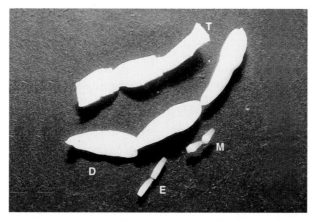

Fig. 1.97. Mature tapeworm segments passed in the feces may be observed by owners and presented for identification. The size and shape of these segments are quite characteristic: *Taenia* segments (T) are square to rectangular in shape, *Dipylidium* segments (D) are more barrel shaped, and *Mesocestoides* has club-shaped segments (M). Both *Mesocestoides* and *Echinococcus* (E) segments are small and are often overlooked. Identification can be confirmed by examining eggs from the segments.

PARASITE: ***Diphyllobothrium latum*** (Fig. 1.99)
Common name: Broad fish tapeworm.

Taxonomy: Cestode. Dogs and cats can also be infected with *D. dendriticum*.

Geographic Distribution: Northern Hemisphere and South America.

Location in Host: Small intestine of dogs, cats, pigs, humans, and various other fish-eating mammals.

Life Cycle: Eggs passed in the feces of the final host hatch coracidia, which are ingested by freshwater copepods (first intermediate hosts). Fish eat the copepods containing the next larval stage (procercoids), which develop into the plerocercoids (infective stage) in the fish. Predatory fish can acquire plerocercoids through ingestion of infected smaller fish. Mammalian definitive hosts acquire infections through the ingestion of plerocercoids contained in the tissues of fish.

Laboratory Diagnosis: The eggs can be detected in feces using a sedimentation technique. Lengths of reproductively spent segments are occasionally passed in the feces.

Size: Eggs 58–76 × 40–51 μm

Clinical Importance: Uncommon in pets in North America. Infections are generally subclinical in dogs and cats. Dogs and cats do not serve as direct sources of infection for humans. Human infection with this tapeworm may lead to the development of vitamin B_{12} deficiency.

PARASITE: ***Spirometra*** spp. (Fig. 1.100)
Common name: Zipper tapeworm.

Taxonomy: Cestode.

Geographic Distribution: *Spirometra mansonoides* occurs in North and South America, and *S. erinaceieuropaei* occurs in Europe and Asia.

Location in Host: Small intestine of cats, dogs, and wild animals.

Life Cycle: Dogs and cats acquire infections by the ingestion of frogs, snakes, rodents, or birds containing plerocercoids (known as spargana). Eggs passed in the feces of dogs and cats hatch coracidia, which are eaten by freshwater copepods and develop into procercoids. The second intermediate hosts (frogs, snakes, etc.) acquire plerocercoids by feeding on the copepods.

Laboratory Diagnosis: The yellow-brown eggs can be detected in feces using a sedimentation technique but are also often recovered in flotation procedures. Lengths of reproductively spent segments are occasionally passed in the feces.

Size: Eggs 65–70 × 35–37 μm

Clinical Importance: Infections in the definitive hosts are usually subclinical. Cats can also serve as a paratenic host, with plerocercoids surviving in various tissues (sparganosis) and causing clinical signs depending on their location.

Fig. 1.98. Within hours of passing from the host, tapeworm segments lose their motility and dry up. Clients may find dried tapeworm segments in resting areas of dogs and cats. The dried segments still retain their characteristic shape. Shown in this photo are *Taenia* (T), *Echinococcus* (E), *Dipylidium* (D), and *Mesocestoides* (M) segments.

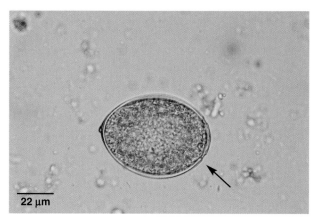

Fig. 1.99. Unlike common tapeworms, *Diphyllobothrium* eggs lack hooks and resemble trematode eggs. They are light brown and operculate (*arrow*). They contain an undifferentiated embryo surrounded by yolk cells that completely fill the space within the eggshell. A pore in the shell wall at the pole opposite to the operculum is often visible due to the slight bit of protein protruding from it.

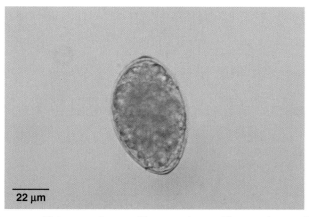

Fig. 1.100. The operculate eggs of *Spirometra* also resemble trematode eggs. They contain an undifferentiated embryo and yolk cells that completely fill the space within the eggshell. The eggs are asymmetrical about the long axis. The operculum in this egg is at the lower end.

PARASITE: *Alaria* **spp.** (Figs. 1.101–1.103)

Taxonomy: Trematode.

Geographic Distribution: Worldwide.

Location in Host: Small intestine of dogs, cats, and various wild carnivores.

Life Cycle: Eggs are passed in the feces of the mammalian host. Following larval development in a snail intermediate host, a second intermediate host (frog) is infected. Infection of dogs and cats occurs by ingestion of frogs or various paratenic hosts harboring the larval stage (mesocercaria). Transmammary transmission has been reported in cats.

Laboratory Diagnosis: The most reliable method is detection of eggs by sedimentation examination of feces, although sometimes eggs may be detected on fecal flotation.

Size: 98–134 × 62–68 µm

Clinical Importance: Infections are generally nonpathogenic in dogs and cats. *Alaria* is a potentially serious zoonotic risk to humans through the ingestion of raw or improperly cooked frogs containing mesocercaria.

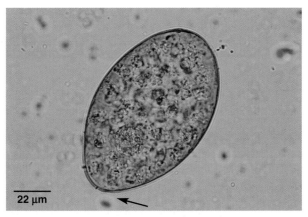

Fig. 1.101. *Alaria* eggs are large, operculate, yellow-brown in color and contain an undifferentiated embryo surrounded by yolk cells. The operculum in this egg is difficult to see but is marked by a discontinuity in the shell (*arrow*).

Fig. 1.102. Sometimes *Alaria* spp. eggs are detected using the centrifugal flotation technique; however, egg morphology may be altered: the eggs appear collapsed or folded due to the osmotic pressure associated with the high specific gravity of the flotation solution.

Fig. 1.103. The large size of *Alaria* spp. eggs is evident in this fecal sample containing eggs of *Alaria* (*arrow*), *Toxocara*, and *Ancylostoma*.

PARASITE: *Paragonimus kellicotti* (Fig. 1.104)

Taxonomy: Trematode.

Geographic Distribution: North America. Other similar species of *Paragonimus* that infect domestic animals, humans, and wildlife occur in South and Central America, Africa, and Asia.

Location in Host: Lung parenchyma of cats, dogs, pigs, goats, minks, and various other wild mammals.

Life Cycle: Snails are infected by the larval stage emerging from eggs released in the feces of definitive hosts. Crayfish serve as the second intermediate host. Dogs and cats acquire infection by ingesting the metacercaria in the tissues of crayfish or paratenic hosts.

Laboratory Diagnosis: A sedimentation technique (recommended) or fecal flotation (less reliable) can be used to detect the yellow-brown, operculate eggs, which have a thickened ridge in the shell wall along the line of the operculum.

Size: 75–118 × 42–67 μm

Clinical Importance: Infection may be subclinical or cause eosinophilic bronchitis and granulomatous pneumonia, resulting in chronic cough and lethargy. Infections can be fatal.

PARASITE: *Heterobilharzia americana* (Figs. 1.105 and 1.106)

Taxonomy: Trematode.

Geographic Distribution: Southeastern United States.

Location in Host: Mesenteric and hepatic portal veins of dogs and various wildlife species.

Life Cycle: Eggs released in the feces of dogs produce ciliated larvae (miracidia) that develop in a snail intermediate host. Cercariae that are released from the snail intermediate host infect dogs and wildlife through direct skin penetration.

Laboratory Diagnosis: Eggs can be detected by sedimentation examination of feces in saline (or 5% formol-saline). It is important to use saline in the procedure because eggs are stimulated to hatch when they contact water. The free-swimming miracidia larvae can be observed by placing the sediment in water after performing the sedimentation procedure with saline.

Size: Eggs 74–113 × 60–80 μm

Clinical Importance: Infection with *H. americana* in dogs is uncommon in most areas. Infection can cause chronic diarrhea, anorexia, and emaciation. *Heterobilharzia* also has zoonotic importance as one of the causal agents of cercarial dermatitis (swimmer's itch) in humans.

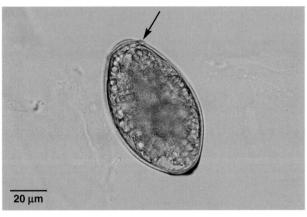

20 μm

Fig. 1.104. *Paragonimus* eggs are undifferentiated when passed in the feces. The yellow-brown, operculate eggs can be differentiated by the characteristic thickened ridge in the shell wall along the line of the operculum (*arrow*). Collapsed eggs may be seen in flotation preparations.

34 μm

Fig. 1.105. The large, elliptical eggs of *Heterobilharzia americana* have a smooth, thin shell wall and contain a fully formed miracidium. The shell wall of the egg lacks an operculum. Photo courtesy of Dr. Bruce Hammerberg and Dr. James Flowers, College of Veterinary Medicine, North Carolina State University, Raleigh, NC.

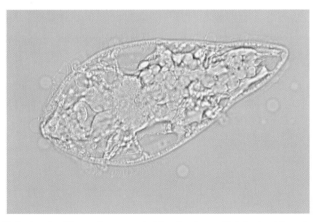

Fig. 1.106. On contact with freshwater, *H. americana* eggs hatch, releasing a ciliated miracidium stage. To prevent hatching of the eggs, a sedimentation procedure for diagnosis should be performed using saline instead of water. Photo courtesy of Dr. Bruce Hammerburg and Dr. James Flowers, College of Veterinary Medicine, North Carolina State University, Raleigh, NC.

PARASITE: ***Nanophyetus salmincola*** (Fig. 1.107)
Common name: Salmon poisoning fluke.

Taxonomy: Trematode.

Geographic Distribution: Pacific Northwest region of North America.

Location in Host: Small intestine of dogs, cats, and various other piscivorous carnivores.

Life Cycle: Dogs and cats are infected by the ingestion of metacercariae in the tissues of salmonid fish (second intermediate hosts). Snails serve as the first intermediate host.

Laboratory Diagnosis: Eggs can be detected by sedimentation examination of feces.

Size: 72–97 × 35–55 μm

Clinical Importance: *Nanophyetus salmincola* serves as a vector for the causal agent of salmon poisoning disease (*Neorickettsia helminthoeca*) and Elokomin fluke fever (*Neorickettsia* sp.). Salmon poisoning disease is extremely pathogenic in dogs.

PARASITE: ***Platynosomum concinnum*** (Figs. 1.108 and 1.109)

Taxonomy: Trematode.

Geographic Distribution: Southeastern United States, South America, West Africa. Other flukes that may be found in the bile or pancreatic ducts in North America include *Eurytrema procyonis* and *Fasciola hepatica*.

Location in Host: Gall bladder and bile ducts of cats.

Life Cycle: Adult worms produce eggs that are passed in the feces of cats. The life cycle is complex, involving snail, crustacean, and amphibian or reptile intermediate hosts. Cats are infected following ingestion of lizards or amphibians containing larvae.

Laboratory Diagnosis: A sedimentation procedure is most effective for recovering the relatively small, operculate eggs of *Platynosomum*.

Size: 34–50 × 20–35 μm

Clinical Significance: Light infections are asymptomatic. Heavily infected cats may show signs of weight loss and hepatomegaly.

Fig. 1.107. The operculated eggs of *Nanophyetus* contain an undifferentiated embryo surrounded by yolk cells.

Fig. 1.108. The small brown eggs of *Platynosomum* have an operculum at one end, contain a fully formed miracidium, and may not be seen with routine flotation procedures.

Fig. 1.109. Cats in the eastern United States are rarely infected with the pancreatic fluke *Eurytrema procyonis* and their eggs may be detected in feces. Small brown eggs can be seen within the body of this adult pancreatic fluke.

PARASITE: *Cryptocotyle lingua* (Fig. 1.110)

Taxonomy: Trematode.

Geographic Distribution: Worldwide in northern temperate marine coastal regions.

Location in Host: Intestine.

Life Cycle: Snails are infected by larval stages emerging from eggs released in the feces of infected definitive hosts. Fish serve as the second intermediate host. Dogs, cats, and birds become infected by ingesting metacercariae, visible as small black spots on the skin of fish.

Laboratory Diagnosis: A sedimentation technique (recommended) or fecal flotation (less reliable) can be used to detect these small, undifferentiated, yellow-brown, operculate eggs. The eggs are elliptical shaped with one end narrower than the other. The operculum occurs at the narrower end and is difficult to see.

Size: 32–50 × 18–25 µm

Clinical Significance: Clinical disease due to infection with this intestinal fluke appears to be rare. Enteritis may occur in cases of heavy infections. Cats appear to be less susceptible to infection.

Dogs and cats may also be rarely infected with acanthocephalan (*Onicola*, *Macracanthorhynchus*) and pentastomid (*Linguatula*) parasites. Eggs of parasites belonging to these groups are shown in Figures 1.185 and 1.233.

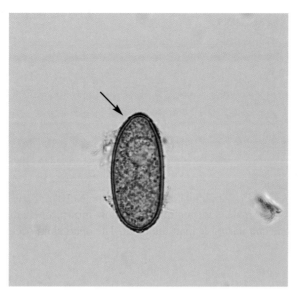

Fig. 1.110. *Cryptocotyle lingua* egg detected on fecal sedimentation of feces from a dog. The operculum of *Cryprocotyle* is difficult to see; it occurs on the narrower pole of the egg (*arrow*). The eggs are undifferentiated when passed in the feces.

Helminth Ova, Larva and Protozoan Cysts
as found in freshly voided feces of
Cattle

ASCARID OVUM

EUCESTODA OVA

Toxocara vitulorum

Moniezia benedeni

Moniezia expansa

OPERCULATED OVA

Dicrocoelium dendriticum

(Fluke Ova Without
Obvious Operculum)

Fascioloides magna

100 μm

Fasciola hepatica

OVA WITH BIPOLAR PLUGS

LARVATED OVUM

Strongyloides papillosus

Trichuris spp.

Capillaria spp. *

MORULATED OVA

'Strongyle' Type Ova

Bunostomum phlebotomum

LARVAL NEMATODE

Nematodirus spp.

PROTOZOA

Eimeria zuernii

Eimeria bovis

Eimeria
auburnensis

Giardia sp.

Cryptosporidium sp.

Dictyocaulus viviparus

ILLUSTRATED BY GARY A. AVERBECK

Fig. 1.111. Common parasites found in bovine feces. *Capillaria* has been reclassified as *Aoncotheca*. Figure courtesy of Dr. Bert Stromberg and Mr. Gary Averbeck, College of Veterinary Medicine, University of Minnesota, Minneapolis, MN.

Helminth Ova, Larva and Protozoan Cysts
as found in freshly voided feces of
Sheep and Goats

OVA WITH BIPOLAR PLUGS

Capillaria spp.

Trichuris spp.

OPERCULATED OVA

100 μm

Dicrocoelium dendriticum

(Fluke Ova Without Obvious Operculum)

Fasciola hepatica

Nematodirus spp.

LARVATED OVA

Strongyloides papillosus

Skrjabinema spp.

MORULATED OVA

'Strongyle' Type Ova

LARVAL NEMATODES

Muellerius capillaris

Protostrongylus spp.

Dictyocaulus filaria

PROTOZOA

EUCESTODA OVA

Moniezia expansa

Thysanosoma actinoides

Eimeria arloingi (Goat)

Eimeria alijevi (Goat)

Eimeria christenseni (Goat)

Eimeria ovinoidalis (Sheep)

Eimeria ahsata (Sheep)

ILLUSTRATED BY GARY A. AVERBECK

Fig. 1.112. Common parasites found in feces of sheep and goats. Figure courtesy of Dr. Bert Stromberg and Mr. Gary Averbeck, College of Veterinary Medicine, University of Minnesota, Minneapolis, MN.

Protozoan Parasites

PARASITE: *Eimeria* **spp.** (Figs. 1.113–1.121, 1.27, 1.131, 1.136)
Common name: Coccidia.

Taxonomy: Protozoa (coccidia).

Geographic Distribution: Worldwide.

Location in Host: Many host-specific species of *Eimeria* infect the intestinal tract of domestic ruminants and camelids.

Life Cycle: Fecal oocysts sporulate in the environment and infect intestinal cells following ingestion. Asexual and sexual reproduction is followed by the production of oocysts that exit the host in manure. Sporulated oocysts can survive for long periods under favorable environmental conditions.

Laboratory Diagnosis: Oocysts are found on routine fecal flotation exam. Species identification is difficult and, in most cases, requires microscopic exam of sporulated (infective) oocysts. Although the number of oocysts in the feces has been used as an indicator of clinical disease, high numbers of oocysts can also be present in the absence of clinical signs.

Size: Approximately 12–45 μm in length (oocyst), depending on species

Clinical Importance: Most ruminants become infected with coccidia at an early age, and low-level infection persists through adulthood. While infection is often subclinical, coccidiosis is a common cause of diarrhea in young ruminants. Signs range from mild diarrhea to severe, bloody diarrhea.

Not all species of *Eimeria* are equally pathogenic. Of 12 species of common bovine *Eimeria*, clinical disease is usually associated with *E. bovis*, *E. zuernii*, or, less commonly, *E. alabamensis*. Similarly, *E. bakuensis*, *E. ahsata*, and *E. ovinoidalis* are pathogenic ovine *Eimeria* species. In goats, *E. airlongi*, *E. caprina*, *E. ninakohlyakimovae*, and *E. christenseni* have been associated with clinical disease. Fewer species of coccidia have been described in camelids than in ruminants, but they all have been reported to cause clinical disease. In the United States, *E. macusaniensis* is considered highly pathogenic in naive animals, including adults.

Fig. 1.113. Ruminants and camelids are infected with a variety of *Eimeria* spp. The oocysts of most of these species are colorless, have a thin wall, and are oval or round. When seen in fresh feces, oocysts contain a single cell.

19 μm

Fig. 1.114. *Eimeria* oocysts undergo sporulation in the environment, resulting in an infective oocyst. Four of the oocysts in this sample are in the four-cell stage, which precedes the development of sporocysts. These oocysts are not infective, because they are not fully sporulated.

Fig. 1.115. In this bovine fecal sample, several fully sporulated *Eimeria* oocysts can be seen. In some cases, examination of the sporulated oocyst is required for confirmation of identification of the *Eimeria* species. In most clinical cases, specific identification is not performed. Photo courtesy of Dr. Aaron Lucas, Virginia-Maryland Regional College of Veterinary Medicine, Virginia Tech, Blacksburg, VA.

27 μm

24 µm

Fig. 1.116. Many, but not all, *Eimeria* species have a cap that covers the micropyle, which can be seen at the upper end of this oocyst. The micropyle cap, if present, is helpful in identifying the genus in dogs that have eaten feces of other animal species. The photo shows the oocyst of *Eimeria intricata*, a parasite of sheep. The oocyst is brown and larger than other ovine *Eimeria*.

Z

B

S

C

35 µm

Fig. 1.117. Oocysts of four species of bovine coccidia are seen in this photo: *Eimeria bovis* (B), *E. subspherica* (S), *E. zuernii* (Z), and *E. cylindrical/ellipsoidalis* (C). *Eimeria bovis* and *E. zuernii* are considered the most pathogenic species and are commonly seen in cattle. Unsporulated oocysts of *E. cylindrical* and *E. ellipsoidalis* cannot be distinguished. Photo courtesy of Dr. Aaron Lucas, Virginia-Maryland Regional College of Veterinary Medicine, Virginia Tech, Blacksburg, VA.

S

P

26 µm

Fig. 1.118. Cattle can be infected with 12 species of *Eimeria*, although only three species are considered pathogenic. This photo illustrates the wide range seen in oocyst size. *Eimera subspherica* (S) is the smallest oocyst (11 µm), and *E. pellita* (P) is one of the largest (40 µm). Photo courtesy of Dr. Aaron Lucas, Virginia-Maryland Regional College of Veterinary Medicine, Virginia Tech, Blacksburg, VA.

Fig. 1.119. Small ruminants are infected with a variety of coccidia species, although few are highly pathogenic. Sheep and goats are considered to be infected by different *Eimeria* spp. (E), although oocysts from the two host species are often indistinguishable. Slightly out of focus in this photo are an egg of *Nematodirus* (N) and a typical strongylid egg (S).

Fig. 1.120. Camelids are hosts to several species of *Eimeria* that produce oocysts similar in appearance to those of common ruminant species. The large brown structures in the photo are probably seeds. The feces of herbivorous animals often contain numerous plant artifacts that can be confused with parasites.

Fig. 1.121. Camelids are also infected with two species of *Eimeria* that produce large brown oocysts that can be confused: *E. macusaniensis* (A) and *E. ivitaensis* (B). The oocysts of *E. macusaniensis* are pear shaped, while those of *E. ivitaensis* are more elongated and elliptical in shape.

93

PARASITE: *Cryptosporidium parvum, C. andersoni* (Fig. 1.122)

Taxonomy: Protozoa (coccidia). The taxonomy of *Cryptosporidium* species is currently undergoing revision.

Geographic Distribution: Worldwide.

Location in Host: *Cryptosporidium parvum* is an intestinal parasite of ruminants, camelids, and other mammals. *Cryptosporidium andersoni* is a parasite of the bovine abomasum and may also infect camelids.

Life Cycle: Ruminants are infected by ingestion of oocysts. Oocysts are infective as soon as they are passed in the manure and are very resistant to environmental conditions.

Laboratory Diagnosis: Very small oocysts are seen with Sheather's sugar centrifugal flotation exam. Fecal smears can also be stained with acid-fast stains or examined by immunodiagnostic techniques. The oocysts of *C. andersoni* are slightly larger than those of *C. parvum*.

| Size: | *C. parvum* | 4–5 µm in diameter |
| | *C. andersoni* | 7×5 µm |

Clinical Importance: Infections with *C. parvum* may be subclinical or cause diarrhea of varying severity in young animals. Some isolates of *C. parvum* can infect both humans and ruminants. *Cryptosporidium andersoni* may cause chronic abomasal infections in cattle, including adults, although it appears to have little economic significance.

PARASITE: **Giardia intestinalis, also identified as G. lamblia, G. duodenalis, G. bovis, etc.** (Figs. 1.123, 1.124, 1.135)

Taxonomy: Protozoa (flagellate). The taxonomy of *Giardia* species is currently undergoing revision. Isolates of the parasite are currently assigned to assemblages based on genetic analysis. Isolates of hoofed stock typically belong to Assemblage E.

Geographic Distribution: Worldwide.

Location in Host: Small intestine of ruminants and camelids.

Life Cycle: *Giardia* cysts passed in the feces infect other animals when ingested in the environment. Following excystation, trophozoites inhabit the small intestine.

Laboratory Diagnosis: Small cysts can be found in fecal samples using centrifugal flotation procedures (33% $ZnSO_4$ flotation solution preferred). Trichrome-stained fecal smears and immunodiagnostic tests can also be used.

| Size: | Cysts | $9–13 \times 7–9$ µm |
| | Trophozoites | $12–17 \times 7–10$ µm |

Clinical Importance: Many animals are infected, particularly when young, but clinical disease is uncommon.

Fig. 1.122. The small oocysts of *Cryptosporidium* are best seen using the high-dry objective (40×) on the microscope. They are highly refractile and often appear to have a single black dot in the center.

Fig. 1.123. Although small, *Giardia* cysts contain internal structures that make them distinctive. A drop of Lugol's iodine on the slide can help in visualizing internal structure. Photo courtesy of Dr. Robert Ridley, College of Veterinary Medicine, Kansas State University, Manhattan, KS.

Fig. 1.124. This fecal sample contains numerous *Giardia* sp. cysts (*arrow*). A strongylid egg is also present in this 40× objective field. Although *Giardia* cysts may be present in large numbers in the feces of ruminants, they are usually not incriminated as a cause of clinical disease.

Helminth Parasites

PARASITE: **Strongylid Parasites of Ruminants and Camelids** (Figs. 1.124–1.128, 1.119, 1.130, 1.131)

Common name: Various, including brown stomach worm, barber pole worm, hookworm, nodular worm, strongyles, trichostrongyles.

Taxonomy: Nematodes (order Strongylida). Numerous genera belong to this group, including *Ostertagia, Haemonchus, Cooperia, Trichostrongylus, Teladorsagia, Mecistocirrus, Oesophagostomum, Bunostomum, Chabertia, Camelostrongylus,* and *Lamanema.*

Geographic Distribution: Worldwide.

Location in Host: Gastrointestinal tract of ruminant and camelid hosts. The genera infecting these hosts are largely the same, although species may vary.

Life Cycle: Adult worms in the gastrointestinal tract produce eggs that develop in manure in the environment. Infective larvae are released onto pasture, where they infect grazing hosts.

Laboratory Diagnosis: Eggs are detected by routine or quantitative fecal flotation procedures. Eggs are similar in appearance and are not easily identified specifically. For diagnosis of genera, culture of feces and identification of infective third-stage larvae are performed. Quantitative egg counts are useful in designing and evaluating parasite control programs.

Size: Approximately 65–100 × 34–50 μm, depending on species

Clinical Importance: Virtually all grazing animals are infected with strongylid parasites, and many infections are asymptomatic. Young, nonimmune animals are most susceptible to subclinical and clinical disease, which may include diarrhea, anemia, hypoproteinemia, reduced growth, and death in severe cases. The species of greatest importance vary with host and region.

Fig. 1.125. The strongylid (also referred to as strongyle or trichostrongyle) egg is the helminth egg seen most often in bovine, small ruminant, and camelid feces. In fresh feces, eggs are thin shelled and oval in shape and contain a grapelike cluster of cells (morula). Development to the first larval stage occurs in the egg, and larvated eggs may be seen in older samples. Identification of eggs to a specific genus or species is not generally considered reliable because of substantial overlap in the sizes and shapes of eggs from different strongylid species.

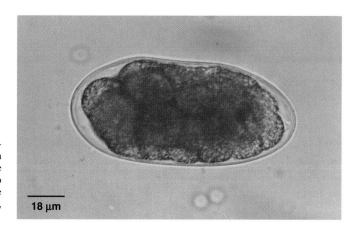

Fig. 1.126. Egg of *Mecistocirrus digitatus*, a parasite of ruminants and pigs in Asia and South America. The parasite produces typical strongylid eggs. Photo courtesy of Dr. Alvin Gajadhar, Centre for Animal Parasitology, CFIA, Saskatoon, Saskatchewan, Canada.

18 μm

Fig. 1.127. Once strongylid eggs are exposed to oxygen and adequate temperature, development to the first larval stage begins. In warm conditions, partially (as seen in this photo) or fully formed larvae may be seen when samples are collected from the ground. In older samples, the eggs will hatch releasing the larvae, which cannot be easily identified.

40 μm

Fig. 1.128. Strongylid eggs must be differentiated from those of *Strongyloides*, an unrelated nematode. *Strongyloides* eggs (*arrow*) are larvated when passed in fresh feces, and they are smaller than strongylid eggs.

38 μm

PARASITE: *Nematodirus* **spp.** (Figs. 1.129–1.131, 1.119)
     Common name: Thread-necked worm.

Taxonomy: Nematode (order Strongylida).

Geographic Distribution: Worldwide.

Location in Host: Several species are found in the small intestine of ruminants and camelids.

Life Cycle: Unlike most other strongylids, larvae develop to the infective stage within the egg. Ruminants are infected when they ingest the hatched infective larvae.

Laboratory Diagnosis: Large eggs present in routine or quantitative fecal flotation exams.

  Size: 152–260 × 67–120 µm, depending on species (a similar egg is produced by *Marshallagia marshalli*, a parasite of sheep in the western United States)

Clinical Importance: Most species of *Nematodirus* do not usually cause clinical disease. *Nematodirus battus*, however, is an important cause of lamb diarrhea in some parts of the world. *Nematodirus* infections may cause disease in young camelids.

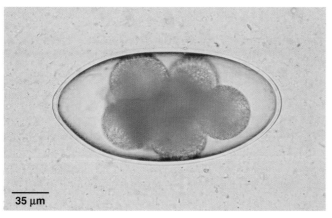

Fig. 1.129. Egg of *Nematodirus* sp. This is one of the few strongylid eggs of ruminants that can be easily identified specifically because of its large size and two to eight distinctive, large cells inside the freshly passed egg. The eggs of *Marshallagia* spp. are similar in size to those of *Nematodirus*. *Marshallagia* spp. are found worldwide, but this genus is less common than *Nematodirus*.

Fig. 1.130. The egg of *Nematodirus battus* (B) is browner than eggs of other *Nematodirus* spp. (N). This sample also contains a typical strongylid egg (S). Photo courtesy of Dr. Gary Zimmerman, Zimmerman Research, Livingston, MT.

Fig. 1.131. Ovine fecal sample containing strongylid eggs (S), a *Nematodirus* sp. egg (N), an *Eimeria intricata* oocyst (I), and *Eimeria* sp. oocysts (E).

PARASITE: ***Trichuris* spp.** (Figs. 1.132 and 1.134)
Common name: Whipworm.

Taxonomy: Nematode (order Enoplida). Several species (*T. ovis*, *T. discolor*, etc.) occur in ruminants.

Geographic Distribution: Worldwide.

Location in Host: Cecum and colon of ruminants and camelids.

Life Cycle: Eggs produced by adults in the large intestine are passed in the feces. After a minimum of 3 weeks in the environment, eggs reach the infective stage and can infect a host when ingested.

Laboratory Diagnosis: Identification of brown, bipolar-plugged eggs in fecal flotation preparations.

Size: 70–80 × 30–42 µm

Clinical Importance: Eggs of *Trichuris* are often found in ruminant fecal samples. Clinical disease (diarrhea) is rare and associated with heavy infection.

PARASITE: ***Aonchotheca* (=*Capillaria*) spp.** (Figs. 1.133–1.135)

Taxonomy: Nematode (order Enoplida). These parasites (*A. bovis* in cattle, *A. longipes* in sheep) were formerly included in the genus *Capillaria*. Camelids are also infected with *Aoncotheca*.

Geographic Distribution: Worldwide.

Location in Host: Small intestine of ruminants and camelids.

Life Cycle: Parasite eggs are shed from the host in manure. Infection follows ingestion of infective eggs in the environment.

Laboratory Diagnosis: Eggs with bipolar plugs are detected by fecal flotation procedures. Although they are similar to *Trichuris* (whipworm) eggs, *Aonchotheca* spp. eggs are smaller.

Size: 45–50 × 22–25 µm

Clinical Importance: *Aonchotheca* infection in ruminants is considered clinically insignificant.

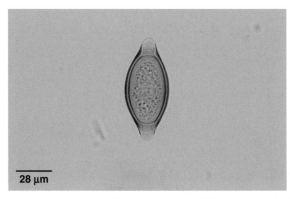

28 µm

Fig. 1.132. *Trichuris* eggs are common in ruminant feces. They have a thick, brown shell and polar plug at each end.

Fig. 1.133. These bipolar *Aonchotheca* (*Capillaria*) eggs can be confused with *Trichuris* eggs but are smaller and less brown in color.

Fig. 1.134. Ruminant fecal sample containing both *Trichuris* (T) and *Aoncotheca* (A) eggs.

Fig. 1.135. Camelids can be infected with *Aoncotheca* sp. but are also parasitized by another capillarid, which produces a distinctively larger egg with asymmetric bipolar plugs. Neither species appears to have clinical significance. A large capillarid egg (C) is shown with a *Moniezia* egg (M).

PARASITE: *Strongyloides papillosus* (Figs. 1.128, 1.136)

Taxonomy: Nematode (order Rhabditida).

Geographic Distribution: Worldwide.

Location in Host: Small intestine of ruminants and camelids.

Life Cycle: Eggs shed in the feces hatch, releasing first-stage larvae. After a period of free-living development in the environment, infective third-stage larvae are produced that infect the host by ingestion or penetration of the skin. Transmammary infection also occurs.

Laboratory Diagnosis: Eggs are detected by routine flotation techniques. They are smaller than strongylid eggs and contain a larva when passed in the feces.

Size: 40–60 × 32–40 µm

Clinical Importance: Infection usually has no clinical significance, although very heavy infection may produce severe diarrhea in young animals.

PARASITE: *Toxocara (Neoascaris) vitulorum* (Fig. 1.137)
　　　　　Common name: Roundworm.

Taxonomy: Nematode (order Ascaridida).

Geographic Distribution: Worldwide, but rare in cattle in North America.

Location in Host: Small intestine of cattle and bison.

Life Cycle: Cattle are infected following the ingestion of larvated eggs in the environment. Larvae migrate into tissues and form a somatic reservoir that is activated in pregnancy. Egg-producing adult infections occur primarily in calves as a result of transmammary transmission.

Laboratory Diagnosis: Detection of typical ascarid-type eggs with flotation procedures.

Size: 75–95 × 60–75 µm

Clinical Importance: Infection with adult worms occurs in calves less than 6 months of age. Small to moderate infection may be tolerated without signs of disease, but diarrhea, weight loss, and death can occur in heavy infection.

PARASITE: *Skrjabinema* spp. (Fig. 1.138)
　　　　　Common name: Pinworm.

Taxonomy: Nematode (order Oxyurida).

Geographic Distribution: Worldwide.

Location in Host: Cecum of sheep, goats, some wild ruminant species, and some camelids.

Life Cycle: Female worms deposit eggs on the perianal skin. Eggs fall off the host, become dispersed in the environment, and are eaten by other animals.

Laboratory Diagnosis: Eggs are rarely seen in routine fecal exams as they are not deposited in feces.

Size: 47–63 × 27–36 µm

Clinical Importance: Clinically insignificant.

Fig. 1.136. *Strongyloides* eggs may be confused with more common strongylid eggs. The two egg types can be easily distinguished because *Strongyloides* eggs are smaller and contain a fully formed larva when passed in the feces. This calf fecal sample contains a larvated *Strongyloides* egg (S) as well as numerous collapsed *Giardia* cysts (G). Several small *Eimeria* oocysts (E) are also present. Most coccidia spp. oocysts are larger than *Giardia* cysts.

Fig. 1.137. *Toxocara vitulorum* eggs have the thick shell typical of ascarids. *Toxocara* is rare in cattle in North America. Photo courtesy of Dr. Gil Myers, Myers Parasitological Service, Magnolia, TN, and Dr. Eugene Lyons, Department of Veterinary Science, University of Kentucky, Lexington, KY.

Fig. 1.138. *Skrjabinema*, the ruminant pinworm. Pinworm eggs often appear flattened on one side. These eggs are rarely found in fecal exams because they are not passed in the feces.

PARASITE: ***Muellerius capillaris, Protostrongylus* spp.** (Figs. 1.139–1.142)

Taxonomy: Nematodes (order Strongylida).

Geographic Distribution: Worldwide.

Location in Host: Lung parenchyma of sheep, goats, and some deer.

Life Cycle: Infection of small ruminants follows ingestion of infected snail or slug intermediate hosts while grazing. Snails are infected when they eat first-stage larvae in the feces.

Laboratory Diagnosis: The Baermann test is used for detection of first-stage larvae. *Muellerius* has a kinked tail with an accessory spine, in contrast to the plain tail of *Protostrongylus*.

Size:	*Muellerius*	300–320 µm
	Protostrongylus	340–400 µm

Clinical Importance: Most cases are asymptomatic. Heavy infections may cause clinical disease, especially in goats infected with *Muellerius*.

Fig. 1.139. Iodine-stained *Muellerius* larva.

Fig. 1.140. *Muellerius* larvae can be easily identified by the presence of a kinked tail and accessory spine (*arrow*) at the end of the tail.

Fig. 1.141. *Protostrongylus* larvae have a plain tail without the kink and accessory spine seen in *Muellerius* larvae. Photo courtesy of Dr. Alvin Gajadhar, Centre for Animal Parasitology, CFIA, Saskatoon, Saskatchewan, Canada.

Fig. 1.142. Higher magnification view of the simple tail of a *Protostrongylus* first-stage larva in feces. Photo courtesy of Dr. Alvin Gajadhar, Centre for Animal Parasitology, CFIA, Saskatoon, Saskatchewan, Canada.

PARASITE: ***Dictyocaulus* spp.** (Figs. 1.143 and 1.144)
Common name: Lungworm.

Taxonomy: Nematode (order Strongylida). Species include *D. viviparus* (cattle, camelids), *D. filaria* (sheep, goat, camel), *D. cameli* (camel).

Geographic Distribution: Worldwide.

Location in Host: Trachea, bronchi, and bronchioles.

Life Cycle: First-stage larvae are passed in the feces of the host. Infective third-stage larvae develop on pasture and are ingested during grazing. Larvae migrate from the intestine to the respiratory tract and become mature.

Laboratory Diagnosis: The Baermann test is used to detect first-stage larvae in fresh feces. Some larvated eggs may also be present in fresh feces.

Size:	*D. viviparus*	300–360 µm
	D. filaria	550–580 µm

Clinical Importance: Heavy infections may cause severe respiratory signs, especially in cattle. Disease is usually seen in young animals before immunity develops.

PARASITE: ***Moniezia* spp.** (Figs. 1.145–1.147)
Common name: Tapeworm.

Taxonomy: Cestode. Species include *M. benedeni* and *M. expansa*.

Geographic Distribution: Worldwide.

Location in Host: Small intestine of ruminants and camelids.

Life Cycle: Tapeworm eggs are shed in segments from the host. Ruminants are infected following ingestion of the intermediate host (free-living pasture mites) containing the tapeworm larvae.

Laboratory Diagnosis: Eggs may be found in fecal flotation tests, but infection is usually recognized when owners see tapeworm segments on the animal or in the environment.

Size: 65–75 µm in diameter

Clinical Importance: In general, little clinical importance, although there are anecdotal reports that heavy infection may cause reduced growth in young animals.

Fig. 1.143. *Dictyocaulus viviparus* first-stage larva. Intestinal cells contain characteristic dark food granules. *Dictyocaulus filaria* larvae have a small knob at the anterior end that is not present in *D. viviparus* larvae.

Fig. 1.144. Although *Dictyocaulus* larvae are most often seen in fecal samples, unhatched eggs may also be found in feces and samples collected from the trachea. The dark food granules are evident even in this unhatched *Dictyocaulus* larva. Photo courtesy of Dr. Jeffrey F. Williams, Vanson HaloSource, Inc., Redmond, WA.

Fig. 1.145. Eggs of *Moniezia* are often square or triangular, unlike the more common round or oval shape of parasite eggs. The presence of the embryo with its six hooks clearly identifies these structures as tapeworm eggs. In this egg, four hooks are visible.

107

PARASITE: ***Thysanosoma, Stilesia*** (Fig. 1.148)

Taxonomy: Cestodes.

Geographic Distribution: *Stilesia* is found in Europe, Africa, and Asia, while *Thysanosoma* is confined to North and South America. In the United States, its distribution appears to be limited to the western states.

Location in Host: Bile ducts of ruminants, especially sheep, and camelids.

Life Cycle: Although these tapeworms have not been extensively studied, it is thought that their intermediate hosts may be oribatid mites. Like *Moniezia*, the definitive host is infected following ingestion of the intermediate host.

Laboratory Diagnosis: Tapeworm segments are passed in the feces and eggs may be found in fecal flotation tests.

Size: Approximately $30 \times 20\,\mu m$

Clinical Importance: These tapeworms have no economic importance unless they are present in large enough numbers to cause liver condemnation.

Fig. 1.146. *Moniezia* sp. eggs and a strongylid egg in an alpaca fecal sample.

Fig. 1.147. Owners may be alarmed by the presence of *Moniezia* segments in the feces of their animals, although tapeworms have little clinical significance. Tapeworm segments are seen most often in the manure of young animals. Photo courtesy of Dr. Jeffrey F. Williams, Vanson HaloSource, Inc., Redmond, WA.

Fig. 1.148. Packet of *Thysanosoma* eggs from a sheep. The eggs lack the pyriform apparatus seen in *Moniezia* eggs. Hooks can be seen in some of the eggs. The entire packet of eggs is $124 \times 62\,\mu$m. Photo courtesy of Dr. Ellis C. Greiner, College of Veterinary Medicine, University of Florida, Gainesville, FL.

PARASITE: ***Fasciola hepatica*** (Fig. 1.149)
      Common name: Liver fluke.

Taxonomy: Trematode.

Geographic Distribution: Worldwide. A similar species, *F. gigantica*, is also found in Africa, Asia, and Hawaii.

Location in Host: Adults in the bile ducts of cattle, sheep, goats, camelids, and a variety of other animals, including dogs, horses, and humans.

Life Cycle: Miracidia hatch from the eggs and invade an appropriate snail host. Cercariae emerging from the snail encyst on vegetation and are ingested by host animals. Larvae leave the gastrointestinal tract and migrate through the liver to reach the bile ducts.

Laboratory Diagnosis: Large brown eggs are detected using a sedimentation procedure. Eggs may be difficult to detect and not indicative of the level of infection in a herd. A commercially available apparatus, the Flukefinder, simplifies the sedimentation procedure (see the section "Fecal Sedimentation").

    Size: 130–150 × 63–90 μm

Clinical Importance: *Fasciola* infections in ruminants may cause significant production losses. Sheep are particularly susceptible, and heavy infection may be fatal. Chronically infected animals can develop anemia and unthriftiness.

PARASITE: ***Paramphistomum* spp.** (Fig. 1.150)
      Common name: Rumen fluke.

Taxonomy: Trematode. Other genera belonging to this family include *Cotylophoron* and *Calicophoron*.

Geographic Distribution: Worldwide.

Location in Host: Adult flukes in the rumen of cattle, sheep, other ruminants, and camelids.

Life Cycle: Eggs passed in the feces of the host animal hatch in water, liberating miracidia, which infect snails. Following development in the snail, cercariae are released, which encyst on vegetation. Definitive hosts are infected by ingesting fluke metacercariae while grazing.

Laboratory Diagnosis: Eggs of paramphistomes are similar to those of *Fasciola*. They are best recovered using a sedimentation procedure, but examination of fecal material will not detect immature flukes, which are the most pathogenic stage of infection.

    Size: Approximately 114–175 × 65–100 μm, depending on species

Clinical Importance: Clinical disease is rare in North America. In other parts of the world, larval paramphistomes in the duodenum and upper ileum are reported to cause enteritis leading to diarrhea, emaciation, and death in severe cases.

PARASITE: ***Dicrocoelium dendriticum*** (Fig. 1.151)

Taxonomy: Trematode.

Geographic Distribution: Europe, Asia, sporadic occurrence in North America.

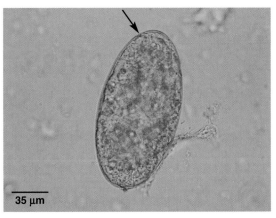

Fig. 1.149. *Fasciola hepatica* egg. These large eggs have an operculum (*arrow*) and look similar to eggs of rumen flukes, although *Paramphistomum* eggs are slightly larger (about 160 μm) and less brown in color.

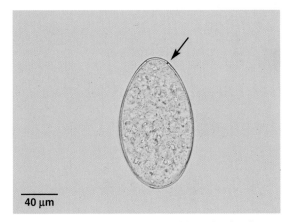

Fig. 1.150. Paramphistome egg. These eggs will not be detected with routine flotation tests. The operculum of this egg can be seen as a discontinuity in the outline of the eggshell (*arrow*). Photo courtesy of Dr. Robert Ridley, College of Veterinary Medicine, Kansas State University, Manhattan, KS.

Fig. 1.151. *Dicrocoelium dendriticum* eggs contain a fully formed miracidium, tend to be flattened on one side, and are smaller than eggs of *Fasciola* and the paramphistome flukes.

Dicrocoelium dendriticum (continued)

Location in Host: Bile ducts of domestic and wild ruminants, pigs, dogs, horses, rabbits.

Life Cycle: Larvae in eggs are ingested by snails. Ants act as the second intermediate host, and the final host is infected while grazing. Larval flukes enter bile ducts directly and do not migrate through the liver.

Laboratory Diagnosis: A sedimentation test will detect the small, brown, operculate eggs in the feces.

Size: 38–45 × 22–30 µm

Clinical Importance: In heavy infections, extensive cirrhosis of the liver can develop, leading to anemia and weight loss.

PARASITE: *Eurytrema pancreaticum* (Fig. 1.152)

Taxonomy: Trematode.

Geographic Distribution: Asia, parts of South America.

Location in Host: Adult flukes are found in the pancreatic ducts of small ruminants, cattle, camels, pigs, and occasionally humans. Flukes are also occasionally found in the bile ducts and small intestine.

Life Cycle: The eggs produced by adult flukes leave the host in manure. Snails are the first intermediate host. A grasshopper or cricket second intermediate host transmits the infection when ingested by the final host.

Laboratory Diagnosis: A sedimentation test will detect the small, brown eggs in the feces.

Size: 44–48 × 23–36 µm

Clinical Importance: Many infections are subclinical. Heavy worm burdens can cause fibrosis of the ducts and pancreatic atrophy, resulting in weight loss and poor condition.

PARASITE: *Schistosoma* spp. (Fig. 1.153)

Taxonomy: Trematode. Several species infect ruminants, camels, horses, and pigs, including *S. bovis*, *S. mattheei*, and *S. japonicum*.

Geographic Distribution: Africa, Asia.

Location in Host: Most important species are found in the portal mesenteric veins of the host.

Life Cycle: Eggs in host feces hatch in water, releasing the miracidia, which enter the snail intermediate host. Cercariae produced by multiplication within the snail are released and penetrate the skin of the definitive host. There is no second intermediate host in the life cycle.

Laboratory Diagnosis: A saline sedimentation procedure is used to detect eggs in manure. Fecal examination is most useful in early infection because egg production declines as infection pro-

Fig. 1.152. The eggs of *Eurytrema* are similar in appearance to those of *Dicrocoelium*. Photo courtesy of Dr. Alvin Gajadhar, Centre for Animal Parasitology, CFIA, Saskatoon, Saskatchewan, Canada.

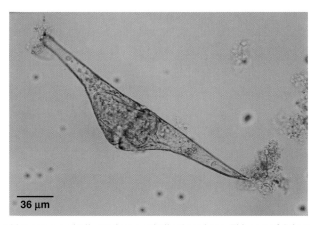

Fig. 1.153. Ruminant schistosomes typically produce a spindle-shaped egg. This egg of *Schistosoma spindale*, an Asian species, has a spine at one end. Photo courtesy of Dr. Alvin Gajadhar, Centre for Animal Parasitology, CFIA, Saskatoon, Saskatchewan, Canada.

gresses. Eggs do not have an operculum and most are spindle shaped. In some species, a spine is present on one end of the egg.

Size: 130–280 × 38–85 μm, depending on species

Clinical Importance: Disease results from the host reaction to the presence of parasite eggs in tissue. Clinical signs may occur in heavy infections, including diarrhea, anemia, and wasting.

Horses

In comparison to dogs and cats and ruminants, the diversity of parasite eggs and oocysts frequently encountered in equine feces is much reduced. The most common finding in equine samples is the strongylid egg. Horses are infected with 54 strongylid species, although individual species cannot be determined. The parasites shown in this section can also infect other equid species. Parasites illustrated in other sections may not be extensively covered here and references are given to figures elsewhere in the book.

Helminth Ova and Protozoan Cysts
as found in freshly voided feces of
Horses

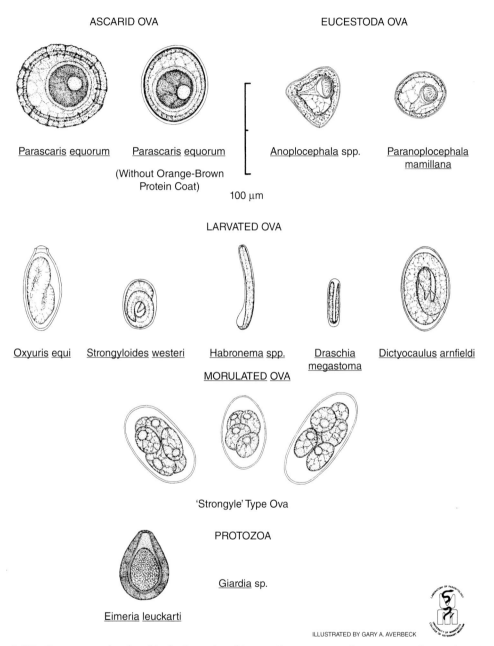

ASCARID OVA

EUCESTODA OVA

Parascaris equorum

Parascaris equorum

(Without Orange-Brown
Protein Coat)

100 μm

Anoplocephala spp.

Paranoplocephala
mamillana

LARVATED OVA

Oxyuris equi

Strongyloides westeri

Habronema spp.

Draschia
megastoma

Dictyocaulus arnfieldi

MORULATED OVA

'Strongyle' Type Ova

PROTOZOA

Giardia sp.

Eimeria leuckarti

ILLUSTRATED BY GARY A. AVERBECK

Fig. 1.154. Common parasites found in fecal samples of horses. Figure courtesy of Dr. Bert Stromberg and Mr. Gary Averbeck, College of Veterinary Medicine, University of Minnesota, Minneapolis, MN.

115

Protozoan Parasites

PARASITE: *Eimeria leuckarti* (Fig. 1.155)

Taxonomy: Protozoa (coccidia).

Geographic Distribution: Worldwide.

Location in Host: Small intestine of horses and donkeys.

Life Cycle: Oocysts leave the host in the manure. Sporulation occurs in the environment, and new hosts are infected by ingestion of infective oocysts.

Laboratory Diagnosis: Infection is diagnosed by finding the large, deep brown oocysts in the feces. A sedimentation procedure has been recommended, but oocysts can also be seen with flotation procedures.

   Size: 80–88 × 55–59 µm

Clinical Importance: Infection appears to have little clinical significance in horses, although rare cases of diarrhea have been reported. Infections are seen only in young animals.

PARASITE: *Giardia intestinalis, Cryptosporidium* **spp.** (Figs. 1.123, 1.124, 1.56, 1.57)

Taxonomy: Protozoa (*Giardia*, flagellate; *Cryptosporidium*, coccidia).

Geographic Location: Worldwide.

Location in Host: Small intestine.

Laboratory Diagnosis: As in other hosts, *Giardia* cysts can be detected with 33% $ZnSO_4$ centrifugal flotation, and *Cryptosporidium* oocysts with Sheather's sugar centrifugal flotation. Both organisms can also be found in fecal smears with appropriate stains and by non-host-specific immunodiagnostic tests.

Clinical Importance: Both infections occur most frequently in young animals but are rarely associated with clinical disease.

Fig. 1.155. The large size and deep brown color of the oocysts of *E. leuckarti* make them very distinctive. They are seen in feces of young horses.

Fig. 1.156. Fecal flotation tests containing iodine-stained *Giardia* cysts.

Fig. 1.157. *Cryptosporidium* oocysts in a sugar flotation preparation.

117

Helminth Parasites

PARASITE: **Equine Strongylid Parasites** (Figs. 1.158–1.160, 1.163, 1.171)
Common name: Various, including bloodworm, small and large strongyle.

Taxonomy: Nematodes (order Strongylida). Numerous genera belong to this group, including the large strongyles (e.g., *Strongylus vulgaris*) the small strongyles (cyathostomes), and *Trichostrongylus axei*.

Geographic Distribution: Worldwide.

Location in Host: Cecum and colon (with the exception of *T. axei*, a parasite of the stomach).

Life Cycle: Eggs released by adult worms in the large bowel develop in feces in the environment. Infective larvae on pasture are ingested by grazing horses. Large and small strongyles undergo a period of development in the intestinal wall (small strongyles) or in extra-intestinal tissue (large strongyles) before maturing in the bowel lumen.

Laboratory Diagnosis: Eggs are detected on routine fecal flotation. Eggs are similar in appearance and are not routinely identified specifically. Quantitative egg counts are useful in designing parasite control programs.

Size: Variable, with considerable overlap among species; eggs approximately 60–120 × 35–60 μm

Clinical Importance: Virtually all grazing horses are infected with strongylid parasites. Many low to moderate infections are subclinical, although they may cause reduced weight gain and performance. Young, nonimmune animals are most susceptible to clinical disease, which may include diarrhea, colic, and hypoproteinemia.

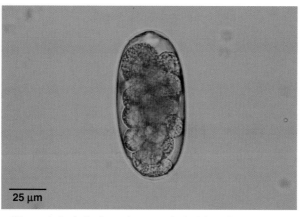

Fig. 1.158. Equine strongylid eggs in fresh fecal samples are typical of the order, with a thin shell surrounding a central group of cells. In warm weather, larvae may form within 1–2 days.

Fig. 1.159. Several equine strongylid eggs are present in this fecal sample. Although egg size is variable, there is too much overlap for size to be a useful characteristic for identification of individual species. Two *Parascaris* (roundworm) eggs are also present.

Fig. 1.160. Equine small strongyle larvae (*arrows*) in manure. These small (less than 2 cm) red larvae may be present in large numbers in manure of horses with acute larval cyathostomiasis.

PARASITE: *Parascaris equorum* (Figs. 1.159, 1.161–1.163)
Common name: Roundworm.

Taxonomy: Nematode (order Ascaridida).

Geographic Distribution: Worldwide.

Location in Host: Small intestine of horses and other equids.

Life Cycle: Infective larvae develop in eggs passed in the feces of horses. Infection occurs by ingestion of larvated eggs. Larvae migrate through the liver and lungs of the host before returning to the small intestine to mature.

Laboratory Diagnosis: Flotation procedures will detect the typical thick-shelled ascarid eggs.

Size: 90–100 µm in diameter

Following treatment with some anthelmintics, adult ascarids may be passed in manure. These worms will be much larger than any other equine helminths, with females reaching 50 cm in length.

Clinical Importance: Adult worms are common in young horses, infrequent in adults. Heavy infections can cause respiratory signs (from migrating larvae), ill-thrift, colic, diarrhea, and intestinal obstruction that may be fatal.

Fig. 1.161. *Parascaris* eggs are typical, thick-shelled ascarid eggs containing a single cell when passed in the feces. Figure 1.159 shows *Parascaris* eggs at a lower magnification.

Fig. 1.162. *Parascaris* eggs may lose the rough, proteinaceous coat on the eggshell, but they can still be identified as ascarid eggs by the thick shell and single cell inside the egg.

Fig. 1.163. Larvated strongylid egg and *Parascaris* egg that has undergone the first cell division. The fecal sample containing these eggs was fresh when collected but was not examined for some time, allowing development to occur.

PARASITE: *Strongyloides westeri* (Figs. 1.128 and 1.164)
                 Common name: Threadworm.

Taxonomy: Nematode (order Rhabditida).

Geographic Distribution: Worldwide.

Location in Host: Small intestine.

Life Cycle: Patent infections develop primarily by transmammary infection of foals. Larvated eggs passed in the feces of foals lead to the development of infective larvae that can penetrate the skin or be ingested. In adult horses, larvae migrate to tissues and form a somatic larval reservoir.

Laboratory Diagnosis: Small, larvated eggs are detected by flotation procedures.

    Size: 40–52 × 32–40 µm

Clinical Importance: Clinical disease occurs only in foals. Heavy burdens can produce severe diarrhea and dehydration. Respiratory signs may develop associated with larval migration.

PARASITE: *Oxyuris equi* (Figs. 1.165 and 1.166)
                Common name: Pinworm.

Taxonomy: Nematode (order Oxyurida). *Probstmayria vivipara* is a less common pinworm of horses.

Geographic Distribution: Worldwide.

Location in Host: Large intestine of horses and other equids.

Life Cycle: Horses ingest infective eggs. Adult female worms migrate to the perianal region and lay clusters of sticky eggs. These eventually are rubbed off the horse and contaminate the environment.

Laboratory Diagnosis: Because eggs are attached to hairs in the perianal region, they are not often seen in flotation tests. A more successful procedure for recovering eggs is the "Scotch tape test." A piece of clear adhesive tape is touched to the skin in the perianal area and then taped onto a microscope slide and examined. Pinworm eggs can easily be seen through the tape.

    Size: 85–95 × 40–45 µm

Clinical Importance: Egg-laying activities of the female worms produce intense pruritus. Horses bite at and rub the perineal region, leading to a "rat-tailed" appearance and possible secondary trauma.

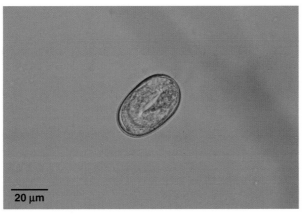

Fig. 1.164. Egg of *Strongyloides westeri*, the horse threadworm. These eggs are usually seen only in the feces of young horses. *Strongyloides* eggs are already larvated when passed in the feces, and they are smaller than strongylid eggs. Figure 1.128 shows both *Strongyloides* and strongylid eggs of ruminants, which have a similar size relationship to the species found in horses.

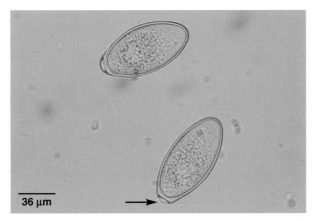

Fig. 1.165. *Oxyuris* eggs are asymmetrical with a polar plug (*arrow*). Eggs embryonate rapidly and may be seen with a larva inside.

Fig. 1.166. Adult pinworms are occasionally seen in the feces of horses. Adult female *Oxyuris* can reach a maximum size of 10 cm and can be recognized by their thin, pointed tails. Male worms are much smaller. Photo courtesy of Dr. Jeffrey F. Williams, Vanson HaloSource, Inc., Redmond, WA.

PARASITE: ***Habronema microstoma, H. muscae, Draschia megastoma*** (Fig. 1.167)

Taxonomy: Nematodes (order Spirurida).

Geographic Distribution: Worldwide.

Location in Host: Stomach of horses and donkeys.

Life Cycle: Adult worms are found in tumorlike masses in the stomach. Larvated eggs are passed in the feces and are ingested by fly larvae intermediate hosts. Infective worm larvae deposited by adult flies around the lips of horses make their way into the mouth and to the stomach.

Laboratory Diagnosis: The larvated eggs passed in the feces are too dense to float in most flotation solutions. A sedimentation procedure is recommended for detection.

Size:	*H. microstoma*	45–59 × 16 μm
	H. muscae	40–50 × 10–12 μm

Clinical Importance: Gastritis resulting in poor growth may develop. If flies deposit third-stage larvae on a wound, a condition known as "summer sore" can occur, in which larvae survive and prevent wound healing. Since the introduction of macrolide anthelmintics, infection with these species has become much less common.

PARASITE: ***Dictyocaulus arnfieldi*** (Figs. 1.168 and 1.169)
              Common name: Lungworm.

Taxonomy: Nematode (order Strongylida).

Geographic Distribution: Worldwide.

Location in Host: Bronchi and bronchioles of horses and donkeys.

Life Cycle: Adult worms in the respiratory tract produce larvated eggs that hatch before or soon after leaving the host. Eggs and/or larvae are coughed up, swallowed, and passed in the feces. Larvae develop to the infective third stage in the environment and are ingested by grazing horses.

Laboratory Diagnosis: Larvated eggs may be detected in feces with flotation tests. However, eggs hatch rapidly or even before leaving the host, so the Baermann test for the first-stage larvae is the preferred technique for diagnosis. While lungworms readily mature in donkeys, they may not mature in horses, making diagnosis more difficult.

Size:	Eggs	74–96 × 46–58 μm
	Larvae	420–480 μm

Clinical Importance: Bronchitis and pneumonia may develop. Infections appear to be tolerated better by donkeys than by horses.

Fig. 1.167. This *Habronema* larva was teased from the uterus of an adult female worm. It will appear in a fecal exam in this form surrounded by a very thin shell.

Fig. 1.168. The only parasitic nematode larvae that would be expected in the fresh feces of horses are those of *Dictyocaulus*. See also Figure 1.144 for *Dictyocaulus* eggs that may be seen in tracheal fluid samples. Photo courtesy of Dr. Craig Reinemeyer, East Tennessee Clinical Research, Knoxville, TN.

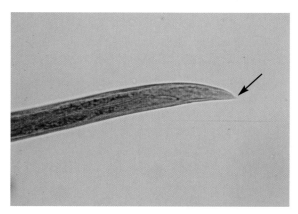

Fig. 1.169. Larvae of *Dictyocaulus arnfieldi*, the equid lungworm, have a small terminal projection at the posterior end (*arrow*) that can be seen with higher magnification.

PARASITE: ***Anoplocephala perfoliata, A. magna,*** **and** ***Paranoplocephala mamillana*** (Figs. 1.170 and 1.171)

> Common name: Tapeworm.

Taxonomy: Cestodes.

Geographic Distribution: Worldwide.

Location in Host: Small intestine of horses and donkeys.

Life Cycle: Eggs passed in the feces are ingested by free-living pasture mites. Horses are infected during grazing when they ingest mites containing tapeworm cysticercoid larvae.

Laboratory Diagnosis: Flotation procedures for detection of eggs in fecal samples are used, but false-negative results are common. An antibody test for detection of *Anoplocephala* infection is available in Europe and the United States.

Size:	*A. perfoliata*	65–80 µm in diameter
	Other species	50–60 µm

Clinical Importance: Most tapeworm infections are asymptomatic. Disease has been associated with *A. perfoliata*. These parasites cluster at the ileo-cecal junction, where heavy infection can cause ulceration leading to perforation or intussusception.

Horses may also be infected with some of the trematode (fluke) parasites that affect ruminants. For information on these parasites, see above.

Fig. 1.170. The egg of the equine tapeworm *Anoplocephala* is similar in appearance to that of the ruminant tapeworm *Moniezia*. The eggs of both genera are often irregularly shaped. A pyriform apparatus surrounds the embryo, which has six hooks (hexacanth).

Fig. 1.171. *Anoplocephala* egg (A) and several equine strongylid eggs.

Swine

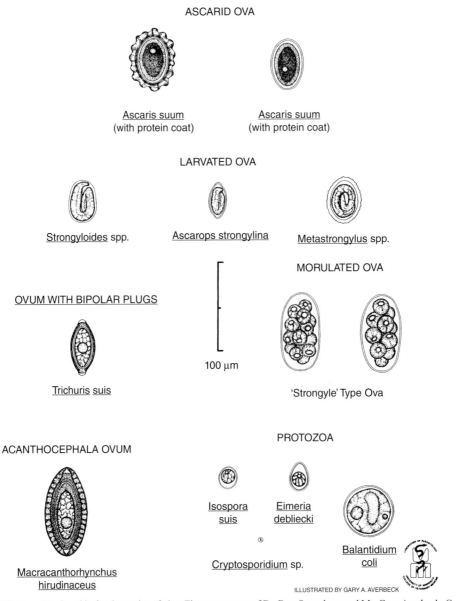

Helminth Ova and Protozoan Cysts
as found in freshly voided feces of
Pigs

ASCARID OVA

Ascaris suum
(with protein coat)

Ascaris suum
(with protein coat)

LARVATED OVA

Strongyloides spp.

Ascarops strongylina

Metastrongylus spp.

MORULATED OVA

OVUM WITH BIPOLAR PLUGS

Trichuris suis

100 µm

'Strongyle' Type Ova

PROTOZOA

ACANTHOCEPHALA OVUM

Isospora
suis

Eimeria
debliecki

Balantidium
coli

Macracanthorhynchus
hirudinaceus

Cryptosporidium sp.

ILLUSTRATED BY GARY A. AVERBECK

Fig. 1.172. Parasites found in fecal samples of pigs. Figure courtesy of Dr. Bert Stromberg and Mr. Gary Averbeck, College of Veterinary Medicine, University of Minnesota, Minneapolis, MN.

Protozoan Parasites

PARASITE: *Eimeria* **spp.,** *Isospora suis* (Fig. 1.173)
Common name: Coccidia.

Taxonomy: Protozoa (coccidia). Eight species of porcine *Eimeria* have been described, including *E. scabra*, *E. deblieki*, and *E. spinosa*.

Geographic Distribution: Worldwide.

Location in Host: Intestinal tract; location depends on species and stage of development.

Life Cycle: Oocysts are shed in the feces and sporulate rapidly in warm weather. Pigs are infected when they ingest sporulated (infective) oocysts. Transmission of *I. suis* is concentrated in the neonatal period of pigs.

Laboratory Diagnosis: *Eimeria* oocysts are detected in feces with flotation procedures. *Isospora suis* oocysts are shed at such a low rate in asymptomatic carriers that detection is very difficult. In clinically affected neonatal pigs, disease usually develops before oocysts are shed, and intestinal mucosal impression smears at necropsy are more effective for diagnosis.

Size: Oocysts vary with species, with a range of $11–35 \times 9–20 \, \mu m$

Clinical Importance: *Eimeria* spp. infections are common in swine but rarely produce clinical disease. In contrast, *I. suis* can produce neonatal diarrhea in pigs (5–10 days of age) that may be severe and cause death.

Swine may also be infected with *C. parvum* and *G. intestinalis*. These two protozoan parasites appear to have little clinical significance but may have zoonotic importance. For further information, see sections related to these parasites in the small animal and ruminant sections.

Fig. 1.173. *Eimeria* spp. are the most common coccidia seen in porcine fecal samples. Although several species can infect pigs, they are of little economic importance. Shown here is a sporulated oocyst of *E. scabra*. Photo courtesy of Dr. David Lindsay, Virginia-Maryland Regional College of Veterinary Medicine, Virginia Tech, Blacksburg, VA.

PARASITE: ***Balantidium coli*** (Figs. 1.174 and 1.175)

Taxonomy: Protozoa (ciliate).

Geographic Distribution: Worldwide.

Location in Host: Large intestine of swine; may also occasionally infect humans and other primates, camels, dogs, and other animals.

Life Cycle: Infection follows ingestion of cysts shed into the environment from infected swine. The only other stage of the life cycle is the motile trophozoite in the intestinal tract.

Laboratory Diagnosis: Motile trophozoites can be seen in direct fecal smears. Flotation tests are more sensitive for detecting cysts. The kidney-bean-shaped macronucleus is a distinctive feature.

Size:	Trophozoites	50–150 µm
	Cysts	40–60 µm

Clinical Importance: *Balantidium* is generally asymptomatic in swine, although bloody diarrhea may occur in some hosts.

Fig. 1.174. *Balantidium coli* trophozoite in a direct smear. The cilia covering trophozoites can be seen as a halo surrounding the organism. Trophozoites are usually destroyed by fecal flotation procedures. Photo courtesy of Dr. Alvin Gajadhar, Centre for Animal Parasitology, CFIA, Saskatoon, Saskatchewan, Canada.

Fig. 1.175. The characteristic kidney-bean-shaped macronucleus of *Balantidium* is faintly visible in this cyst in a porcine fecal sample. The macronucleus is usually easily seen in stained specimens. Photo courtesy of Dr. Alvin Gajadhar, Centre for Animal Parasitology, CFIA, Saskatoon, Saskatchewan, Canada.

Helminth Parasites

PARASITE: ***Ascaris suum*** (Fig. 1.176)
> Common name: Roundworm.

Taxonomy: Nematode (order Ascaridida).

Geographic Distribution: Worldwide.

Location in Host: Small intestine.

Life Cycle: Pigs are infected when they ingest infective eggs in the environment. Following migration through the liver and lungs, adults develop in the small intestine. Like other ascarids, *A. suum* has very resistant eggs that can survive for years in the environment.

Laboratory Diagnosis: Eggs can be detected in feces with routine flotation procedures.

> Size: 50–70 × 40–60 µm

Clinical Importance: *Ascaris suum* is a common and important parasite of swine, even in confinement systems. Larval migration through liver and lung may cause liver condemnation and predispose pigs to bacterial or viral pneumonia. Adult worms in the small intestine may cause reduced growth. Larvae can also migrate and cause disease in other animals and humans.

PARASITE: ***Hyostrongylus rubidus, Oesophagostomum* spp.** (Fig. 1.177)
> Common name: Red stomach worm (*Hyostrongylus*), nodular worm (*Oesophagostomum*).

Taxonomy: Nematodes (order Strongylida).

Geographic Distribution: Worldwide.

Location in Host: Stomach (*Hyostrongylus*) and large intestine (*Oesophagostomum*) of wild and domestic swine.

Life Cycle: These parasites have a direct life cycle; eggs are shed in the feces and hatch in the environment. Swine are infected following ingestion of third-stage larvae.

Laboratory Diagnosis: Typical strongylid eggs are detected in fecal samples by flotation techniques. Eggs of *Hyostrongylus* and *Oesophagostomum* cannot be distinguished from each other or from less common strongylid parasites of swine, including *Trichostrongylus axei* and *Globocephalus*.

> Size: 69–85 × 39–45 µm

Clinical Importance: These parasites are common in pastured swine. *Hyostrongylus* may cause ulcerative gastritis, resulting in anemia and reduced production. Host response to *Oesophagostomum* larvae in the wall of the intestinal tract leads to the development of nodules that, in heavy infections, can lead to enteritis and reduced production.

PARASITE: ***Trichuris suis*** (Fig. 1.178)
> Common name: Whipworm.

Taxonomy: Nematode (order Enoplida).

Geographic Distribution: Worldwide.

Location in Host: Large intestine of wild and domestic pigs.

Fig. 1.176. Like other ascarid eggs, those of *Ascaris suum* contain a single cell surrounded by a thick shell when first passed in the feces. In some cases, the rough, brown outer layer of the shell may be absent, as seen in two of the eggs in this figure. *Ascaris suum* eggs are very similar in appearance to those of the human ascarid, *A. lumbricoides*.

Fig. 1.177. *Hyostrongylus* and *Oesophagostomum* are the most common and important strongylid parasites of swine and produce indistinguishable eggs typical of this group of nematodes. Fecal culture and identification of third-stage larvae are necessary to identify parasite genus.

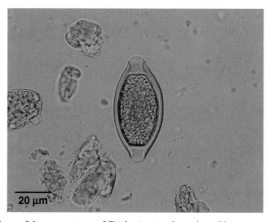

Fig. 1.178. Like other members of the genus, eggs of *Trichuris suis*, the swine whipworm, are football shaped with a polar plug at each end.

Trichuris suis (*continued*)

Life Cycle: *Trichuris* spp. have a direct life cycle. Pigs are infected following ingestion of infective eggs in the environment. Eggs leave the host in manure and are able to survive for long periods in the environment.

Laboratory Diagnosis: Eggs can be detected in routine fecal flotation tests.

   Size: 50–60 × 21–25 μm

Clinical Importance: This common helminth infection of swine may cause severe diarrhea and dehydration. Severe infections can produce bloody diarrhea.

PARASITE: ***Strongyloides ransomi*** (Figs. 1.128, 1.179, 1.180)
         Common name: Threadworm.

Taxonomy: Nematode (order Rhabditida).

Geographic Distribution: Worldwide.

Location in Host: Small intestine.

Life Cycle: Larvated eggs are passed in the feces and hatch in the environment. After a free-living period in the environment, third-stage larvae are produced that infect pigs through either ingestion or skin penetration. Sows carrying larvae in the tissues transmit the parasite through the milk to their litters.

Laboratory Diagnosis: Eggs are detected in fecal samples using flotation techniques. The thin-shelled egg contains a larva in fresh fecal samples.

   Size: 40–50 × 20–35 μm

Clinical Importance: *Strongyloides* causes diarrhea in pigs as young as 10 days of age. Severe infections may be fatal.

PARASITE: ***Metastrongylus* spp.** (Fig. 1.181)
         Common name: Lungworm.

Taxonomy: Nematode (order Strongylida). Several species similar in life cycle and pathogenicity have been described.

Geographic Distribution: Worldwide.

Location in Host: Bronchi and bronchioles of domestic and wild pigs.

Life Cycle: Eggs containing a larva are passed in the feces of pigs. When earthworm intermediate hosts ingest the eggs, they hatch and develop to infective larvae. Swine are infected by ingestion of earthworms containing third-stage larvae.

Laboratory Diagnosis: Larvated eggs are detected in feces by flotation procedures.

   Size: 51–63 × 33–42 μm

Clinical Importance: These parasites are uncommon in intensively raised swine. Heavy infections, especially in young pigs, can cause clinical respiratory disease.

Fig. 1.179. Larvated *Strongyloides* eggs are usually present only in the feces of young pigs. Photo courtesy of Merial.

Fig. 1.180. The *Strongyloides* eggs pictured here could be confused with strongylid eggs, but strongylid eggs are larger and do not contain a larva in fresh fecal samples. Figure 1.128 shows the similar size relationship of ruminant strongylid and *Strongyloides* eggs. Photo courtesy of Dr. T. Bonner Stewart, School of Veterinary Medicine, Louisiana State University, Baton Rouge, LA.

Fig. 1.181. In fresh fecal samples, *Metastrongylus* eggs contain a larva and must be differentiated from other larvated parasite eggs found in swine manure.

PARASITE: ***Physocephalus sexalatus, Ascarops strongylina*** (Figs. 1.182 and 1.183)

Taxonomy: Nematode (order Spirurida).

Geographic Distribution: Worldwide.

Location in Host: Stomach of domestic and wild pigs.

Life Cycle: Eggs containing larvae are passed in the feces, where they are ingested by beetle intermediate hosts. Pigs are infected following ingestion of larvae in the intermediate host.

Laboratory Diagnosis: A sedimentation procedure is recommended for detecting spirurid parasite eggs. The ellipsoidal eggs of both species are indistinguishable and are larvated when passed in the feces.

Size: 39–45 × 17–26 µm

Clinical Importance: Spirurid parasites are uncommon in intensively raised swine. Most infections are asymptomatic, but heavy infections may produce gastritis, leading to weight loss or failure to gain.

PARASITE: ***Fasciola* spp., *Eurytrema pancreaticum, Dicrocoelium dentriticum, Schistosoma* spp.** (Figs. 1.149, 1.151–1.153, 1.184)

Although swine are not considered to be the primary host for most trematodes, pigs may be infected with trematode parasites (*Fasciola* spp., *E. pancreaticum, D. dentriticum, Schistosoma* spp.) that also infect ruminants. Trematode infections of domestic swine would only be seen in pastured pigs because the complicated life cycle of flukes make transmission impossible in confinement operations.

Fig. 1.182. Egg of *Physocephalus*. Photo courtesy of Merial.

Fig. 1.183. *Ascarops* egg. Spirurid eggs are unlikely to be seen if standard flotation procedures are used. Their larvated eggs have a thick shell (easily appreciated in the *Physocephalus* egg), unlike the thin-shelled eggs of *Strongyloides* or *Metastrongylus*. Photo courtesy of Merial.

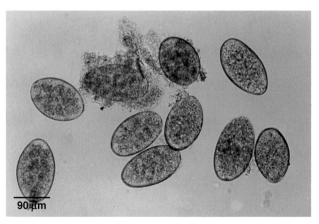

Fig. 1.184. *Fasciola* eggs. Trematode infections are rarely encountered in swine in North America, but are more common in other parts of the world where pigs range freely and infections also occur in other domestic animals. Photo courtesy of Dr. Alvin Gajadhar, Centre for Animal Parasitology, CFIA, Saskatoon, Saskatchewan, Canada.

PARASITE: ***Macracanthorhynchus hirudinaceus*** (Fig. 1.185)
Common name: Thorny-headed worm.

Taxonomy: Acanthocephalan.

Geographic Distribution: Worldwide.

Location in Host: Small intestine.

Life Cycle: Parasite eggs are passed in manure and ingested by beetle intermediate hosts. Swine are infected when they ingest infective larvae (cystacanths) in beetles.

Laboratory Diagnosis: Eggs are not consistently recovered by flotation procedures. A sedimentation procedure should also be performed.

Size: Variable, 67–110 × 40–65 μm

Clinical Importance: Acanthocephalan parasites have a proboscis covered with hooks. Attachment of the proboscis causes damage to the intestinal wall. Clinical signs range from none to diarrhea and weight loss. *Macracanthorhynchus* is unlikely to be present in total-confinement systems.

Fig. 1.185. *Macracanthorhynchus hirudinaceus* egg. The embryo (acanthor) is surrounded by several membranes and contains hooks at one end that are often visible (*arrow*). Common tapeworm eggs also contain hooks, but thorny-headed worm eggs have a more complex membranous structure and an elongated embryo. Photo courtesy of Dr. Alvin Gajadhar, Centre for Animal Parasitology, CFIA, Saskatoon, Saskatchewan, Canada.

Birds

Protozoan Parasites

PARASITE: ***Eimeria* spp., *Isospora* spp.** (Figs. 1.186–1.190, 1.194, 1.196, 1.198, 1.201)
Common name: Coccidia.

Taxonomy: Protozoa (coccidia). *Eimeria* spp. are common in poultry and other Galliformes and Columbriformes. *Isospora coccidia* species are more common in Passeriformes, Psittaciformes, and Piciformes. Species of coccidia are host specific. *Caryospora*, *Sarcocystis*, and *Atoxoplasma* are other coccidian genera that infect some birds.

Geographic Distribution: Worldwide.

Location in Host: Primarily in the gastrointestinal tract.

Life Cycle: These parasites have a typical coccidian life cycle. Birds ingest infective oocysts from the environment. Sexual and asexual multiplication occurs within cells of the intestinal tract (some more unusual species are found in other organs). Development culminates in the production of oocysts, which are passed in the feces.

Laboratory Diagnosis: *Eimeria* oocysts are detected with routine flotation procedures. Sporulation of oocysts may be required for species identification.

Size: Approximately 10–45 μm in length (oocysts), depending on species

Clinical Importance: Coccidia are common parasites of domestic and wild birds. Many infections are asymptomatic, but under some circumstances coccidia may cause severe diarrhea and death. *Eimeria* spp. are among the most important pathogens in modern poultry confinement operations.

Fig. 1.186. *Eimeria* spp. oocysts from a chicken. *Eimeria* species are common parasites of wild and domestic birds. Individual birds may be infected with multiple coccidia species.

Fig. 1.187. After reaching the environment, *Eimeria* oocysts sporulate; the length of time required for this process is determined by temperature but may take only a few days. This field shows several unsporulated oocysts. A sporulated oocyst (*arrow*) contains four sporocysts (three are visible). Sporulated *Isospora* oocysts contain two sporocysts.

Fig. 1.188. *Isospora* spp. can also be found in birds, as seen in this fecal sample from a crow. Sporulated *Isospora* spp. oocysts contain two sporocysts. Photo courtesy of Dr. Alvin Gajadhar, Centre for Animal Parasitology, CFIA, Saskatoon, Saskatchewan, Canada.

Fig. 1.189. *Caryospora* oocyst. The sporulated oocyst of this genus contains a single sporocyst with eight sporozoites. Photo courtesy of Dr. David Baker, School of Veterinary Medicine, Louisiana State University, Baton Rouge, LA.

PARASITE: *Cryptosporidium* **spp.** (Fig. 1.191)

Taxonomy: Protozoa (coccidia). Avian species of this genus include *C. baileyi* and *C. meleagridis*. The latter species has been found to be infective for humans and some other mammals, as well as birds.

Geographic Distribution: Worldwide.

Location in Host: Gastrointestinal, respiratory, and/or urinary tracts depending on host.

Life Cycle: Infection of the bird host follows ingestion of the infective oocyst. Development and reproduction occur in the epithelial cells of the gastrointestinal and respiratory tract primarily. In some bird species, the urinary tract is affected.

Laboratory Diagnosis: Oocysts can be detected with the Sheather's sugar flotation procedure. Acid-fast or other staining procedures of fecal smears can also be used, as well as fecal immuno-diagnostic tests.

Size: 4–6 µm in diameter

Clinical Importance: Depending on the body systems affected, birds may show diarrhea, coughing, sneezing, and dyspnea or renal disease. Severe infection may cause death. *Cryptosporidium meleagridis* can infect humans.

PARASITE: **Gastrointestinal Flagellates** (Figs. 1.192 and 1.193; see also Figs. 1.50–1.56 for illustrations of *Giardia*)

Taxonomy: Protozoa (flagellates). Several genera are found in the avian digestive tract, including *Trichomonas*, *Cochlosoma*, *Histomonas*, *Giardia*, *Spironucleus* (=*Hexamita*), and *Chilomastix*.

Geographic Distribution: Worldwide.

Location in Host: *Trichomonas gallinae* is found in the upper digestive system; *Histomonas* in the cecum and liver; and *Cochlosoma*, *Giardia*, and *Spironucleus* in the intestines.

Life Cycle: Most avian flagellates have only a trophozoite stage. They are transmitted from bird to bird by direct contact and contaminated food or water. Feeding of young birds by adults can also transmit *T. gallinae*, while *Histomonas* can be carried in the eggs of the cecal roundworm, *Heterakis*. *Giardia* trophozoites encyst in the intestinal tract. Cysts passed in the feces are ingested by birds. *Chilomastix* also forms cysts.

Laboratory Diagnosis: *Trichomonas* trophozoites have anterior flagella and an undulating membrane. They can usually be detected in smears made from exudates or lesions in the oral cavity, esophagus, and crop. *Giardia* cysts can be recovered by $ZnSO_4$ centrifugal flotation. *Chilomastix* cysts are rarely found in feces. *Giardia*, *Spironucleus*, and *Cochlosoma* trophozoites may be seen in very fresh fecal smears. *Spironucleus* has no sucking disk, unlike *Giardia* and *Cochlosoma*. *Histomonas* is unlikely to be detected in fecal smears.

Size:		
	Trichomonas	8–14 µm in length, depending on species
	Giardia trophozoites	10–20 × 5–15 µm
	Giardia cysts	10–14 × 8–10 µm
	Cochlosoma	6–10 × 4–6.5 µm
	Spironucleus	5–12 × 2–7 µm
	Chilomastix	6–24 × 3–10 µm

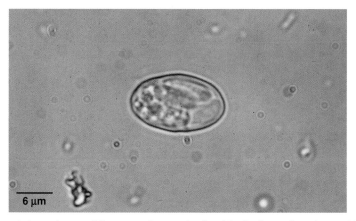

Fig. 1.190. *Sarcocystis* is another coccidian genus that may be found in the feces of carnivorous birds that act as the definitive host of the parasite. Oocysts sporulate in the host, and small sporocysts (approximately 10–12 μm) are passed in the feces.

Fig. 1.191. *Cryptosporidium* spp. oocysts in birds are similar in appearance to those of mammalian species. Slides should be examined using the 40× lens of the microscope.

Fig. 1.192. *Trichomonas* spp. in birds have an undulating membrane and several anterior flagella. They can be seen in smears made from lesions in the upper gastrointestinal (GI) tract. The presence of caseous lesions in the esophagus and crop is also helpful in diagnosis.

143

Gastrointestinal Flagellates (*continued*)

Clinical Importance: Pigeons and raptors are particularly susceptible to trichomoniasis of the upper digestive tract. Affected birds may show depression and weakness with characteristic plaques and accumulation of cheesy material in the mouth, esophagus, and crop. Severe infections may be fatal. Although many *Giardia* infections are asymptomatic, the parasite can cause diarrhea, depression, and debilitation, particularly in young psittacines. Feather picking associated with infection has also been described. *Histomonas* is the cause of blackhead in turkeys. Other flagellates may also produce diarrhea, but many infections are asymptomatic. None of these avian flagellates has zoonotic importance.

Helminth Parasites

PARASITE: **Avian Ascarids** (Figs. 1.194 and 1.195)
Common name: Roundworm, cecal worm (*Heterakis*).

Taxonomy: Nematodes (order Ascaridida). *Ascaridia* spp. and *Heterakis* spp. are common in poultry and many wild bird hosts. *Porrocecum* spp. and *Contracecum* spp. are also found in a variety of bird hosts.

Geographic Distribution: Worldwide.

Location in Host: Intestinal tract; *Heterakis* spp. parasitize the ceca of birds.

Life Cycle: Eggs are passed in the feces of the bird host and develop to the infective stage in the environment. Birds become infected when they ingest infective eggs. Earthworms may act as transport hosts.

Laboratory Diagnosis: Thick-shelled eggs are detected with flotation procedures. Eggs of *Ascaridia* and *Heterakis* are similar in size and morphology and are not easily differentiated.

Size:	*Ascaridia*	77–94 × 43–55 μm
	Heterakis	66–79 × 41–48 μm

Clinical Importance: Larvae of *Ascaridia* appear to be the most pathogenic stage and may cause enteritis in the prepatent period. Heavy burdens of adult worms can cause enteritis and intestinal obstruction. *Heterakis* is primarily important in poultry as a vector of *Histomonas meleagridis* (blackhead), which can be a serious disease of turkeys. The protozoan is carried from bird to bird in the eggs and larvae of *Heterakis*. Fatal infections of *Heterakis isolonche* due to nodular typhlitis have been reported in pheasants.

Fig. 1.193. *Giardia* trophozoites found in smears of avian feces are very similar in appearance to these mammalian parasites.

Fig. 1.194. A smooth, thick shell is seen in both *Ascaridia* spp. and *Heterakis* spp. eggs. This sample from a chicken shows both an ascarid egg and a much smaller *Eimeria* oocyst.

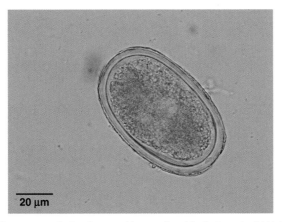

Fig. 1.195. *Ascaridia* egg from a peacock. Another ascarid genus found in ducks and wild birds is *Porrocecum*, which has eggs with a rough shell similar in appearance to that of many mammalian ascarid species.

PARASITE: *Capillaria* **spp.** (Figs. 1.196, 1.197, 1.199)

Taxonomy: Nematode (order Enoplida). A variety of species can be found in domestic and wild birds.

Geographic Distribution: Worldwide.

Location in Host: Various locations in the gastrointestinal tract, depending on species.

Life Cycle: Eggs are passed in the feces of the host and become infective in the environment. Some species, such as *C. obsignata*, have a direct life cycle, while others have been shown to use an earthworm intermediate host.

Laboratory Diagnosis: Bipolar-plugged eggs can be detected in the feces with flotation techniques.

   Size: Approximately 45–70 μm in length, depending on species

Clinical Importance: *Capillaria* spp. can cause severe inflammation wherever species occur in the digestive tract, including the esophagus, crop, and intestines. Heavy infections may be fatal.

PARASITE: *Trichostrongylus tenuis*, *Amidostomum* **spp., and Other Avian Strongylids** (Fig. 1.198)

Taxonomy: Nematodes (order Strongylida). *Trichostrongylus tenuis* and *Amidostomum* spp. occur in domestic and game birds.

Geographic Distribution: Worldwide.

Location in Host: Cecum and intestines of game birds, poultry, and wild birds.

Life Cycle: Eggs are passed from the host in the feces. First-stage larvae hatch from the eggs, develop to the infective stage in the environment, and develop to the adult stage when ingested by the avian host.

Laboratory Diagnosis: Typical thin-shelled strongylid eggs can be detected with flotation procedures.

Size:	Varies with species	
	T. tenuis eggs	65–75 μm × 35–42 μm
	Amidostomum anseri eggs	85–110 × 50–82 μm

Clinical Importance: Heavy infections of *T. tenuis* can produce severe enteritis with resulting hemorrhagic diarrhea, weight loss, and death.

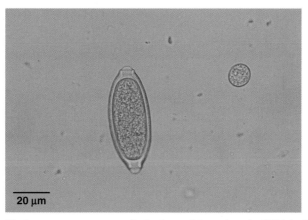

Fig. 1.196. Eggs of *Capillaria* spp. are very common in the feces of domestic and wild birds. The bipolar-plugged eggs have a thick shell and are typically yellowish. This *Capillaria* egg and *Eimeria* oocyst were present in a fecal sample from a backyard chicken flock. *Capillaria* spp. are uncommon in poultry maintained in total-confinement systems.

Fig. 1.197. *Capillaria* sp. egg in an owl (*arrow*). The larger, browner egg belongs to *Trichosomoides* sp., a parasite of the bladder of rats. Because parasite eggs of prey are sometimes found in predator feces, it is important to appreciate the normal array of parasites found in a host so spurious parasites can be correctly identified. Photo courtesy of Dr. Stephen Smith, Virginia-Maryland Regional College of Veterinary Medicine, Virginia Tech, Blacksburg, VA.

Fig. 1.198. Strongylid egg and coccidia oocysts in an avian fecal sample.

147

PARASITE: *Syngamus* **spp.** (Figs. 1.199 and 1.200)
Common name: Gapeworm.

Taxonomy: Nematode (order Strongylida).

Geographic Distribution: Worldwide.

Location in Host: Trachea and bronchi of numerous domestic and wild birds. Species of a similar genus, *Cyathostoma*, are found in some aquatic birds and birds of prey.

Life Cycle: Eggs are produced by females in the trachea and are coughed up, swallowed, and passed out of the host in the feces. Infective larvae may be eaten directly from the environment by the avian host, or they may be ingested by an earthworm or molluscan transport host that is eaten, in turn, by a bird.

Laboratory Diagnosis: Ellipsoidal, bipolar eggs are seen in the feces with flotation procedures.

Size: 80–110 × 40–50 μm

Clinical Importance: Young birds are most severely affected. Large numbers of parasites and exudate obstruct the airways and can suffocate the host. The parasite's common name originates from the gaping and gasping of infected birds as they attempt to breathe. *Syngamus* is uncommon in total-confinement poultry systems.

PARASITE: *Dispharynx, Echinuria, Tetrameres, Subulura, Cheilospiura (Acuaria), Serratospiculum,* **and Others** (Figs. 1.201 and 1.202)

Taxonomy: Nematodes (order Spirurida).

Geographic Distribution: Worldwide.

Location in Host: Species are found throughout the digestive tract. *Serratospiculum* parasitizes the respiratory tract of some wild birds.

Life Cycle: Adults (except *Serratospiculum*) are located in the digestive tract. Eggs are passed in the feces and are ingested by various arthropod intermediate hosts. Birds are infected by ingesting an intermediate host carrying infective larvae.

Laboratory Diagnosis: Flotation and sedimentation techniques can be used to detect the relatively small, larvated eggs in feces.

Size: Approximately 30–55 × 20–35 μm, depending on species

Clinical Importance: Most infections with this group of parasites are not highly pathogenic. However, *Tetrameres* and *Dispharynx* in large numbers in the proventriculus may cause weight loss and reduced production. In poultry, members of this group of parasites are rare in total-confinement management systems.

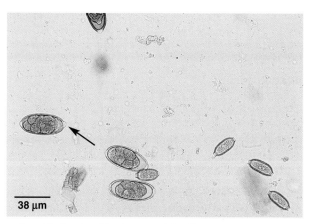

Fig. 1.199. *Syngamus* eggs have bipolar plugs like the eggs of *Capillaria* spp. However, the eggs of *Syngamus* are larger and contain several well-defined cells (morula) when passed in the feces. In this specimen, both *Syngamus* and *Capillaria* eggs are present. The polar plugs of *Syngamus* can be seen in some of the eggs (*arrow*). Photo courtesy of Dr. Robert Ridley, College of Veterinary Medicine, Kansas State University, Manhattan, KS.

Fig. 1.200. *Cyathostoma bronchialis* is a species similar to *Syngamus* that is found in the respiratory system of some aquatic birds. Other species parasitize raptors. The polar plugs in this species are not prominent. The eggs shown here are inside the uterus of a female worm removed from a goose.

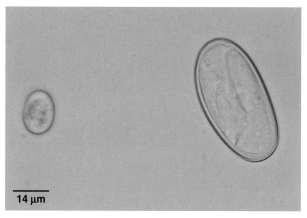

Fig. 1.201. *Tetrameres* egg in the feces of a homing pigeon. Like other spirurid eggs, this *Tetrameres* egg is larvated when passed in the feces, but further specific identification is difficult. Also pictured is a coccidia oocyst. Photo courtesy of Dr. Robert Ridley, College of Veterinary Medicine, Kansas State University, Manhattan, KS.

PARASITE: *Echinostoma* **spp.,** *Echinoparyphium,* *Prosthogonimus* **spp., and Others** (Figs. 1.203 and 1.204)

Common name: Fluke.

Taxonomy: Trematode.

Geographic Distribution: Worldwide.

Location in Host: Domestic and wild birds are parasitized by many fluke species. Adults can be found in various body systems, including the intestines and respiratory and reproductive tracts.

Life Cycle: Adult worms produce eggs that leave the host principally via the digestive tract. The first intermediate host is a mollusk, and a variety of animals act as second intermediate host depending on the fluke species (with the exception of schistosome flukes, which do not require a second intermediate host).

Laboratory Diagnosis: Fluke eggs in feces are best detected with a sedimentation technique because of their higher density. Fluke eggs are typically operculated and brown.

Size: Highly variable with species, approximately 20–100 μm in length

Clinical Importance: Many fluke infections are of low pathogenicity. Some genera of importance in domestic poultry are *Echinostoma* and *Echinoparyphium*, which may cause enteritis, and *Prosthogonimus*, a parasite of the oviduct, which can cause abnormal egg production and peritonitis. Because of their complex life cycles, flukes will be seen only in birds with access to intermediate hosts and will not occur in poultry confinement operations.

Fig. 1.202. Spirurid egg in the feces of a red-tailed hawk. The larva within the egg is clearly visible. Photo courtesy of Dr. Stephen Smith, Virginia-Maryland Regional College of Veterinary Medicine, Virginia Tech, Blacksburg, VA.

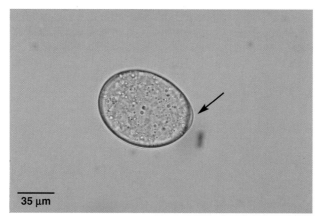

Fig. 1.203. Fluke egg in the feces of a screech owl. The operculum is marked by an arrow.

Fig. 1.204. The developing miracidium can be seen inside this avian trematode egg found in feces from a bird of prey.

PARASITE: *Davainea* **spp.,** *Choanotaenia* **spp.,** *Raillietina* **spp.,** *Hymenolepis* **spp., and Others** (Figs. 1.205–1.207)

Common name: Tapeworm.

Taxonomy: Cestodes.

Geographic Distribution: Worldwide.

Location in Host: Small intestine of a wide variety of domestic and wild birds.

Life Cycle: Eggs are passed in the feces. Insects are the most common intermediate hosts, but other invertebrates may also be used by some species (e.g., the intermediate host of *Davainea* is a mollusk).

Laboratory Diagnosis: Although proglottids are intermittently passed in the feces, detection of eggs by fecal exam is unreliable, and diagnosis is usually made at necropsy.

Size: Varies with species; individual eggs of many species are approximately 50–80 μm; some species have large egg packets

Clinical Importance: Many tapeworm infections are asymptomatic. However, some are serious pathogens; for example, *Davainea proglottina* and *Raillietina echinobothrida* can cause severe enteritis and death in domestic poultry. Tapeworms are common in unconfined poultry with access to the intermediate hosts.

Fig. 1.205. Avian tapeworm egg. Several embryonic hooks are clearly visible, and this characteristic is very helpful in identification. Photo courtesy of Dr. Stephen Smith, Virginia-Maryland Regional College of Veterinary Medicine, Virginia Tech, Blacksburg, VA.

Fig. 1.206. Tapeworm eggs from a magpie. Scattered among the cestode eggs are occasional coccidia oocysts (*arrows*). Photo courtesy of Dr. Alvin Gajadhar, Centre for Animal Parasitology, CFIA, Saskatoon, Saskatchewan, Canada.

Fig. 1.207. Tapeworm eggs from a canary. Photo courtesy of Dr. Ellis C. Greiner, College of Veterinary Medicine, University of Florida, Gainesville, FL.

PARASITE: ***Polymorphus* spp., *Filicollis* spp., and Others** (Figs. 1.208 and 1.209)
Common name: Thorny-headed worm.

Taxonomy: Acanthocephalan.

Geographic Distribution: Worldwide.

Location in Host: Digestive system.

Life Cycle: Eggs are passed in the feces of the host. Infective larvae develop in arthropod intermediate hosts and infect birds when they are ingested.

Laboratory Diagnosis: Eggs are not consistently recovered by flotation procedures. A sedimentation procedure should also be performed.

Size: Approximately 50–100 μm in length, depending on species

Clinical Importance: Thorny-headed worms are primarily parasites of free-ranging and wild birds because of their complex life cycles. Heavy infections may cause diarrhea and debilitation.

Fig. 1.208. Egg of a thorny-headed worm (*Centorhynchus*) from the feces of a barred owl. Acanthocephalan eggs have several internal layers surrounding the larva (acanthor). Photo courtesy of Dr. Ellis C. Greiner, College of Veterinary Medicine, University of Florida, Gainesville, FL.

Fig. 1.209. Acanthocephalan eggs in the feces of a blue jay. Photo courtesy of Dr. Thomas Nolan, School of Veterinary Medicine, University of Pennsylvania, Philadelphia, PA.

Rodents and Rabbits

Protozoan Parasites

PARASITE: *Eimeria* **spp.** (Figs. 1.210–1.212)
   Common name: Coccidia.

Taxonomy: Protozoa (coccidia).

Geographic Distribution: Worldwide.

Location in Host: A variety of species parasitize the intestinal tract of rodents and rabbits. *Eimeria stiedae* is found in the bile ducts of rabbits.

Life Cycle: Oocysts passed in the feces can sporulate quickly and infect the host when ingested. Asexual and sexual reproduction occurs in cells of the gastrointestinal tract.

Laboratory Diagnosis: Oocysts can be detected in feces by centrifugal or simple flotation techniques. Oocysts are elliptical to spherical shaped.

   Size: Approximately 10–45 × 10–30 μm, depending on species

Clinical Importance: Some species are nonpathogenic. Pathogenic intestinal coccidia can cause anorexia, weight loss, profuse diarrhea, and death. *Eimeria stiedae* infection of the rabbit liver can cause anorexia, diarrhea, distended abdomen, and death.

   Rodents may also be infected with species of *Giardia* and *Cryptosporidium* (see Figs. 1.47 and 1.50–1.56).

Fig. 1.210. *Eimeria* oocysts have smooth, clear cyst walls and contain a single round cell when freshly passed. The oocysts in this figure are *Eimeria nieschulzi*, a parasite of rats. Photo courtesy of Dr. George Conder, Pfizer Veterinary Medicine Pharmaceuticals Clinical Development, Pfizer, Inc., Kalamazoo, MI.

Fig. 1.211. Rodent and rabbit hosts may be infected with multiple species of coccidia. Oocysts of more than one species of rabbit *Eimeria* were detected in this sample.

Fig. 1.212. Once in the environment, oocysts undergo sporulation to the infective stage. Sporulated oocysts of *Eimeria* contain four sporocysts, each containing two sporozoites (individual organisms). The sporocysts can clearly be seen inside this rabbit *Eimeria* sp. oocyst. Surrounding the oocyst are several elongated nonpathogenic yeast organisms that are very common in rabbit feces.

Helminth Parasites

PARASITE: **Syphacia obvelata** (Fig. 1.213)
Common name: Pinworm.

Taxonomy: Nematode (order Oxyurida).

Geographic Distribution: Worldwide.

Location in Host: Large intestine of mice and gerbils.

Life Cycle: Eggs passed in the feces quickly become infective. Rodents develop infection following ingestion of larvated eggs.

Laboratory Diagnosis: When present in the feces, eggs can be detected by routine flotation techniques. Eggs are normally found on the skin in the perineal region of infected animals.

Size: 100–142 × 30–40 μm

Clinical Importance: Infections are typically subclinical.

PARASITE: **Aspicularis tetraptera** (Fig. 1.214)
Common name: Pinworm.

Taxonomy: Nematode (order Oxyurida).

Geographic Distribution: Worldwide.

Location in Host: Large intestine of mice.

Life Cycle: The life cycle is similar to that of *Syphacia oblevata*. Adult pinworms develop following ingestion of infective eggs.

Laboratory Diagnosis: Eggs can be detected in feces by centrifugal or simple flotation techniques. The eggs are ellipsoidal with a distinctive double shell wall and contain an undifferentiated embryo in fresh feces.

Size: 70–98 × 29–50 μm

Clinical Importance: Infections are usually subclinical.

PARASITE: **Passalurus ambiguus** (Fig. 1.215)
Common name: Pinworm.

Taxonomy: Nematode (order Oxyurida).

Geographic Distribution: Worldwide.

Location in Host: Cecum of rabbits.

Life Cycle: Eggs are passed in the feces of infected rabbits. The eggs become infective within a short period and infect the next host when ingested.

Laboratory Diagnosis: Eggs can be detected in feces by flotation techniques. The eggs have a smooth, clear shell wall that is flat on one side.

Size: 95–103 × 43 μm

Clinical Importance: Infections are usually subclinical.

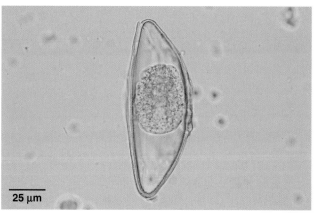

Fig. 1.213. *Syphacia* egg in feces from a gerbil. Eggs of *Syphacia* have a smooth, clear shell wall; are flat on one side; and contain an undifferentiated morula in fresh fecal samples.

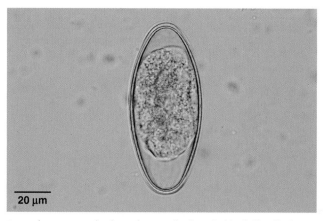

Fig. 1.214. *Aspicularis* eggs have narrowed poles and a smooth, clear, double shell wall. Pinworms are common in rodents.

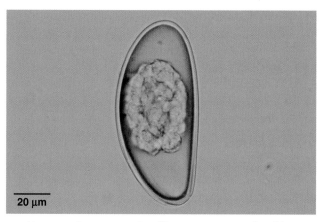

Fig. 1.215. *Passalurus ambiguus* eggs have an operculum-like structure at one end, and the eggs contain an undifferentiated morula in fresh fecal samples.

PARASITE: *Paraspidodera uncinata, Heterakis spumosa* (Fig. 1.216)

Taxonomy: Nematodes (order Ascaridida).

Geographic Distribution: Worldwide.

Location in Host: Cecum of guinea pigs (*Paraspidodera*) and rats (*Heterakis*).

Life Cycle: Eggs passed in the feces develop to the infective stage and infect the host when they are ingested.

Laboratory Diagnosis: Fecal flotation procedures can be used to recover these thick-shelled eggs.

Size:	*Heterakis*	55–60 × 40–55 μm
	Paraspidodera	43 × 31 μm

Clinical Importance: Infection is usually subclinical. These parasites are seen primarily in wild rats and guinea pigs raised on dirt.

PARASITE: *Heligmosomoides polygyrus, Nippostrongylus braziliensis, Obeliscoides cuniculi, Graphidium strigosum* (Fig. 1.217)

Taxonomy: Nematodes (order Strongylida).

Geographic Distribution: Worldwide.

Location in Host: Stomach (*Obeliscoides, Graphidium*) of rabbits; small intestine of rats (*Nippostrongylus*) and mice (*Heligmosomoides*).

Life Cycle: Eggs passed in the feces develop into first-stage larvae, which hatch and continue development in the environment. In most cases, the definitive host is infected by ingesting third-stage larvae, but larvae of *Nippostrongylus braziliensis* usually penetrate the skin of the final host.

Laboratory Diagnosis: Fecal flotation procedures will recover the typical strongylid eggs produced by these parasites.

Size: 52–106 × 28–58 μm (eggs), depending on species

Clinical Importance: Parasites belonging to this group of nematodes are unlikely to occur in caged rabbits and rodents but are common in wild animals. Infection is usually subclinical.

PARASITE: *Hymenolepis* spp. (Figs. 1.218 and 1.219)
    Common name: Dwarf tapeworm of humans (*Hymenolepis nana*).

Taxonomy: Cestode. The most common species in domestic rodents is *Hymenolepis* (=*Vampirolepis*) *nana*. Other species infecting rodents are *H. diminuta* and *H. microstoma*.

Geographic Distribution: Worldwide.

Location in Host: Small intestine of rodents (mouse, rat, hamster). Humans and other primates also serve as hosts for *H. nana*.

Life Cycle: Eggs passed in the feces of definitive hosts are ingested by beetle intermediate hosts. Rodents and humans are infected following ingestion of the intermediate host containing cysticercoids. Infection with adult *H. nana* can also follow ingestion of the egg.

Fig. 1.216. Specimens of *Paraspidodera uncinata*, the cecal worm of guinea pigs. The eggs produced by this cecal nematode of rodents are similar to those of the avian cecal worm, *Heterakis* (Fig. 1.194). Photo courtesy of Dr. David Baker, School of Veterinary Medicine, Louisiana State University, Baton Rouge, LA.

Fig. 1.217. These *Heligmosomoides* eggs are similar to eggs produced by other strongylid nematodes of rabbits and rodents. Photo courtesy of Dr. David Baker, School of Veterinary Medicine, Louisiana State University, Baton Rouge, LA.

Fig. 1.218. *Hymenolepis nana* infects rodents and primates. Eggs are elliptical in shape with a smooth, clear shell wall and contain an embryo with six hooks. There are two knoblike protrusions at each end of the embryo. Like eggs of other common tapeworms, hooks are visible within the embryo.

Hymenolepis (*continued*)

Laboratory Diagnosis: Eggs with six embryonic hooks are detected by either centrifugal or simple fecal flotation examination.

Size:	*H. nana*	40–45 × 34–37 μm
	H. diminuta	60–88 × 52–81 μm

Clinical Importance: Infections are usually subclinical. Heavy infections, particularly in young animals, can result in poor growth and rarely intestinal impaction and death.

PARASITE: ***Cittotaenia* spp.** (Fig. 1.220)
Common name: Rabbit tapeworm.

Taxonomy: Cestode.

Geographic Distribution: Worldwide.

Location in Host: Small intestine of rabbits and hares.

Life Cycle: Eggs are ingested by free-living oribatid mites and develop into the cysticercoid larval stage. Rabbits are infected when they ingest the infected mites.

Laboratory Diagnosis: Fecal flotation procedures will recover *Cittotaenia* eggs.

Size: 64 μm in diameter

Clinical Importance: Heavy infections may cause weight loss.

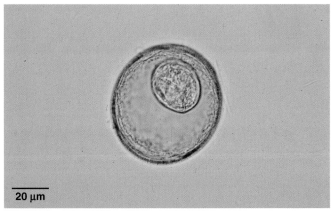

20 µm

Fig. 1.219. Other species of *Hymenolepis* found in rodents have larger, rounder eggs than *H. nana*. Hymenolepid eggs are seen occasionally in fecal samples of dogs and cats that have recently eaten rodents.

16 µm

Fig. 1.220. *Cittotaenia* eggs are quite similar in appearance to *Hymenolepis* eggs. The hooks in the tapeworm embryo are usually easily seen.

Reptiles

PARASITE: ***Entamoeba, Cryptosporidium, Eimeria, Isospora,* and *Caryospora*** (Figs. 1.221–1.223)

Taxonomy: Protozoa.

Geographic Distribution: Worldwide.

Location in Host: Gastrointestinal tract.

Life Cycle: Reptiles are infected by ingestion of cysts (*Entamoeba*) or oocysts that are passed in host feces.

Laboratory Diagnosis: *Eimeria, Caryospora,* and *Cryptosporidium* oocysts can be detected by fecal flotation techniques (the centrifugal flotation procedure with Sheather's sugar solution is recommended for *Cryptosporidium*). Wet mounts of feces or colonic washings can be examined for *Entamoeba* trophozoites and cysts. Fecal smears may also be stained with Wright's stain or Giemsa stain.

Clinical Importance: *Cryptosporidium serpentis* may cause chronic hypertrophic gastritis in snakes, associated with weight loss and regurgitation. *Entamoeba invadens* can cause bloody diarrhea and hepatitis in snakes and some tortoise and lizard hosts. Weight loss and enteritis may accompany infection with *Eimeria* (all reptiles) and *Caryospora* (primarily snakes).

14 µm

Fig. 1.221. Sporulated *Eimeria* oocyst in the feces of a king snake. Oocysts of prey coccidia species may also be found in the feces of carnivorous reptiles. Photo courtesy of Dr. Robert Ridley, College of Veterinary Medicine, Kansas State University, Manhattan, KS.

N

5 µm

Fig. 1.222. *Entamoeba invadens* trophozoite in a stained fecal smear from a Burmese python. A single nucleus (N) is seen in the trophozoite, and they are approximately 16 µm in size. Trophozoite movement can be seen in a wet mount of fresh feces. Photo courtesy of Dr. Ellis C. Greiner, College of Veterinary Medicine, University of Florida, Gainesville, FL.

N

10 µm

Fig. 1.223. Cyst of *Entamoeba invadens* in an iodine-stained smear of reptile feces. Two of the four nuclei (N) present in the cyst can be seen (*arrow*). Cysts are 11–20 µm. Photo courtesy of Dr. Thomas Nolan, School of Veterinary Medicine, University of Pennsylvania, Philadelphia, PA.

PARASITE: **Reptile Helminths** (Figs. 1.224–1.233)

Taxonomy: Nematodes, cestodes (tapeworms), trematodes (flukes), acanthocephalans (thorny-headed worms), and pentastomid parasites.

Geographic Distribution: Worldwide.

Location in Host: Helminth parasites can be found in a variety of body systems, although those detected by fecal exam are primarily gastrointestinal or respiratory system parasites.

Life Cycle: Life cycle varies widely depending on the species. Some nematodes have a direct life cycle. Other nematodes and the remaining helminth groups all require at least one intermediate host.

Laboratory Diagnosis: Eggs are detected in feces by flotation or sedimentation procedures.

Clinical Importance: As in other hosts, low levels of helminth infection are usually well tolerated by reptiles. Heavy infections may result in clinical disease, especially in young or immunosuppressed animals. The complex life cycles of most flukes, tapeworms, and thorny-headed worms make these parasites uncommon in reptiles bred in captivity.

40 µm

Fig. 1.224. Reptiles may be infected with the same groups of helminth parasites that infect other vertebrates. The photo shows examples of reptile capillarid and ascarid eggs.

Fig. 1.225. Pinworm eggs are frequently encountered in reptile feces. These eggs are usually elongated and may appear flat on one side. The eggs shown here are from a bearded dragon.

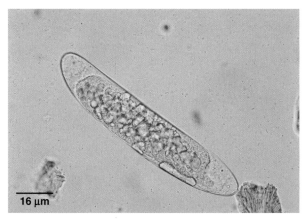

Fig. 1.226. Pinworm egg from a turtle.

Fig. 1.227. *Kalicephalus* sp. egg from a python. This is one of the genera of strongylid nematodes parasitizing reptiles. Eggs of this nematode group are thin shelled. In fresh feces, reptile strongylid eggs may be larvated or contain a morula (cluster of cells), like the one shown here. Photo courtesy of Dr. Ellis C. Greiner, College of Veterinary Medicine, University of Florida, Gainesville, FL.

Fig. 1.228. *Rhabdias* egg in the feces of a rat snake. Eggs containing a larva are passed in the feces and are smaller than strongylid eggs.

Fig. 1.229. Tapeworm egg from a water moccasin. This egg is surrounded by a gelatinous layer with one hook of the hexacanth embryo visible (*arrow*).

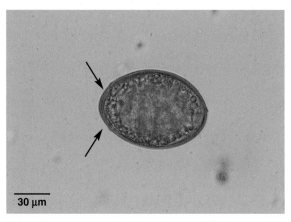

Fig. 1.230. Fluke (trematode) infections are common in wild reptiles, especially those associated with water. The operculum is clearly visible (*arrows*) in this fluke egg from a turtle.

Fig. 1.231. Spirorchid egg detected on sedimentation of feces from a wood turtle. Spirorchids are blood flukes infecting various species of turtles. The large eggs lack an operculum and contain a fully formed miracidium. Note the two black eye spots in this miracidium.

Fig. 1.232. Acanthocephalans (thorny-headed worms) are also common in wild reptiles. This egg was found in mammalian feces but shows the complex layered shell that would also be seen in the eggs of thorny-headed worms of snakes.

Fig. 1.233. Pentastomid egg in feces from a Boelon's python. Pentastomids are an unusual group that shows some arthropod characteristics. Adults are parasites of the respiratory tract. Large eggs (over 100 μm) passed in the feces are often surrounded by a capsule. Larvae within the eggs have legs bearing hooklets (*arrow*) and could be mistaken for mite eggs. An intermediate host is required for completion of the life cycle. Photo courtesy of Dr. Ellis C. Greiner, College of Veterinary Medicine, University of Florida, Gainesville, FL.

169

Detection of Protozoan and Helminth Parasites in the Urinary, Reproductive, and Integumentary Systems and in the Eye

TECHNIQUES FOR PARASITE RECOVERY

Parasites of the Urinary System

Several organisms parasitize the urinary tract, and their eggs and cysts can be detected by routine urine sedimentation. Samples collected by cystocentesis are preferred because voided urine samples could be contaminated with fecal material containing parasite eggs or larvae from the intestinal or respiratory systems.

Urine Sedimentation

1. Centrifuge 5–10 mL of urine in a conical-tip centrifuge tube for 5 minutes at 1500–2000 rpm (approximately $100 \times g$).
2. Decant the supernatant fluid, leaving 0.5 mL. Resuspend the sediment.
3. Transfer a drop of sediment to a slide, add a coverslip, and examine.

Parasites of the Reproductive Tract

Organisms that are primary parasites of the reproductive tract are not important pathogens of common domestic species in North America, with the exception of *Tritrichomonas foetus*. In South America, the Middle East, and parts of Africa, *Trypanosoma equiperdum* causes serious disease in horses and is transmitted venereally. However, this parasite is difficult to recover from tissue fluids or blood, and immunodiagnostic tests are usually used for confirmation of infection. Several other parasites can affect reproduction as a part of general systematic effects, including *Neospora*, *Toxoplasma*, and *Sarcocystis*. These parasites also would not be recovered and identified in the live animal.

Tritrichomonas foetus is a parasite of cattle found in the uterus and vagina of cows and the prepuce of bulls. Diagnosis of infection is usually by identification of the organisms in preputial samples from bulls, although vaginal or cervical secretions from cows can also be tested. It is recommended that samples be collected in lactated Ringer's solution and submitted to a laboratory for culture in Diamond's medium. There is also a commercial kit available that provides a plastic pouch containing a medium into which the sample can be inoculated and cultured (InPouch® TF, BioMed Diagnostics, Inc., White City, OR, www.biomeddiagnostics.com/).

Bovine Preputial Sample Collection

1. Attach a dry 21-in. infusion pipette to a 20-cc syringe and insert into the prepuce of the bull. The tip of the pipette is scraped back and forth across the epithelium while suction is applied.
2. Examine the collected sample microscopically immediately if desired and then inoculate into Ringer's solution (or the commercial InPouch) and refrigerate for transport to the laboratory for culture.
3. Samples not placed directly into nutritive medium should not be held for more than 48 hours in Ringer's or other balanced-salt solution.

Helminth Parasites of the Integumentary System

Several filarid nematode parasites produce microfilariae that are found in the subcutaneous tissue. These larvae can be detected in fresh skin biopsies or on examination of fixed and stained biopsy tissue sections. For recovery of microfilariae from fresh biopsies, the biopsy is macerated and allowed to incubate in saline for several hours at room temperature. Following incubation, the saline is examined microscopically for the presence of microfilariae. Free-living nematodes that occasionally invade the skin may also be seen in fresh or fixed and stained skin biopsies.

PARASITE: ***Dioctophyme renale*** (Fig. 2.1)

Common name: Giant kidney worm.

Taxonomy: Nematode (order Enoplida).

Geographic Distribution: North America and Europe.

Location in Host: Kidney and occasionally peritoneal cavity of dogs, mink, and other domestic and wild animals.

Life Cycle: Adult worms in the kidney produce eggs that are passed in the urine. The first intermediate host is an annelid worm; the second intermediate host is a fish. The final host becomes infected when it eats a fish containing infective parasite larvae.

Laboratory Diagnosis: Eggs with a thick, rough shell are detected in the urine.

Size: $60–80 \times 39–46\,\mu m$

Clinical Importance: The spectacular adult worms (females may reach 100 cm in length) enter the renal pelvis and eventually destroy the kidney, leaving only the capsule. Typically, only one kidney (usually the right) is affected. Most infections are asymptomatic, despite the loss of a kidney, although hematuria and dysuria may occur. *Dioctophyme renale* is a rare finding in dogs in North America.

28 mm

Fig. 2.1. *Dioctophyme* eggs are larger than those of *Pearsonema* and have a thicker eggshell with a rougher surface.

URINARY SYSTEM PARASITES

PARASITE: ***Pearsonema (=Capillaria) plica, P. feliscati*** (Figs. 2.2 and 2.3)

Taxonomy: Nematode (order Enoplida). These parasites were previously included in the genus *Capillaria*.

Geographic Distribution: Worldwide.

Location in Host: Adult worms in the bladder of dogs and foxes (*P. plica*) and cats (*P. feliscati*).

Life Cycle: Parasite eggs passed in the urine become infective in the environment. Although the life cycle is not known with certainty, the final host is probably infected by ingesting an earthworm intermediate host or a transport host, such as a bird.

Laboratory Diagnosis: Typical capillarid eggs are detected in urine sediment. Cystocentesis is preferred for collecting urine samples since fecal material containing similar eggs of other capillarid species may contaminate voided urine samples.

Size: 51–65 × 24–32 μm

Clinical Importance: Many infections are asymptomatic, although infected animals may develop cystitis.

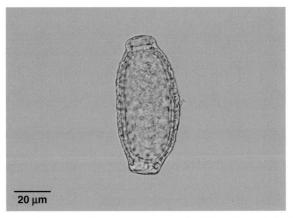

20 μm

Fig. 2.2. *Pearsonema feliscati* egg in a urine sedimentation procedure. Methylene blue stain is often added to these preparations, which will stain the eggs purple. Like other capillarids, *P. feliscati* eggs are elongated and bipolar plugged.

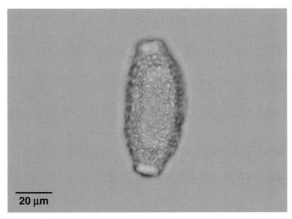

20 μm

Fig. 2.3. If the microscope is focused on the shell wall of the *Pearsonema* egg, a thick globular pattern of ridges can be seen.

PARASITE: ***Stephanurus dentatus*** (Fig. 2.4)
Common name: Kidney worm.

Taxonomy: Nematode (order Strongylida).

Geographic Distribution: Tropical and subtropical regions.

Location in Host: Adults are found in the wall of the ureters and the pelvis of the kidney as well as in the peritoneal fat of swine.

Life Cycle: Parasite eggs leave the host via the urine. Like other strongylids, first-stage larvae of *S. dentatus* hatch from the eggs and develop to the infective third stage. The pig definitive host is infected by ingestion of infective larvae or of an earthworm transport host or by skin penetration by infective larvae. Once in the host, larvae migrate through the liver before moving to the perirenal tissues, where development is completed.

Laboratory Diagnosis: Diagnosis is made by detection of eggs in urine sedimentation tests or from clinical signs. However, disease may be present before the infection is patent (prepatent period is 4–6 months).

Size: 90–114 × 53–65 μm

Clinical Importance: The damage associated with larval migration through the liver is an important component of disease caused by the parasite. Pigs may show reduced growth or weight loss and general loss of condition. *Stephanurus dentatus* is unlikely to occur in modern swine confinement systems.

PARASITE: ***Trichosomoides crassicauda*** (Figs. 2.5 and 1.197)

Taxonomy: Nematode (order Enoplida).

Geographic Distribution: Worldwide.

Location in Host: Adult female worms are found in the wall of the bladder of wild and laboratory rats. Male worms exist as hyperparasites in the reproductive tract of the females.

Life Cycle: Eggs leave the host in the urine. Infection occurs when eggs are ingested by the host.

Laboratory Diagnosis: Infection is often detected by identification of adults in the bladder or during histologic examination of bladder sections, but diagnosis may also be made by finding eggs in the urine. *Trichosomoides* eggs are brown with bipolar plugs.

Size: 60–70 × 30–35 μm

Clinical Importance: Infection is typically subclinical but is undesirable in laboratory rats.

18 µm

Fig. 2.4. *Stephanurus dentatus* adults produce typical strongylid eggs that can be seen in urine. However, disease may develop before the infection becomes patent. Photo courtesy of Dr. T. Bonner Stewart, School of Veterinary Medicine, Louisiana State University, Baton Rouge, LA.

20 µm

Fig. 2.5. The brown eggs of *Trichosomoides* have bipolar plugs. Photo courtesy of Dr. Stephen Smith, Virginia Maryland Regional College of Veterinary Medicine, Virginia Tech, Blacksburg, VA.

REPRODUCTIVE SYSTEM PARASITES

PARASITE: ***Tritrichomonas foetus*** (Fig. 2.6)

Taxonomy: Protozoa (flagellate).

Geographic Distribution: Worldwide, but uncommon where artificial insemination is widely practiced.

Location in Host: Preputial cavity of bulls, uterus and vagina of cows.

Life Cycle: Organisms are transmitted during breeding. The trophozoite in the reproductive tract is the only form of the organism.

Laboratory Diagnosis: Organisms are detected in vaginal or uterine discharges or in preputial scrapings. The prepuce is the site most frequently sampled. Organisms may be present in small numbers, and culture is recommended using Diamond's medium or the commercial InPouch system available in North America. *Tritrichomonas* is easily recognized by its undulating membrane and three anterior flagella. A polymerase chain reaction (PCR) test is also available.

Size: $10–25 \times 3–15\,\mu m$

Clinical Importance: The presence of *T. foetus* in a cattle herd produces chronic abortion and infertility and can have a serious economic impact on production.

PARASITES OF OTHER SYSTEMS (EXCLUDING ARTHROPODS)

PARASITE: ***Onchocerca* spp., *Stephanofilaria* spp.** (Figs. 2.7 and 2.8)

Taxonomy: Nematodes (order Spirurida).

Geographic Distribution: *Onchocerca cervicalis* and *O. gutterosa* are found worldwide. Other species have more limited distribution, primarily in Africa but also in the Middle East and Asia. *Stephanofilaria* spp. are found worldwide.

Location in Host: *Onchocerca cervicalis* is found in the equine nuchal ligament. Other species are bovine parasites. *Onchocerca gutterosa* parasitizes the nuchal and gastrosplenic ligament, while *O. gibsoni* is found in subcutaneous and intermuscular nodules and *O. armillata* is found in the wall of the thoracic aorta. *Stephanofilaria* spp. live in the subcutaneous tissue of the ventrum in cattle.

Life Cycle: Depending on the parasite species, *Culicoides* (midges), *Simulium* (black flies), *Haematobia* (horn flies), and *Musca* species act as the intermediate host and transmit the parasite during feeding.

Laboratory Diagnosis: Diagnosis is made by skin biopsy of affected areas and examination for microfilariae following saline incubation or histopathologic examination. Examination of tissues from lesions caused by *Stephanofilaria* will reveal both adults and microfilariae.

Size:	*Onchocerca* microfilariae	approximately 200 to >300 μm in length, depending on species
	Stephanofilaria microfilariae	approximately 50 μm

Clinical Importance: *Onchocerca* spp. are not generally considered to be highly pathogenic parasites, although equine *O. cervicalis* infection can be associated with dermatitis in horses, and some of the bovine species cause skin or connective tissue lesions that must be trimmed at slaughter. In North America, localized ventral midline dermatitis caused by *Stephanofilaria* is relatively common in adult cattle but has no clinical significance.

Fig. 2.6. *Tritrichomonas foetus* organisms from culture. The undulating membrane (U) and anterior flagella can be seen in several of the organisms. In culture, living organisms move in a jerky motion, and the rippling undulating membrane can be seen with the 40× objective. Photo courtesy of Dr. Alvin Gajadhar, Centre for Animal Parasitology, CFIA, Saskatoon, Saskatchewan, Canada.

Fig. 2.7. Microfilariae of *Onchocerca gutterosa* (*arrow*) in bovine skin. Diagnosis can be made more rapidly by incubating skin biopsies in saline and examining the fluid several hours later for moving microfilariae that have migrated out of the skin. Photo courtesy of Dr. Fernando Paiva, Universidade Federal de Mato Grosso do Sul, Campo Grande, MS, Brazil.

Fig. 2.8. Horn flies (*Haematobia irritans*) feeding on a *Stephanofilaria stilesi* lesion on the ventrum of a bovine host. The flies are the intermediate host of the parasite and ingest microfilariae in the lesion during feeding. *Stephanofilaria stilesi* is common, but unimportant, in North America. Photo courtesy of Dr. Jeffrey F. Williams, Vanson HaloSource, Inc., Redmond, WA.

PARASITE: *Dracunculus insignis* (Fig. 2.9)

Taxonomy: Nematode (order Spirurida).

Geographic Distribution: North America.

Location in Host: Adults occur in the subcutaneous tissue, usually on the limbs. Raccoons, other wild animals, and occasionally dogs are infected.

Life Cycle: The female worm creates an ulcer on the skin of a limb. When the limb is placed in water, the female extrudes a portion of the uterus, which ruptures, releasing first-stage larvae into the water. Larvae are ingested by a copepod, *Cyclops*, that acts as the intermediate host. The definitive host becomes infected by drinking water containing the infected intermediate host.

Laboratory Diagnosis: The diagnosis is usually made by examination of the skin lesion and removal of the worm.

Size: First-stage larva 608 μm

Clinical Importance: *Dracunculus* occurs infrequently in dogs but can cause a chronic ulcer that may develop secondary bacterial infection.

PARASITE: *Pelodera strongyloides* (Fig. 2.10)

Taxonomy: Nematode (order Rhabditida).

Geographic Distribution: Worldwide.

Location in Host: Skin.

Life Cycle: *Pelodera strongyloides* is a free-living nematode that may invade the skin of animals. It is usually seen as a pathogen where animals are confined to areas with moist bedding high in organic material that will support growth and development of the nematodes.

Laboratory Diagnosis: Parasite infection can be diagnosed by finding first-stage (rhabditiform) larvae in skin scrapings from affected areas.

Clinical Importance: *Pelodera* is an uncommon cause of dermatitis in a variety of animal species.

PARASITE: *Thelazia* spp. (Fig. 2.11)

Common name: Eye worm.

Taxonomy: Nematode (order Spirurida).

Geographic Distribution: Worldwide.

Location in Host: Conjunctival sac and lacrimal duct of cattle, horses, dogs.

Life Cycle: Muscid flies act as intermediate hosts and ingest first-stage larvae released by adult worms into the tears. Development to the third larval stage occurs in the fly, which deposits the infective larvae on the host during feeding.

Laboratory Diagnosis: Laboratory diagnosis is unnecessary since the worms can be seen during examination of the eyes of the host.

Size: Adult worms 1–2 cm

Clinical Importance: Worms may cause tearing and conjunctivitis, but many chronic cases are asymptomatic.

Fig. 2.9. First-stage larvae of *Dracunculus insignis*. These distinctive larvae with their long, thin tails can be teased from the uterus of a worm removed from a skin ulcer and confirm the diagnosis of *Dracunculus* infection.

Fig. 2.10. All stages of the life cycle from egg to adult are present in this agar plate culture of *Pelodera*. Only larvae would be present in scrapings of skin infected with this free-living nematode.

Fig. 2.11. *Thelazia* in the eye of a cow. Photo courtesy of Dr. Jeffrey F. Williams, Vanson HaloSource, Inc., Redmond, WA.

PARASITE: ***Besnoitia* spp.** (Figs. 2.12 and 2.13)
Common name: Elephant skin disease (cattle).

Taxonomy: Protozoa (coccidia).

Geographic Distribution: *Besnoitia besnoiti* (cattle, goats) is found worldwide but is of greatest importance in Africa. *Besnoitia bennetti* (horses and donkeys) occurs primarily in Africa, southern Europe, and South America but is also found in North America.

Location in Host: Cysts are seen in the subcutaneous tissue and scleral conjunctiva of livestock.

Life Cycle: The definitive host of this coccidian parasite is the cat. Oocysts are shed in cat feces and are ingested by the intermediate host (cattle, horses, etc.). Parasites multiply in the endothelial cells and finally form large cysts in the subcutaneous tissue of intermediate hosts.

Laboratory Diagnosis: *Besnoitia* spp. often form cysts ("pearls") in the scleral conjunctiva that can easily be seen with the naked eye. Diagnosis can also be made by examining stained sections of skin biopsies for the presence of subcutaneous cysts.

Clinical Importance: Many cases are asymptomatic. However, an acute febrile illness can develop, followed by thickening and wrinkling of skin that makes the hide unsuitable for leather production. Affected animals may recover slowly. Although *Besnoitia* occurs in North America, its extent is unknown, and it rarely seems to cause clinical disease.

Fig. 2.12. Extensive skin thickening and wrinkling caused by *Besnoitia besnoiti*. This disease is most prevalent in Africa. Photo courtesy of Dr. Jeffrey F. Williams, Vanson HaloSource, Inc., Redmond, WA.

Fig. 2.13. Scleral "pearls," or cysts, of *Besnoitia bennetti* in the eye of a donkey in North America. Photo courtesy of Dr. Hany M. Elsheikha and Dr. Charles Mackenzie, College of Veterinary Medicine, Michigan State University, East Lansing, MI.

CHAPTER 3

Detection of Parasites in the Blood

Various pathogenic and nonpathogenic protozoa and nematodes may be detected in blood samples from domestic animals. Most of these parasites are ingested by arthropod vectors during feeding and are present in the bloodstream of their mammalian hosts as a normal part of their life cycles.

IMMUNOLOGIC DETECTION OF BLOOD PARASITES

Although the focus of this book is the morphologic diagnosis of parasitism, it is important to recognize that immunologic tests are now widely used in conjunction with or in place of microscopic examination of blood smears for some blood-borne parasites, and the use of these tests can be expected to increase in the future. Immunologic tests offer increased sensitivity compared with morphologic techniques in many cases and are especially valuable in some chronic hemoprotozoan infections and in canine and feline heartworm infection. In both cases, many infections are undetectable by routine microscopic tests. The commercial immunologic tests used most widely are the indirect fluorescent antibody (IFA) test and the enzyme-linked immunosorbent assay (ELISA). For additional discussion of the basis and use of immunodiagnostic and molecular diagnostic procedures in veterinary parasitology, particularly in the United States, see Chapter 4.

MICROSCOPIC EXAMINATION OF BLOOD FOR PROTOZOAN PARASITES

Most hemoprotozoan parasites are intracellular in erythrocytes or white blood cells and may cause anemia. A routine thin blood smear is therefore useful both for assessing erythrocyte abnormalities and for detecting the presence of parasites. Parasites are most likely to be detected in blood smears during acute infection. Once infections become chronic, immunologic diagnostic techniques are usually more sensitive.

For microscopic examination of blood smears for hemoprotozoa, Giemsa stain is most effective, but Wright's stain can also be used in most cases. Commercial stain kits used in many veterinary practices (an example is Dip Quick Stain, Jorgensen Laboratories, Loveland, CO, www.jorvet.com) will also stain hemoprotozoa when used as directed, but the stain will be of poorer quality. The following procedure can be followed when Giemsa stain is used.

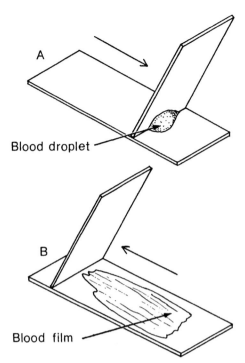

Fig. 3.1. Technique for making a blood smear. (A) Bring a spreader slide back at an angle until it touches the drop of blood; wait until the drop flows laterally. (B) Draw the spreader slide away from the drop, maintaining an angle. The blood will spread into a smooth, thin film.

To prepare a thin blood smear, place a drop of blood on one end of a microscope slide and draw the blood into a thin film as shown in Figure 3.1.

Giemsa Stain

1. Air-dry the blood film, protecting it from flies and other insects if it is not to be stained immediately.
2. Fix in absolute methanol for 5 minutes and air-dry.
3. Dilute stock Giemsa stain 1:20 with distilled water and flood the film (or place slide in staining jar). Fresh stain should be prepared at least every 2 days.
4. Stain for 30 minutes.
5. Wash stain away gently with tap water.
6. Air-dry; parasite cytoplasm will stain blue, and nuclei will stain magenta.

The stained blood film can be scanned using the 40× objective of the microscope with use of the oil immersion lens for greater detail when suspected parasites are found.

The dimensions of blood parasites are best determined by means of an ocular micrometer (see Chapter 1). A micrometer is highly recommended for accurate measurement of parasites in blood and fecal samples. If a micrometer is not available, the size of the parasite on a blood film may be approximated by comparison with the dimensions of host erythrocytes (Table 3.1).

Table 3.1. **Average diameters of erythrocytes**

Animal	Erythrocyte Diameter (μm)
Horse	5.5
Cattle	5.8
Sheep	4.5
Goat	3.2
Dog	7.0
Cat	5.8
Chicken	7.0×12.0

Source: Measurements from Weiss and Wardrop (2010).

MICROSCOPIC EXAMINATION OF BLOOD FOR NEMATODE PARASITES

Many species of parasitic worms enter the bloodstream of the host to reach certain organs, where they develop to maturity. These parasites usually stay in the blood only minutes or hours; thus, they are seldom seen in blood samples taken for diagnostic purposes. There are some filarial nematodes, however, whose larvae (microfilariae) are normally found in the peripheral blood. The microfilarial stage of these parasite species remains in the circulation until ingestion by the bloodsucking intermediate host. Microfilaria testing is most often performed for detection of canine heartworm infection, and the following discussion of techniques for microfilaria detection is directed specifically to heartworm testing. However, all species of microfilariae in the blood could be detected by the same microscopic techniques.

Although the techniques for microscopic detection of heartworm microfilariae are presented below, the ELISA adult-female antigen test for diagnosis of canine heartworm infection is the preferred screening test and has largely supplanted microfilaria tests. Antigen tests are significantly more sensitive than microfilaria tests because many heartworm infections are amicrofilaremic. The absence of microfilariae may be due to low or single-sex worm burdens or immune clearance of microfilariae. Moreover, the macrolide heartworm preventatives are microfilaricidal and sterilize existing heartworm infections after several months of administration.

The American Heartworm Society and the European Scientific Counsel Companion Animal Parasites (ESCCAP) currently recommend annual testing using an antigen test as the primary method of heartworm diagnosis for all dogs in endemic areas. Any dog testing positive on an antigen test should also be tested for microfilariae to determine if microfilaricidal treatment is necessary. If a microfilaria test is used alone for heartworm testing, one of the concentration techniques (Knott's or filter test) must be used.

Antigen tests currently available in the United States are available in ELISA and immunochromatographic formats. Although differences in sensitivity among these tests have been found experimentally, they are not statistically significant. False-negative results are uncommon and are usually the result of lab error, although a small number (<1%) of antigen-negative dogs will be microfilaremic. Available tests are also highly specific.

Diagnosis of heartworm infection in cats is more difficult than in dogs. Several of the antigen tests can be used in cats, but they can produce false-negative results because of the low worm burdens usually found in cats. Similarly, cats are rarely microfilaremic and may develop disease before the adult stage, detectable by antigen testing, is present. To improve the sensitivity of heartworm detection in cats, heartworm antibody tests have been developed. These tests can detect

BLOOD

infection earlier than antigen tests but may only indicate exposure to the parasite rather than active infection. Care should be taken in interpreting a feline antibody test, and the results of that test alone should not be used to establish a diagnosis of heartworm infection. In a cat showing clinical signs consistent with heartworm infection, both antigen and antibody tests should be performed as part of the diagnostic workup.

For current recommendations of the American Heartworm Society and the European Scientific Counsel Companion Animal Parasites relating to diagnosis and treatment of heartworm infection in dogs and cats, consult the websites of the two organizations: www.heartwormsociety.org and www.esccap.org.

Tests for Canine Heartworm Microfilariae in Blood Samples

The following techniques can be used to detect microfilariae in blood samples. The canine heartworm, *Dirofilaria immitis*, is found throughout the world. In North America, dogs may also be infected with *Acanthocheilonema* (=*Dipetalonema*) *reconditum* or, rarely, with *Dirofilaria striata*, a parasite of wild felids in North and South America. In parts of Europe, Asia, and Africa, *Dirofilaria repens*, *Acanthocheilonema dracunculoides*, and *Cercopithifilaria* (=*Acanthocheilonema*) *grassi* parasitize dogs. When a microfilaria test is used for heartworm diagnosis, the microfilariae of other species must be differentiated from those of *D. immitis*.

Size is an important characteristic in identification of microfilariae (Table 3.2) and should be measured with an eyepiece micrometer (see Chapter 1 for micrometer calibration procedure). Other criteria can also be used to discriminate between species, but they are less dependable. Determination of the length, width, and shape of the head of a microfilaria should allow identification of most canine microfilariae. The standard measurements of these microfilariae were determined with formalin-fixed specimens; use of other fixatives or lysing solutions may alter the size of the organisms. Similarly, storage of whole blood for more than 3 days may cause some *D. immitis* microfilariae to shrink in length to the size of *A. reconditum*.

Direct Smear

The direct smear is the simplest and most rapid of the procedures to be described for microfilariae. It is not a very sensitive technique but can be used in conjunction with an adult heartworm antigen test to determine if microfilariae are present or to evaluate the pattern of movement of microfilariae when attempting to differentiate between *Dirofilaria* and *Acanthocheilonema*:

1. Place one drop of venous blood onto a clean microscope slide and coverslip.
2. Examine the coverslip area under low magnification (10×) of the microscope. Look for undulating movements of larvae, which may retain motility for as long as 24 hours.

Hematocrit Test

This technique is only slightly more sensitive than the direct smear:

1. Draw fresh whole blood into a microhematocrit tube.
2. Spin for 3 minutes in a hematocrit tube centrifuge.
3. Examine the plasma portion of the separated blood, while still in the tube, under low magnification (10×). Moving microfilariae will be present in the plasma above the buffy coat.

Table 3.2. Characteristics of *Dirofilaria* spp. and other microfilariae found in canine blood based on formalin-fixed specimens

	Dirofilaria immitis	*Dirofilaria repens*	*Dirofilaria striata*	*Acanthocheilonema reconditum*	*Cercopithifilaria grassi*	*Acanthocheilonema dracunculoides*
Length (μm)	295–325	268–360	360–385	250–288	570	189–230
Width (μm)	5–7.5	5–8	5–6	4.5–5.5	12–25	5–6
Head	Tapered	Blunt	Tapered	Blunt		Blunt
Tail	Straight	Variable—straight or hooked	Curved	Variable—hooked (30%) or curved	Slightly bent	Sharp and extended
Body shape	Straight		S shaped	Curved		
Motion (live)	Stationary		Stationary	Progressive		
Relative number	Few to many		Few	Few		
Location of adult	Pulmonary arteries, right heart	Subcutaneous intramuscular tissues	Subcutaneous and intramuscular tissue	Subcutaneous tissues	Subcutaneous tissue	Peritoneum
Geographic location	Worldwide	Europe, Middle East, Africa, Asia, North America (?)	North and South America	Africa, Europe, North America	Southern Europe, Africa	Africa, Europe, India

The direct smear and microhematocrit techniques may not detect infections with only small numbers of microfilariae. Therefore, if a microfilariae test is used as a screening procedure for heartworm infection, one of the following concentration techniques is preferred.

Modified Knott's Test

The modified Knott's technique is the preferred concentration method for the detection and identification of microfilariae in blood:

1. Draw a sample of blood into a syringe containing anticoagulant such as EDTA or heparin.
2. Mix 1 mL of the blood with 9 mL of a 2% formalin solution. If not well mixed, the red cells will not be thoroughly lysed by the hypotonic formalin solution, making the test much more difficult to read. Microfilariae, but not red cells, will be fixed by 2% formalin. If 10% formalin is used (the concentration used for fixation of tissues), red cells will also be fixed and not lysed.
3. Centrifuge the mixture at 1200 rpm for 5 minutes (or as for fecal flotation procedures) and discard the supernatant.
4. Add one drop of 0.1% methylene blue to the sediment, mix well, and transfer the stained sediment to a microscope slide using a Pasteur pipette to collect the entire sample.
5. Examine using the 10× microscope objective. Microfilariae will be fixed in an extended position with nuclei stained blue.

An alternative procedure using the same amount of blood is the filter test, which traps microfilariae on a filter that is examined with the microscope. This technique can be performed more quickly than the modified Knott's test, but microfilariae are not easily measured for identification.

Filter Test

Kits containing filter apparatus, filters, lysing solution, and stain are commercially available (Difil-Test®, EVSCO Pharmaceuticals, Buena, NJ). Components of the test can also be purchased. Use of 2% formalin as the lysing solution is recommended, since other lysing solutions may cause significant changes in the size of microfilariae:

1. Mix 1 mL of blood with 9 mL lysing solution in a syringe.
2. Attach the syringe to the filter holder containing a filter with a 5-μm pore size and empty the syringe.
3. Refill syringe with water and pass it through the filter to wash away remaining small debris.
4. Refill syringe with air, reattach to the filter apparatus, and express.
5. Unscrew the filter assembly, remove the filter with forceps, and place the filter on a microscope slide.
6. Add one drop of 0.1% methylene blue, coverslip, and examine at 10×.

BLOOD

BLOOD PARASITES OF DOGS AND CATS

Parasite: ***Hepatozoon* spp.** (Fig. 3.2)

Taxonomy: Protozoa (hemogregarine).

Geographic Distribution: *Hepatozoon canis* occurs worldwide, while the distribution of *Hepatozoon americanum* appears to be limited to the southeastern United States.

Location in Host: Gamonts are found in polymorphonuclear leukocytes (*H. americanum, H. canis*) and meronts in skeletal muscle (*H. americanum*) or various organs (*H. canis*) of dogs, cats, and various wild carnivores.

Life Cycle: The tick intermediate host acquires infection during feeding. Dogs become infected by ingesting infected ticks. *Hepatozoon americanum* is transmitted by *Amblyomma maculatum* (the Gulf Coast tick), and the vector of *H. canis* is *Rhipicephalus sanguineus* (the brown dog tick).

Laboratory Diagnosis: Sausage-shaped *Hepatozoon* gamonts can be detected in polymorphonuclear leukocytes in Wright- or Geimsa-stained blood smears. Although this method of diagnosis can be used for *H. canis, H. americanum* is rarely found on blood smears, and a molecular diagnostic test may be used. Morphologic diagnosis of this species generally occurs by the detection of meronts in skeletal muscle biopsies or on histopathology after necropsy.

Size: Gamonts 8–12 × 3–6 µm

Clinical Importance: *Hepatozoon americanum* can cause severe disease, with fever, depression, joint pain, myositis, periosteal bone proliferation, and chronic wasting while *H. canis* infections are usually subclinical.

10 µm

Fig. 3.2. *Hepatozoon* gamont in a polymorphonucleocyte. The parasite is sausage shaped with a centrally compact nucleus that stains only faintly in this specimen (*arrow*). *Hepatozoon americanum* is rarely present in blood films, and muscle biopsies are more commonly used for diagnosis.

BLOOD

PARASITE: ***Babesia canis* and *B. gibsoni*** (Figs. 3.3 and 3.4)

Taxonomy: Protozoa (piroplasm). *Babesia gibsoni* consists of more than one genetically distinct but morphologically identical species.

Geographic Distribution: *Babesia* mostly occurs in the tropical and subtropical regions of the world. *Babesia canis* is worldwide in distribution; in the United States, it occurs in the southeast. *Babesia gibsoni* infects canids in North Africa and the Far East and has recently been reported in various states in the United States.

Location in Host: Canine red blood cells. *Babesia* spp. have been described in cats but are not widely distributed and do not appear to be present in North America.

Life Cycle: In North America, dogs acquire *B. canis* and *B. gibsoni* infections from the brown dog tick, *Rhipicephalus sanguineus*. Other tick vectors include *Dermacentor reticulatus* in Europe and *Haemaphysalis leachi* in Africa.

Laboratory Diagnosis: Piroplasms can be detected in erythrocytes on Wright- or Giemsa-stained blood smears. Immunologic and molecular diagnostic tests can also be used and are a more sensitive diagnostic technique in chronic infections. *Babesia canis* is pear shaped and usually occurs in pairs; *B. gibsoni* is round to oval shaped.

Size:	*B. canis*	4–5 μm
	B. gibsoni	1–3 μm

Clinical Importance: Severity of clinical disease may range from mild to life threatening. Anemia, hemolytic crisis, and multi-organ failure can occur. North American and European strains appear to be less pathogenic than those infecting dogs in Africa and Asia.

BLOOD

Fig. 3.3. Erythrocyte containing pear-shaped *Babesia canis* piroplasms. The parasite is usually found in pairs; as many as eight piroplasms may be found in a single red blood cell.

Fig. 3.4. *Babesia gibsoni* (*arrow*) is a smaller organism than *B. canis*. The pear shape seen so clearly with *B. canis* is much less distinct with *B. gibsoni*. Photo courtesy of Dr. Kurt Zimmerman, Virginia-Maryland Regional College of Veterinary Medicine, Virginia Tech, Blacksburg VA.

PARASITE: *Cytauxzoon felis* (Figs. 3.5 and 3.6)

Taxonomy: Protozoa (piroplasm).

Geographic Distribution: Southern United States.

Location in Host: Merozoites occur in red blood cells, and schizonts occur in histiocytes of bobcats and cats.

Life Cycle: Infection transmission occurs through the blood-feeding activities of the tick vectors. *Dermacentor variabilis* has been used to transmit infections experimentally.

Laboratory Diagnosis: Merozoites are detected in red blood cells (1–4 merozoites/erythrocyte) in Wright- or Giemsa-stained blood smears. Schizonts are detected in mononuclear cells in bone-marrow aspirates. A molecular diagnostic test is also available.

  Size: 1–2 μm

Clinical Importance: *Cytauxzoon felis* is highly pathogenic in cats. Infections are usually fatal; cats die within a few days of the onset of clinical signs. Anemia, depression, high fever, icterus, hepatomegaly, and splenomegaly occur.

PARASITE: *Leishmania* spp. (Figs. 3.7 and 3.8)
      Common name: Visceral and cutaneous leishmaniasis.

Taxonomy: Protozoa (hemoflagellate). Species include *L. donovani*, *L. tropica*, *L. infantum*, *L. chagasi*, *L. braziliensis*, *L. mexicana*.

Geographic Distribution: Worldwide.

Location in Host: Amastigotes occur in macrophages and cells of the reticuloendothelial system of various organs (skin, spleen, liver, bone marrow, lymph nodes).

Life Cycle: Blood-feeding sand flies (*Lutzomyia*, *Phlebotomus*) serve as intermediate hosts.

Laboratory Diagnosis: Diagnosis occurs by detection of amastigotes in macrophages in stained smears made from needle aspirate biopsies of lymph node, bone marrow, or spleen or in impression smears of skin lesions. Amastigotes are rarely seen in stained peripheral blood smears. Serologic and polymerase chain reaction (PCR) techniques are also used in diagnosis.

  Size: 2.5–5.0 × 1.5–2.0 μm

Clinical Importance: Infection in dogs is often subclinical. However, disease may develop involving various visceral organs and skin, resulting in cutaneous lesions, lethargy, progressive weight loss, and anorexia that may end in death. Infection with *L. infantum* has recently been found to be widespread in foxhounds in the United States. Cats are rarely infected. Leishmaniasis is a serious, potentially fatal disease in humans. Dogs serve as an important reservoir host of the parasite in some parts of the world.

Fig. 3.5. Small *Cytauxzoon felis* merozoites in infected erythrocytes (*arrow*) have a dark nucleus and a light blue cytoplasm on Wright- or Giemsa-stained blood smears. Photo courtesy of Dr. Karen F. Snowden, College of Veterinary Medicine, Texas A&M University, College Station, TX.

Fig. 3.6. Mononuclear cell containing a *Cytauxzoon felis* schizont. Photo courtesy of Dr. Kurt Zimmerman, Virginia-Maryland Regional College of Veterinary Medicine, Virginia Tech, Blacksburg VA.

Fig. 3.7. *Leishmania* spp. amastigotes in a lymph node impression smear. Photo courtesy of Dr. Karen F. Snowden, College of Veterinary Medicine, Texas A&M University, College Station, TX.

PARASITE: ***Trypanosoma cruzi*** (Fig. 3.9)
Common name: Chagas disease.

Taxonomy: Protozoa (hemoflagellate). Dogs and cats can also be infected with *T. brucei*, *T. congolense*, and *T. evansi*, trypanosome species more commonly associated with large animals (see below).

Geographic Distribution: North and South America.

Location in Host: Trypomastigotes occur in the blood; amastigotes and epimastigotes occur in skeletal muscle, reticuloendothelial cells, and various other tissues of humans, dogs, cats, and many wildlife mammalian species.

Life Cycle: Triatomids (kissing or assassin bugs) pass trypomastigotes in the feces during blood feeding on the vertebrate definitive host. Parasites enter the definitive host through mucous membranes or through the triatomid bite-wound site.

Laboratory Diagnosis: Trypomastigotes are detected on Wright- or Giemsa-stained blood smears early in infection. Diagnosis in chronic or light infections may require serologic tests, culture, or xenodiagnosis.

Size: 16–20 µm

Clinical Importance: Infection with *T. cruzi* is highly pathogenic, causing acute and chronic cardiac disease. Lymphadenopathy, pale mucous membranes, lethargy, ascites, hepatomegaly, splenomegaly, anorexia, diarrhea, and neurologic signs may be seen. Infection in dogs and cats is relatively uncommon in North America.

PARASITE: ***Dirofilaria immitis*** (Figs. 3.10–3.12)
Common name: Heartworm.

Taxonomy: Nematode (order Spirurida).

Geographic Distribution: Worldwide. *Dirofilaria striata* is a rare parasite of dogs in the southeastern United States.

Location in Host: Adult worms are found in the pulmonary arteries and right ventricle of dogs, wild canids, and ferrets. Cats are much less likely than dogs to become infected, and feline infections are rarely patent.

Life Cycle: Mosquitoes serve as intermediate hosts, acquiring microfilariae and transmitting infective third-stage larvae while blood feeding. The prepatent period in dogs is about 6 months.

Laboratory Diagnosis: The most sensitive technique for heartworm diagnosis is detection of antigen using one of the various commercial antigen kits for use with serum, plasma, and/or whole blood. Less sensitive is testing for microfilariae in blood samples using the Knott's test or a filter test, which is equal in ability to detect microfilariae. However, the Knott's test should be used for specific identification of microfilariae (on the basis of size and morphology).

Size: 295–325 × 5–7.5 µm

Clinical Importance: Heartworm infection is highly pathogenic and is an important medical health issue in both canine and feline medicine. Chronic heartworm infection in dogs can lead to fatal right-sided congestive heart failure. A liver failure (or Caval) syndrome occurs in some dogs with heavy worm burdens (>100) that, without treatment, leads to a rapidly fatal hemolytic crisis. Heartworm infection in cats can be subclinical or result in serious chronic disease (respiratory or vomiting/gastrointestinal) or cats may die acutely.

Fig. 3.8. *Leishmania* amastigote (*arrow*) in a macrophage from a canine lymph node. The small round kinetoplast can be seen adjacent to the nucleus in this amastigote. Photo courtesy of Dr. Bernard Feldman, Virginia-Maryland Regional College of Veterinary Medicine, Virginia Tech, Blacksburg, VA.

Fig. 3.9. Stained trypomastigote of *Trypanosooma cruzi* in a blood smear from an infected dog. The organisms often assume a C shape in blood smears. The dark-staining kinetoplast can easily be seen in this specimen. Photo courtesy of Dr. Karen F. Snowden, College of Veterinary Medicine, Texas A&M University, College Station, TX.

Fig. 3.10. Microfilariae of *Dirofilaria immitis* recovered from a blood sample using the modified Knott's technique. Photo courtesy of Dr. Thomas Nolan, School of Veterinary Medicine, University of Pennsylvania, Philadelphia, PA.

PARASITE: *Acanthocheilonema (=Dipetalonema) reconditum* (Figs. 3.13 and 3.14)

Taxonomy: Nematode (order Spirurida). The genus *Dipetalonema* has been revised in recent years and the correct name for *D. reconditum* is now considered to be *Acanthocheilonema reconditum*.

Geographic Distribution: United States, South America, Africa, southern Europe, Asia.

Location in Host: Subcutaneous tissues of dogs and various wild canids.

Life Cycle: Dogs acquire infections from fleas (*Ctenocephalides*, *Pulex*) and lice (*Linognathus*, *Heterodoxus*). Arthropods ingest microfilariae in the blood (*Ctenocephalides*, *Pulex*, *Linognathus*) or skin (*Heterodoxus*) of infected canids.

Laboratory Diagnosis: Diagnosis is by detection of microfilariae as for *D. immitis*. Canine heartworm antigen tests do not give a positive reaction in the presence of *Acanthocheilonema* infection. Microfilariae of *A. reconditum* have a blunt anterior end, and the tails of some individuals may form a small hook or U shape, usually referred to as a "buttonhook."

Size: 250–288 × 4.5–5.5 μm

Clinical Importance: Infections with *A. reconditum* are subclinical. The accurate diagnosis of *A. reconditum* infections in dogs is important in order to prevent misdiagnoses of heartworm infection.

Fig. 3.11. Microfilariae of *Dirofilaria immitis* have gently tapered heads (A) and relatively straight tails (B).

Fig. 3.12. Microfilariae are at an earlier developmental stage than first-stage larvae and do not contain a digestive tract. Only dark-staining cell nuclei can be seen in this *D. immitis* microfilaria. Photo courtesy of Dr. Dwight Bowman, College of Veterinary Medicine, Cornell University, Ithaca, NY.

Fig. 3.13. Microfilariae of *Acanthocheilonema* (*Dipetalonema*) *reconditum* in a modified Knott's test. The anterior end (*arrow*) is blunter than that of *D. immitis*. Photo courtesy of Dr. Thomas Nolan, School of Veterinary Medicine, University of Pennsylvania, Philadelphia, PA.

PARASITE: **_Dirofilaria repens_** (Figs. 3.14–3.16)

Taxonomy: Nematode (Spirurida)

Geographic Distribution: Various countries in Europe, Asia, and Africa. Introduction into North America is considered a possibility.

Location in Host: Subcutaneous tissues of canids, felids, and various other carnivores.

Life Cycle: Transmission occurs by introduction of infective third-stage larvae through the bite of culicid mosquito intermediate hosts. After a prepatent period of 6–8 months, microfilariae are produced and circulate in the blood of infected hosts.

Laboratory Diagnosis: Microfilariae are detected in circulating blood by the modified Knott's test or by the use of filter tests. PCR tests have also been used. When detected by the modified Knott's examination, the _D. repens_ microfilariae have a relatively blunt anterior end, and the tail may show the buttonhook preservation artifact as occurs with _A. reconditum_. The larger _D. repens_ microfilariae are easily differentiated from _D. immitis_ and _A. reconditum_ based on size (see Table 3.2).

   Size: 268–360 × 5–8 μm

Clinical Importance: Infection in dogs and cats in usually subclinical. Infection can result in dermatitis with focal alopecia, pruritis, erythema, and crusting. Human infection can also occur.

BLOOD

Fig. 3.14. The tails of some individual microfilariae of *Acanthocheilonmea reconditum* and *Dirofilaria repens* may form a buttonhook shape when fixed. See Table 3.2 for a comparison of morphologic characteristics of microfilariae found in dogs.

42 μm

Fig. 3.15. *Dirofilaria repens* microfilariae. This filarid species is expanding its range in Europe, and microfilariae can be difficult to distinguish from those of *Dirofilaria immitis*.

Fig. 3.16. The head of *Dirofilaria repens* is blunt in comparison to the tapering head of *D. immitis* (Fig. 3.11).

BLOOD PARASITES OF LIVESTOCK AND HORSES

PARASITE: ***Babesia* spp. of ruminants** (Fig. 3.17)
Common name: Redwater, Texas fever, tick fever.

Taxonomy: Protozoa (piroplasm).

Geographic Distribution: Worldwide, particularly in tropical regions.

Location in Host: Red blood cells of cattle (at least six species, including *B. bovis*, *B. divergens*, *B. bigemina*, *B. major*) and sheep and goats (*B. motasi*, *B. ovis*).

Life Cycle: A variety of tick genera, including *Ixodes* and *Rhipicephalus*, act as intermediate hosts of *Babesia* spp. Ticks acquire the parasite during feeding.

Laboratory Diagnosis: In acute infection, blood smears stained with Giemsa or Wright's stain can be examined for parasites in red blood cells. In chronic infection, parasites are difficult to find in peripheral blood, and therefore, antibody tests, including IFA and ELISA tests, are used for diagnosis. *Babesia* typically appears as pairs of organisms in red blood cells, although erythrocytes may also contain single organisms.

Size: 1.5–4.5 × 0.4–2.0 µm, depending on species (*B. bigemina*: 4.5 × 2.5 µm; *B. bovis*: 2.4 × 1.5 µm)

Clinical Importance: In susceptible animals, infection can lead to the development of anemia, hemoglobinuria, and fever, with death often occurring during the acute phase of infection. Unlike many parasitic diseases, young animals are less likely to develop disease than adults. Bovine babesiosis has been eradicated from the United States.

PARASITE: ***Babesia caballi*, *Babesia* (=*Theileria*) *equi*** (Figs. 3.18 and 3.19)

Taxonomy: Protozoa (piroplasm). *Babesia equi* has recently been reassigned to the genus *Theileria*.

Geographic Distribution: Equine babesiosis is endemic in Central and South America, Africa, southern Europe, the Middle East, and parts of Asia.

Location in Host: Equine erythrocytes. Tick intermediate hosts include species of *Rhipicephalus*, *Hyalomma*, and *Dermacentor*.

Life Cycle: Similar to ruminant *Babesia* spp.

Laboratory Diagnosis: Blood smears are examined in acute infection. Chronic carriers are unlikely to show parasites in the peripheral blood. ELISA and IFA tests are used for detecting antibody to parasites in chronic infection.

Size: *B. equi*   2 µm
            B. caballi   2.5–4 µm

Clinical Importance: Equine babesiosis can cause anemia, hemoglobinuria, and edema. *Babesia caballi* may cause incoordination and paralysis.

Fig. 3.17. *Babesia bigemina* can be seen in this bovine blood smear. The teardrop-shaped organisms are present in pairs in several erythrocytes. *Babesia trautmanni*, a cause of porcine babesiosis in parts of Europe and Africa, has a similar morphology. Photo courtesy of Dr. Alvin Gajadhar, Centre for Animal Parasitology, CFIA, Saskatoon, Saskatchewan, Canada.

8 µm

Fig. 3.18. Composite photo showing *Babesia equi* in equine red blood cells. The definitive diagnostic tetrad form is seen in the top right. Also shown in the photo are the small rings (*arrow*) that are most commonly seen in low parasitemia (carrier state). Photo courtesy of Dr. Patricia Holman, College of Veterinary Medicine and Biomedical Sciences, Texas A&M University, College Station, TX.

Fig. 3.19. Composite photo of *Babesia caballi*. The definitive diagnostic form is the joined pair form, in contrast to the tetrad form of *Babesia equi* (Fig. 3.18). Also shown are other forms of the organism. The different large forms of the two species demonstrate the difficulty of distinguishing *B. caballi* from *B. equi* in the absence of paired piriforms in the former and tetrads in the latter. Photo courtesy of Dr. Patricia Holman, College of Veterinary Medicine and Biomedical Sciences, Texas A&M University, College Station, TX.

PARASITE: **_Theileria_ spp.** (Figs. 3.20 and 3.21)
Common name: East Coast fever, corridor disease, African Coast fever.

Taxonomy: Protozoa (piroplasm).

Geographic Distribution: Species of greatest importance are _T. parva_ in East Central and South Africa and _T. annulata_ in North Africa and southern Europe.

Location in Host: Bovine erythrocytes and lymph nodes.

Life Cycle: _Rhipicephalus_ (_T. parva_) and _Hyalomma_ (_T. annulata_) ticks are infected when they ingest host red blood cells. Following development in the tick, sporozoites are passed to cattle during feeding and enter lymphocytes, where schizogony occurs, releasing merozoites that infect red blood cells.

Laboratory Diagnosis: Schizonts can be seen in smears of lymph node biopsies and, in the case of _T. annulata_, infection may be diagnosed by finding infected red blood cells in a blood smear. _Theileria parva_ is unlikely to be present in blood smears except in advanced cases. IFA and ELISA tests are available, but because of the acute nature of clinical disease, these tests are of greater use in assessing host response in recovered animals.

| Size: | Piroplasms in red blood cells | $1.5–2.0 \times 0.5–1.0\,\mu m$ |
| | Schizonts in lymphocytes | approximately $8\,\mu m$ |

Clinical Importance: Susceptible animals develop fever, lymphadenopathy, depression, and nasal discharge; there is high mortality in nonimmune animals. Chronic disease is associated with a variety of signs, including diarrhea and reduced production.

PARASITE: **_Trypanosoma_ spp.** (Figs. 3.22–3.27)
Common name: Nagana, sleeping sickness, surra, dourine.

Taxonomy: Protozoa (flagellate).

Geographic Distribution: Clinically important livestock species, including _T. congolense_, _T. brucei brucei_, _T. simiae_, _T. vivax_, and _T. evansi_, are all found in Africa. _Trypanosoma evansi_ and _T. vivax_ are also found in South America and parts of Asia. _Trypanosoma theileri_ (cattle only) and _T. melophagium_ (sheep only) occur worldwide. Another species, _T. equiperdum_ (horses), is found in tropical and subtropical regions.

Location in Host: Bloodstream of ruminants, horses, swine, and other domestic animals. _Trypanosma brucei_ can also be found in other tissues, including the heart and central nervous system and _T. equiperdum_ is found in the urethra of stallions and vagina of mares.

Life Cycle: Trypanosomes are transmitted to the host by biting flies. The intermediate host of _T. congolense_, _T. vivax_, _T. brucei_, and _T. simiae_ is the tsetse fly (_Glossina_) in Africa. In other areas, tabanid and other biting flies transmit _T. vivax_ and _T. evansi_. Tabanid flies are also the intermediate host of _T. theileri_ in cattle, while the sheep ked (_Melophagus ovinus_) is the intermediate host of _T. melophagium_. The exception to fly transmission is _T. equiperdum_, which is transmitted venereally.

Laboratory Diagnosis: In acute infection, most trypanosome species can usually be detected in wet mounts of blood. Species of trypanosomes can be differentiated based on size, presence or absence of a free flagellum, location and size of the kinetoplast, and characteristics

Fig. 3.20. *Theileria parva* multinucleated schizont in a lymphocyte. The species of *Theileria* are difficult to differentiate morphologically. Photo courtesy of Dr. Andrew Peregrine, Ontario Veterinary College, University of Guelph, Guelph, Ontario, Canada.

Fig. 3.21. *Theileria* sp. erythrocytic forms in a blood smear (*arrow*). Photo courtesy of Dr. Karen F. Snowden, College of Veterinary Medicine, Texas A&M University, College Station, TX.

Fig. 3.22. *Trypanosoma brucei* and *T. congolense* are found in domestic mammals in Africa. *Trypanosoma brucei* has a prominent undulating membrane (U) and a kinetoplast that is located subterminally (K). Photo courtesy of Dr. Andrew Peregrine, Ontario Veterinary College, University of Guelph, Guelph, Ontario, Canada.

Trypanosoma (*continued*)

of the undulating membrane. An ELISA antigen test and DNA probes have been developed for detection of African trypanosomiasis in cattle. *Trypanosoma equiperdum* infection is diagnosed by a complement fixation test.

	Size:		
		T. vivax	20–26 μm
		T. brucei	12–35 μm
		T. congolense	9–18 μm
		T. evansi	15–35 μm
		T. theileri	60–70 μm, may be up to 120 μm
		T. melophagium	50–60 μm
		T. simiae	13–18 μm

Clinical Importance: The principal clinical signs of trypanosomiasis are anemia accompanied by fever, edema, and loss of condition. Mortality may be high, especially if other disease agents are also present. *Trypanosoma equiperdum* produces the disease known as dourine in horses, which is marked by genital and ventral edema, abortion, nervous system disease, and emaciation.

Fig. 3.23. *Trypanosoma congolense* has a subterminal kinetoplast that is on the margin of the trypanosome (K). Its undulating membrane is not distinctive. Photo courtesy of Dr. Andrew Peregrine, Ontario Veterinary College, University of Guelph, Guelph, Ontario, Canada.

Fig. 3.24. *Trypanosoma vivax* is found in Africa and other parts of the world. Its kinetoplast is at the end of the organism (*arrow*), and its undulating membrane is not distinctive. Photo courtesy of Dr. Andrew Peregrine, Ontario Veterinary College, University of Guelph, Guelph, Ontario, Canada.

Fig. 3.25. *Trypanosoma theileri* is found worldwide in cattle, and a similar parasite, *T. melophagium*, occurs in sheep. Parasites are occasionally seen in blood smears but rarely are of clinical importance. These species can be distinguished from the pathogenic trypanosome species by their large size (50 μm or more). This blood smear from a calf demonstrates the wide size variation that can occur with *T. theileri*.

Fig. 3.26. *Trypanosoma evansi* is an important pathogen of horses and camels in parts of Africa, Asia, and Latin America. It is difficult to distinguish from *T. brucei* microscopically. Photo courtesy of Dr. Jeffrey F. Williams, Vanson HaloSource, Inc., Redmond, WA.

Fig. 3.27. *Trypanosoma simiae* is a parasite of African warthogs that is transmitted by the tsetse fly to domestic pigs and camels. Swine may also be infected with other trypanosome species. Photo courtesy of Dr. Andrew Peregrine, Ontario Veterinary College, University of Guelph, Guelph, Ontario, Canada.

Trypanosoma melophagium and *T. theileri* are widespread nonpathogenic species that may occasionally be seen in blood smears.

PARASITE: ***Setaria* spp.** (Fig. 3.28)

Taxonomy: Nematode (order Spirurida).

Geographic Distribution: Worldwide.

Location in Host: Adult worms are found primarily in the peritoneal cavity of ruminants and equids.

Life Cycle: Microfilariae in the blood are ingested by mosquitoes. The infective third larval stage develops in the mosquito; transmission to the definitive host occurs during feeding.

Laboratory Diagnosis: Detection of sheathed microfilariae in blood smears.

Size: Approximately 200–300 μm in length

Clinical Importance: *Setaria* has no clinical importance, with the exception of rare cases of abnormal migration of parasites in the nervous system.

BLOOD PARASITES OF BIRDS

PARASITE: ***Leucocytozoon* spp.** (Figs. 3.29 and 3.30)

Taxonomy: Protozoa (hemosporozoa).

Geographic Distribution: Important species include *L. simondi*, which is found worldwide in domestic and wild ducks and geese; *L. smithi* in North American and European domestic and wild turkeys; and *L. caulleryi* in chickens in Asia.

Location in Host: Gamonts (microgamonts and macrogamonts) occur in leukocytes and erythrocytes.

Life Cycle: Black flies (*Simulium* spp. and other simulids) transmit infections to birds during blood feeding.

Laboratory Diagnosis: Gamonts are detected in white and red blood cells on Wright- or Giemsa-stained blood smears. Meronts are detected in stained tissue sections.

Size: Gamonts 14–22 μm

Clinical Importance: *Leucocytozoon* is pathogenic in ducks, geese, and turkeys, especially in younger birds. Clinical signs vary somewhat with species but can include lethargy, emaciation, and acute or chronic fatalities.

Fig. 3.28. Microfilariae of *Setaria* spp. may occasionally be seen in ruminant or equine blood samples but have no clinical significance. A clear sheath can often be seen projecting beyond the end of the larva, although it is not evident in this specimen. Photo courtesy of Dr. Jeffrey F. Williams, Vanson HaloSource, Inc., Redmond, WA.

Fig. 3.29. Host leukocytes and erythrocytes containing the sausage-shaped *Leucocytozoon* gamonts appear elongated, with the remnants of the nucleus pushed to one side and the cytoplasm extending beyond the parasite and forming "horns." Photo courtesy of Dr. David Baker, School of Veterinary Medicine, Louisiana State University, Baton Rouge, LA.

Fig. 3.30. Birds may be infected with more than one species of protozoa. Both *Leucocytozoon* (L) and *Plasmodium* (P) are present in this hawk. Photo courtesy of Dr. David Baker, School of Veterinary Medicine, Louisiana State University, Baton Rouge, LA.

PARASITE: *Haemoproteus* **spp.** (Fig. 3.31)

Taxonomy: Protozoa (hemosporozoa).

Geographic Distribution: Worldwide (except *H. meleagridis*, which occurs only in North America).

Location in Host: Gamonts (microgamonts and macrogamonts) occur in erythrocytes of pigeons and doves (*H. columbae*, *H. sacharovi*), wild and domestic turkeys (*H. meleagridis*), and wild and domestic ducks and geese (*H. nettionis*).

Life Cycle: Birds acquire infections from blood-feeding hippoboscid flies, midges (*Culicoides*), and deer flies (*Chrysops* spp.), which act as intermediate hosts.

Laboratory Diagnosis: Gamonts are detected in red blood cells on Wright- or Giemsa-stained blood smears. The gamonts of *Haemoproteus* may vary in size and contain pigment granules. They appear morphologically identical to those of *Plasmodium* spp.

   Size: Approximately 7 μm

Clinical Importance: Infections are usually subclinical.

PARASITE: *Plasmodium* **spp.** (Figs. 3.30 and 3.32)
        Common name: Malaria.

Taxonomy: Protozoa (hemosporozoa).

Geographic Distribution: Worldwide.

Location in Host: Erythrocytes and various other tissues in a wide variety of birds.

Life Cycle: Mosquitoes act as the intermediate host for *Plasmodium*. The parasite is transmitted during insect feeding.

Laboratory Diagnosis: Gamonts, merozoites, and meronts are detected in red blood cells on Wright- or Giemsa-stained blood smears. Gamonts of *Plasmodium* appear morphologically identical to those of *Haemoproteus* spp.

   Size: Gamonts 7–8 μm

Clinical Importance: Most species are nonpathogenic. Exceptions are *P. cathemerium* and *P. matutinum* in canaries; *P. gallinaceum* and *P. juxtanucleare* in chickens; *P. hermani* in turkeys; and *P. relictum* in pigeons. Birds infected with these species may become anemic, with high fatality rates possible.

BLOOD

Fig. 3.31. Gamonts of *Haemoproteus* in a Swainson's hawk. The gamonts are often crescent shaped and wrapped around the nucleus of the host erythrocyte. Pigment granules can be seen inside the gamont. Photo courtesy of Dr. Robert Ridley, College of Veterinary Medicine, Kansas State University, Manhattan, KS.

Fig. 3.32. The appearance of multiple stages of the parasite (signet-ring stage, meronts, and gamonts) in infected erythrocytes differentiates *Plasmodium* infection from *Haemoproteus* (in which only gamonts are found). In this sample from a cockatoo, several stages of the parasite are present (*arrows*). Photo courtesy of Dr. David Baker, School of Veterinary Medicine, Louisiana State University, Baton Rouge, LA.

CHAPTER 4

Immunodiagnostic and Molecular Diagnostic Tests in Veterinary Parasitology

Karen F. Snowden

IMMUNODIAGNOSTIC METHODS

Immunodiagnostic methods for a range of parasitologic infections are increasingly available at fee-for-service diagnostic laboratories and as point-of-use tests that can be conducted in a clinical setting.

There are two basic approaches in designing an immunologic test. **Antigen detection** tests identify specific parasite-associated compounds in blood, serum, or fecal suspensions that indicate the presence of the organism in the host. Alternatively, **antibody detection** tests show the host immune response to a parasite through the production of specific antibodies. To have a positive test result, it is assumed that the host animal is immunologically competent to react to the pathogen and that a sufficient time of exposure has occurred for the animal to produce detectable antibodies.

There are a variety of test formats for immunodiagnostic tests. The enzyme-linked immunosorbent assay (ELISA) is designed with a series of wells in a plate or tray with an end result indicated colorimetrically (Fig. 4.1). The lateral-flow immunochromatographic assay uses similar principles and reagents in a cassette format, and works by capillary action with a series of reagents moving along a membrane with the end result indicated as a colored dot or line on the membrane (Fig. 4.2). Both of these test formats can be designed as antigen or as antibody detection assays, and both test formats have been developed for use with blood, serum, or feces. Most ELISA tests are designed for processing sample batches in a diagnostic lab setting. However, selected ELISA tests as well as the immunochromatographic tests are available as point-of-use tests that can be performed in a clinical setting on one or several samples in a relatively rapid time frame.

The third commonly used format is the indirect fluorescent antibody (IFA) test, which is an antibody detection test designed for use with serum or plasma (IFA is compared with ELISA antibody test in Fig. 4.3). These tests are routinely performed in the diagnostic lab setting because a compound microscope equipped with appropriate barrier filters and a UV light source is needed to evaluate the test. Other less common immunodiagnostic test formats include direct or indirect hemagglutination (HA or IHA), complement-fixation (CF) tests, and Western blot tests.

In the United States, two of the most widely used immunodiagnostic tests in companion animal medicine are the heartworm antigen test, which detects antigens primarily found in adult female worms of *Dirofilaria immitis* in blood, serum or plasma, and the fecal antigen test for *Giardia intestinalis* (Table 4.1)

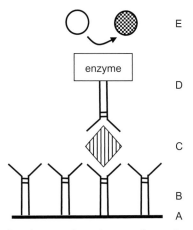

Fig. 4.1. Schematic of ELISA antigen detection procedures: A, test surface: polystyrene well; B, parasite-specific capture antibody (may be monoclonal or polyclonal); C, parasite antigen in serum of the animal patient; D, detecting reagent parasite-specific antibody labeled with an enzyme; E, visualizing step: if enzyme is present, it acts on soluble substrate to produce color, which can be evaluated visually or measured spectrophotometrically.

Fig. 4.2. Schematic of antigen detection using an immunochromatographic lateral flow test.

A much wider variety of antibody detection tests are available in fee-for-service veterinary diagnostic laboratories (Table 4.1). The test result is typically expressed as a "titer," and the IgG antibody isotype is usually the immunoglobulin that is detected in the test. The titer value is the reciprocal of the highest dilution of serum/plasma where the test remains positive. Different test formats (ELISA vs. IFA most commonly) have different thresholds of antibody detection. Therefore, the positive/negative cutoff value for each standardized assay should be provided by the laboratory performing the test in order to adequately interpret the meaning of the antibody titer as positive/negative or high/low. For example, the cutoff value for an IFA test might be a 1 : 10 dilution, while a similar test in an ELISA format might have a 1 : 100 dilution cutoff value as positive.

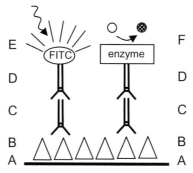

Fig. 4.3. Comparison of common antibody detection procedures: indirect fluorescent antibody (IFA, *left*) test and enzyme-linked immunosorbent assay (ELISA, *right*). A, test surface: glass slide (IFA) or polystyrene well (ELISA); B, parasite antigen: whole parasite, such as cultured tachyzoites and promastigotes (IFA), or soluble parasite antigen, which can be a crude homogenate, a purified protein, or a recombinant protein (ELISA); C, serum of the animal patient, which may contain parasite-specific antibodies; D, detecting reagent for host-specific antibody: host-specific antibody labeled with a fluorochrome such as fluorescein (IFA) or host-specific antibody labeled with an enzyme (ELISA); E, visualizing step: specific UV wavelength light from microscope causes fluorescein (FITC) to emit yellow-green fluorescence (IFA); F, visualizing step: if enzyme is present, it acts on soluble substrate to produce color, which can be evaluated visually or measured spectrophotometrically.

Table 4.1. **Immunodiagnostic and molecular diagnostic tests for parasites available in the United States**[a]

Pathogen	Host	POU[b]	Lab
Antigen detection			
Cryptosporidium spp.	C, E, F, Ru (fecal)		X
Dirofilaria immitis	C, F (blood)	X	X
Giardia intestinalis	C, F (fecal)	X	X
Antibody detection			
Anoplocephala perfoliata	E		X
Babesia canis, B. gibsoni	C		X[c]
Babesia bovis, B. bigemina	B		X[c]
Babesia caballi, B. (Theileria) equi	E		X[c]
Dirofilaria immitis	F	X	X
Encephalitozoon cuniculi	C, Ro, Rb		X
Leishmania donovani complex	C		X
Neospora caninum	C, B		X
Sarcocystis neurona (EPM)	E		X
Toxoplasma gondii	F		X
Trypanosoma cruzi	C		X
Other tick-borne bacterial/rickettsial pathogens such as *Ehrlichia, Anaplasma, Borrelia*	C	X	X
Molecular			
Babesia spp.	C		X
Cryptosporidium spp.	C, F		X
Cytauxzoon felis	F		X
Giardia spp.	C, F		X
Hepatozoon americanum	C		X
Leishmania spp.	C		X
Neospora caninum	B, C		X
Sarcocystis neurona (EPM)	E		X
Toxoplasma gondii	C, F		X
Tritrichomonas spp.	F, B		X
Other tick-borne bacterial/rickettsial pathogens such as *Ehrlichia, Anaplasma, Borrelia*	C		X

[a] Molecular and immunodiagnostic tests for a number of internationally important parasitic diseases such as *Trypanosoma brucei* and *Theileria parva* are not readily available in North America.
[b] Performed at site of patient care.
[c] Serologic tests for canine babesias are not federally regulated, but bovine and equine babesias are reportable to the United States Department of Agriculture (USDA) Animal and Plant Health Inspection Service (APHIS) and are reportable in some states; therefore, serologic testing is regulated (www.aphis.usda.gov/vs/nahss/disease_status.htm).
B, bovine; C, canine; E, equine; F, feline; Ro, rodent; Rb, rabbit; Ru, ruminant; POU, point-of-use tests; EPM, equine protozoal myeloencephalitis.

It is important to have an understanding of the life cycle and pathogenicity of a specific parasite in order to interpret antibody titers in a specific test. For instance, having antibodies can indicate protection against disease. If a cat has a significant antibody titer against *Toxoplasma gondii*, that animal is very unlikely to shed oocysts, and it is a low-risk animal as a pet for an immunocompromised or pregnant owner. On the other hand, having a measurable antibody titer can be of significant diagnostic value in confirming a parasite infection as the cause of clinical disease. For example, if a dog has chronic dilitative cardiac disease with a titer to *Trypanosoma cruzi*, a probable diagnosis is Chagas' disease. In a third scenario, having an antibody titer may indicate exposure but not necessarily active parasite infection. An example of this situation is a domestic cat with an antibody titer to *Dirofilaria immitis*. The cat can produce antibodies to the parasite after exposure to larvae from an infected mosquito bite, but those parasites do not necessarily develop successfully to adult worms causing a patent infection.

MOLECULAR DIAGNOSTIC METHODS

The advent of molecular diagnostic methods has resulted in an expanding selection of sensitive and specific tests for a range of infectious organisms and genetic diseases. Molecular diagnostic assays can be performed with many types of samples including blood, urine, tissues, feces, and other body fluids as well as environmental samples. Regardless of the sample matrix, the first step in a protocol is to isolate the nucleic acid (DNA, RNA) for testing. The accuracy of the test depends on the quality and quantity of DNA or RNA extracted as well as the presence/absence of inhibitors. A typical assay uses that DNA, along with appropriate primers, enzymes, and nucleotides, in a polymerase chain reaction (PCR) to amplify short specific DNA sequences that identify a particular gene or section of target DNA. In some cases, the assay is considered positive if the appropriately sized DNA amplicon is visualized by gel electrophoresis or detected by fluorescence. In other cases, the amplified DNA fragment must be sequenced to determine nucleic acid sequence variations that are characteristic of various genetic mutations.

An expanding variety of veterinary applications are available on a fee-for-service basis. The most common assays detect a variety of viral or bacterial pathogens in blood or other body fluids, tissues, or feces of the host animal. Other tests are designed to detect specific targeted genetic variations in the host animal that are markers of diseases or anomalies. Although experimental molecular diagnostic tests are increasingly reported in the scientific literature, few specific tests are commercially available to detect parasitic pathogens.

The parasitologic molecular diagnostic test used most widely in the United States at this time detects the venereal protozoan of cattle, *Tritrichomonas foetus*, in preputial swabs or specialized short-term cultures. Since this parasite has become a regulatory issue in many states, the validation and comparison of molecular and *in vitro* culture methods has become a topic of interest to many diagnostic laboratories, and to veterinary practitioners and their clients as well.

Both canine and feline tick-borne disease agent panels that include hemoprotozoan parasites are offered as well by a number of commercial and university-associated diagnostic laboratories on a fee-for-service basis.

At the present time, use of PCR diagnostics for parasitic infections is not widely applied due to difficulties in extracting quality DNA or RNA from tissue, blood, or fecal samples for testing. Molecular diagnosis undoubtedly will become commonplace as automated procedures for nucleic acid extraction improve, facilitating the use of these tests. The high sensitivity and specificity of these tests make them especially attractive in cases of low parasite burden. The parasitic infections that currently can be detected with molecular diagnostic methods in the United States are listed in Table 4.1.

CHAPTER 5

Diagnosis of Arthropod Parasites

Ellis Greiner, contributing author

The phylum Arthropoda contains many species that parasitize domestic and wild animals and humans. The most familiar of these parasites are ticks, mites (class Arachnida, subclass Acari), and insects (class Insecta). Aquatic animals are parasitized by many crustaceans that also belong to this phylum (see Chapter 6). All arthropods have jointed appendages and exoskeletons. The organisms pictured in this chapter represent a selection of arthropods that are common or important in domestic animals.

SUBCLASS ACARI (MITES AND TICKS)

The bodies of mites and ticks are divided into two parts: the gnathosoma, which contains the mouthparts on a false head (basis capituli), and the idiosoma, which comprises the remainder of the animal and to which the legs are attached. After hatching from the egg, mites and ticks pass through larval and nymphal stages before becoming adults. Larvae of ticks and mites have six legs; while nymphs and adults have eight legs. Nymphal ticks and mites usually closely resemble the adults but are smaller and lack a genital opening.

Mite Identification

Parasitic mites are usually microscopic, rarely exceeding 1 mm in length. Female mites are usually larger than males. Mites are covered by a relatively soft integument through which the smaller forms respire. The larger forms breathe through openings called stigmata, sometimes used in identification. Scales, spines, or setae (hairs) on the body and claws or suckers on the legs (Fig. 5.1) are used in identifying the organisms. Many common mange, itch, and scab mites resemble one another, but they can be differentiated on the basis of the characteristics outlined in Table 5.1.

Most common mite infestations are diagnosed by deep or superficial skin scrapings. For a deep skin scraping, a dulled, rounded scalpel blade (#10) and the area of skin to be scraped are coated with mineral oil. The site selected for scraping should be at the periphery of a lesion or the predilection site of the suspected parasite. The blade should be scraped back and forth over the skin until capillary bleeding is evident (a shallower scraping is done for surface-dwelling mites). For collection of *Demodex*, the follicle mite, a skin fold should be squeezed between the fingers to express

Fig. 5.1. An important characteristic for identification of a number of common mites is length and segmentation of the stalk (pedicle) connecting a sucker to the leg. In *Sarcoptes* spp. mites (A), the stalk is long and unjointed (*arrow*). *Psoroptes* has a long, jointed pedicle (B).

Table 5.1. **Microscopic characteristics of some mange, itch, and scab mites**

Genus	Egg-Laying Female	Male	Anus
	Leg Characteristics		
Sarcoptes	Suckers on long, unsegmented stalks on pairs 1, 2; pointed scales on dorsum	Suckers on long unsegmented stalks on pairs 1, 2, 4; few pointed scales on dorsum	Terminal
Notoedres	Suckers as above; many prominent rounded scales on dorsum	Suckers as above; few rounded scales on dorsum	Dorsal
Knemidokoptes	No suckers	Suckers on unsegmented stalks on pairs 1, 2, 3, 4	Terminal
Psoroptes	Suckers on long, segmented stalks on pairs 1, 2, 4	Suckers on long, segmented stalks on pairs 1, 2, 3	Terminal
Chorioptes	Suckers on short, unsegmented stalks on pairs 1, 2, 4	Suckers on short, unsegmented stalks on pairs 1, 2, 3, 4; pair 4 rudimentary	Terminal
Otodectes	Suckers on short, unsegmented stalks on pairs 1, 2; pair 4 rudimentary	Suckers on short, unsegmented stalks on pairs 1, 2, 3, 4	Terminal
Trixacarus	Suckers on long, unsegmented stalks on pairs 1, 2		Dorsal

the mites before the scraping is done. The debris collected on the scalpel blade is then placed on a microscope slide, coverslipped, and examined using the 10× microscope objective. Several slides may need to be examined before mites are found, especially in cases of *Sarcoptes* infestation.

To recover surface mites, such as *Cheyletiella*, a superficial scraping that does not cause bleeding is made with a scalpel blade coated in mineral oil. Alternatively, clear acetate tape can be used to collect material. The sticky side of the tape is pressed to the hair coat in an affected area and then placed on a microscope slide, trapping skin debris and mites against the slide and allowing microscopic examination. Brushings from the hair coat may also be examined.

If mites must be shipped to an acarologist or veterinary laboratory for identification, they should be stored in 70% alcohol. Skin scrapings and mites that are stored dry cannot usually be successfully identified.

PARASITE: *Sarcoptes scabiei* (Figs. 5.2–5.5)
Common name: Itch mite (often called scabies mite in dogs).

Taxonomy: Mite (family Sarcoptidae).

Host: Host-specific varieties of *Sarcoptes* are found on a wide range of domestic animals, including dogs, ruminants, horses, rodents, swine, and camelids. Humans also have their own strain of *Sarcoptes*.

Geographic Distribution: Worldwide.

Location on Host: Hairless or thin-skinned areas of the body are usually the first to be affected, but large portions of the skin can be involved in severe cases.

Life Cycle: Transmission of *Sarcoptes* is by direct contact with an infested animal or fomites. Female mites tunnel into the epidermis, where eggs are deposited and where development of mites occurs. The life cycle from egg to adult occurs in about 3 weeks.

Laboratory Diagnosis: Deep skin scrapings are used for diagnosis. However, mites may be difficult to recover, and several scrapings should be collected from suspected cases. Many cases are treated presumptively when no mites are recovered. Fecal examination may reveal mites and mite eggs swallowed during grooming. In swine, *Sarcoptes* can often be found in scabs in the ears of chronically infected animals. To diagnose these infections on the farm, scab material can be removed and broken up over dark paper. Tiny, moving specks will be mites. Scabs can also be digested with 10% sodium hydroxide and the remaining material examined with the microscope. Characteristics of the terminal suckers used in identification are found in Table 5.1.

Size: Females approximately 400 μm; males approximately 250 μm

Clinical Importance: Mange caused by *Sarcoptes* is a highly pruritic condition accompanied by alopecia, thickening of the skin, and crust formation. In North America, infestations are most often encountered in dogs and swine, while other domestic animals are only rarely infested. *Sarcoptes* mites from animals can transiently infest humans and produce lesions.

125 μm

Fig. 5.2. *Sarcoptes* and related mites are typically round bodied. The third and fourth pairs of legs are short and often do not project beyond the margin of the body.

ARTHROPODS

Fig. 5.3. Pruritic mite infestations may stimulate intense grooming by the host, resulting in the presence of both mites and their eggs in the feces. Arrows indicate an egg in a female sarcoptic mite and other eggs outside mites in this skin scraping. These eggs are much larger than common helminth eggs (about 200 μm).

Fig. 5.4. *Sarcoptes scabiei* is a common cause of the condition called "scabies" in dogs. Lesions on the face and along the margin of the ear are common early in infestation. Photo courtesy of Dr. Jeffrey F. Williams, Vanson HaloSource, Inc., Redmond WA.

Fig. 5.5. Sarcoptic mange in an alpaca. In chronic sarcoptic mange, affected skin is hairless, thickened, and wrinkled. These nonspecific changes also occur in other chronic skin diseases. Photos courtesy of Dr. Jeffrey F. Williams, Vanson HaloSource, Inc., Redmond, WA.

PARASITE: ***Notoedres* spp.** (Fig. 5.6)
            Common name: Ear mange mite (rodents).

Taxonomy: Mite (family Sarcoptidae).

Host: *Notoedres cati* occurs on cats. Other species occur on rodents, rabbits, and some wild animals.

Geographic Distribution: Worldwide.

Location on Host: The head is usually infested first, but mites may spread to other regions of the body.

Life Cycle: Similar to *Sarcoptes*.

Laboratory Diagnosis: Mites are observed with deep skin scrapings.

   Size: *N. cati* approximately 225 µm; rodent species are larger

Clinical Importance: Feline notoedric mange is usually confined to the head and neck. Infestations are rarely seen in North America.

PARASITE: ***Knemidokoptes* spp.** (Figs. 5.7 and 5.8)
            Common name: Scaly leg or scaly face mite.

Taxonomy: Mite (family Knemidokoptidae).

Host: Birds, including domestic poultry and pet birds.

Geographic Distribution: Worldwide.

Location on Host: Nonfeathered portions of the body, including feet, legs, and face.

Life Cycle: Like *Sarcoptes*, transmission occurs by direct contact with infested birds or fomites, and all stages of the mite are found on the host.

Laboratory Diagnosis: Mites can be found in skin scrapings collected from the periphery of lesions. Typically, the exudative lesions produced by the mites contain numerous small holes, giving them a honeycombed appearance.

   Size: Approximately 400 µm

Clinical Importance: *Knemidokoptes* species burrow under the scales on the legs or nonfeathered portions of the face, inducing a serous exudate that hardens into crusts. These proliferative lesions eventually may cause trauma and disfigurement leading to the death of the host.

ARTHROPODS

58 μm

Fig. 5.6. *Notoedres* mites are similar in appearance to *Sarcoptes*. However, the anus of *Notoedres*, unlike that of *Sarcoptes*, is located on the dorsal surface rather than the ventral. *Notoedres* also has scalloped scales on the dorsum rather than the sawtooth scales on *Sarcoptes*. The suckers on the front legs of *Notoedres* and *Sarcoptes* are attached to the legs by long, unjointed stalks.

88 μm

Fig. 5.7. *Knemidokoptes* is a round-bodied mite, generally similar in appearance to sarcoptic mites.

Fig. 5.8. Budgerigar with a deformed beak resulting from the proliferative lesion produced by *Knemidokoptes* infestation. Photo courtesy of Dr. Jeffrey F. Williams, Vanson HaloSource, Inc., Redmond WA.

PARASITE: **_Trixacarus_ spp.** (Fig. 5.9)

Taxonomy: Mite (family Sarcoptidae).

Host: Guinea pigs (_Trixacarus caviae_) and rats (_T. diversus_).

Geographic Distribution: Europe and North America.

Location on Host: Lesions begin on the head, neck, and back but can spread to other areas.

Life Cycle: Similar to _Sarcoptes_. Mites are readily transferred from the dam to young animals in the neonatal period.

Laboratory Diagnosis: Mites are identified in skin scrapings.

   Size: Approximately 200 μm

Clinical Importance: _Trixacarus_ is the sarcoptic mange mite of guinea pigs. Infestation is associated with pruritus, alopecia, and hyperkeratosis and can become a serious problem in guinea pig colonies. Humans in contact with infested guinea pigs may develop transient lesions.

PARASITE: **_Psoroptes_ spp.** (Figs. 5.10–5.13)
   Common name: Scab or scabies mite (ruminants).

Taxonomy: Mite (family Psoroptidae).

Host: _Psoroptes ovis_ is the cause of psoroptic mange in ruminants; _P. cuniculi_ (now thought to be a strain of _P. ovis_) is found on rabbits and ruminants. _Psoroptes_ spp. can also be found on horses and some wildlife hosts. The number of species within the genus is currently undergoing revision.

Geographic Distribution: Worldwide.

Location on Host: _Psoroptes cuniculi_ is found in the ears of rabbits, sheep, goats, and horses. Other _Psoroptes_ infestations are often first detected on the dorsum of the host but may spread to other areas.

Life Cycle: Transmission is by direct contact or fomites. Unlike sarcoptic mites, _Psoroptes_ spp. do not burrow, and all stages are found on the skin surface. The life cycle can be completed in as little as 10 days. Mites may survive for several days off the host.

Laboratory Diagnosis: Superficial skin scrapings should be collected from the periphery of skin lesions. Alternatively, skin scabs can be broken apart or digested and the residue examined microscopically. Crusts from the ears can be treated similarly when infestations of _P. cuniculi_ are suspected. Psoroptic mites are more oval in shape and have longer legs than sarcoptic mites.

   Size: Approximately 750 μm

Clinical Importance: _Psoroptes_ is a highly contagious, economically important cause of skin disease in ruminants worldwide. Infestation leads to exudative dermatitis and hair loss. In the United States, the strain of _P. ovis_ affecting sheep has been eradicated, and the bovine strain has diminished in importance since the introduction of macrolide endectocide drugs. In severe cases, _P. cuniculi_ lesions on rabbits may extend beyond the ears to the face, neck, and back.

ARTHROPODS

Fig. 5.9. Like other sarcoptic mites, *Trixacarus* is a round-bodied mite with short legs. *Trixacarus caviae* causes sarcoptic mange in guinea pigs.

Fig. 5.10. Psoroptic mites have a more oval shape and longer legs than sarcoptic mites. Terminal suckers are connected to the legs by long, segmented stalks (Table 5.1). Photo courtesy of Dr. Robert Ridley, College of Veterinary Medicine, Kansas State University, Manhattan, KS.

Fig. 5.11. *Psoroptes* may be up to 800 μm in length. Shown here are specimens of *Psoroptes cuniculi* from rabbit ears. Figure 5.1B shows a closer view of the jointed pedicle on some of the legs of *Psoroptes*. Photo courtesy of Dr. David Baker, School of Veterinary Medicine, Louisiana State University, Baton Rouge, LA.

PARASITE: ***Chorioptes bovis*** (Figs. 5.14 and 5.15)
Common name: Foot mange, leg mange, itchy heel.

Taxonomy: Mite (family Psoroptidae).

Host: Varieties of *C. bovis* are found on ruminants, horses, and rabbits.

Geographic Distribution: Worldwide.

Location on Host: *Chorioptes* are found primarily on the lower body of the host. In horses, the mites are seen more often in breeds with feathered legs. In cattle, the rear legs, base of the tail, and back of the udder are most often affected.

Life Cycle: Transmission is by direct contact or fomites. *Chorioptes* mites spend their entire life cycle on the skin surface. The life cycle can be completed in about 3 weeks.

Laboratory Diagnosis: Mites are observed in skin scrapings. *Chorioptes* has short, unsegmented stalks bearing the suckers on the legs (see Table 5.1).

Size: Approximately 300 μm

Clinical Importance: Infestation may be asymptomatic or cause only mild lesions in some animals. As mite populations increase, pruritus, alopecia, and crusting may develop.

Fig. 5.12. Psorptic mange or "scab" can be a serious infestation in ruminants. In sheep, mite activity causes an exudate that forms a crust on the surface of the skin, with the resulting loss of the fleece over affected areas.

Fig. 5.13. Psoroptic ear mange in a rabbit. Photo courtesy of Dr. Jeffrey F. Williams, Vanson HaloSource, Inc., Redmond, WA.

100 μm

Fig. 5.14. *Chorioptes* mite. The two "eyes" on the posterior end of this *Chorioptes* male are actually copulatory suckers. Photo courtesy of Dr. Jeffrey F. Williams, Vanson HaloSource, Inc., Redmond, WA.

PARASITE: ***Otodectes cynotis*** (Figs. 5.16 and 5.17)
Common name: Ear mite.

Taxonomy: Mite (family Psoroptidae).

Host: Dogs, cats, and ferrets.

Geographic Distribution: Worldwide.

Location on Host: Ear canal.

Life Cycle: Mites complete their life cycle in the ear. Transmission occurs by direct contact or fomites. Kittens and puppies are easily infested by contact with the dam.

Laboratory Diagnosis: Routinely diagnosed by otoscope or microscopic examination of aural exudate collected with cotton swabs.

Size: Approximately 300 μm

Clinical Importance: These mites are a common cause of otitis externa. Bacterial decomposition of otic secretions and exudate leads to the formation of black, waxy cerumen. Infested animals often suffer severe pruritus that may lead to self-inflicted trauma. Heavy infestations may spread outside the ear to the face, neck, and back.

ARTHROPODS

Fig. 5.15. *Chorioptes* mites are very similar in appearance to *Psoroptes* spp. The two genera can be accurately differentiated by the length and segmentation of the stalks (pedicles) carrying the suckers on the legs (Table 5.1). The suckers of *Chorioptes* are found on short, unsegmented stalks (*arrow*). See Figure 5.1B for the pedicle of *Psoroptes*.

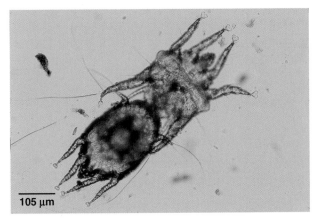

105 µm

Fig. 5.16. Mating *Otodectes cynotis* mites from a ferret. *Otodectes* is another psoroptic mite with an oval-shaped body and long legs. They are similar in size and appearance to *Chorioptes*. In heavy infestations, it is common to find copulating mites in ear swab preparations. The short unsegmented stalks carrying the suckers can be seen in this photo.

Fig. 5.17. *Otodectes cynotis* infestation in a cat. The mites cause the production of black "coffee ground" exudate. Photo courtesy of Dr. Jeffrey F. Williams, Vanson HaloSource, Inc., Redmond, WA.

PARASITE: **_Demodex_ spp.** (Figs. 5.18–5.22)
Common name: Follicle mite.

Taxonomy: Mite (family Demodicidae).

Host: Species of _Demodex_ have been identified from many hosts, including dogs, cats, pigs, horses, cattle, goats, sheep, laboratory animals, humans, and other species.

Geographic Distribution: Worldwide.

Location on Host: Sebaceous glands and hair follicles.

Life Cycle: Mites are usually transferred from the dam to offspring in the neonatal period. All stages of the life cycle are found on the host.

Laboratory Diagnosis: Deep skin scrapings are required for diagnosis. A skin fold should be squeezed before scraping to express mites from follicles and sebaceous glands. Finding a high proportion of immature mites on a skin scraping is indicative of a more serious infestation than is a predominance of adult mites. _Demodex_ and its eggs may be ingested during grooming by pruritic animals and be seen in fecal flotation tests.

Size: 100–400 μm, depending on species

Clinical Importance: Most infested animals do not develop clinical disease. Dogs are the host most likely to be clinically affected. Generalized demodectic mange in dogs has a genetic component and is thought to be associated with an immune deficiency. Demodecosis is rare in livestock species.

75 μm

Fig. 5.18. _Demodex_ spp. are usually described as looking like cigars with short legs. _Demodex canis_, shown in this photo, reaches a length of about 390 μm.

ARTHROPODS

Fig. 5.19. Many animals are parasitized by *Demodex* spp. Shown here is *Demodex* from a gerbil. Hosts rarely show clinical signs of infestation. Photos courtesy of Dr. David Baker, School of Veterinary Medicine, Louisiana State University, Baton Rouge, LA.

Fig. 5.20. *Demodex* egg in a canine skin scraping. Both mites and eggs may be detected in feces when pruritic animals swallow the parasites during grooming.

Fig. 5.21. *Demodex* is most often seen as a clinical problem in dogs. Lesions often appear first on the face or forelegs. Photo courtesy of Dr. Jeffrey F. Williams, Vanson HaloSource, Inc., Redmond, WA.

PARASITE: ***Cheyletiella* spp.** (Figs. 5.23 and 5.24)
Common name: Walking dandruff.

Taxonomy: Mite (family Cheyletiellidae).

Host: *Cheyletiella parasitovorax*, *C. yasguri*, and *C. blakei* are seen on rabbits, dogs, and cats, respectively.

Geographic Distribution: Worldwide.

Location on Host: *Cheyletiella* infestations are usually seen on the back. In cats, the head is also often affected.

Life Cycle: Transmission is by direct contact or fomites. *Cheyletiella* can be carried from one animal to another by fleas (*Ctenocephalides*). Mites can live up to 10 days in the environment.

Laboratory Diagnosis: *Cheyletiella* is a fur mite and not a skin dweller, so only superficial skin scrapings are required for diagnosis. Alternatively, if material combed from the hair is examined against a dark background, mites can be seen as moving white dots ("walking dandruff"). The distinctive feature of the mite is the large palpal claws.

Size: Approximately 400 μm

Clinical Importance: Many infested animals do not show clinical signs. Young animals are most likely to show evidence of infestation, including crusting, increased skin scurf, and pruritus. In heavy infestations, hair loss may occur. Owners may develop lesions in areas of close contact with their animals.

Fig. 5.22. In goats and cattle, clinical demodecosis is usually associated with the formation of pustules. Photo courtesy of Dr. Jeffrey F. Williams, Vanson HaloSource, Inc., Redmond, WA, and Dr. C. S. F. Williams, Langley, WA.

Fig. 5.23. *Cheyletiella* is a surface mite that can be collected by brushing the hair coat or collecting material with sticky tape. In heavy infestations, mites may be found throughout the hair coat.

Fig. 5.24. *Cheyletiella* spp. are easily identified microscopically by the presence of large palpal claws (*arrow*). Small combs are found on the legs instead of the suckers seen in some other species of parasitic mites.

PARASITE: *Lynxacarus radovskyi* (Fig. 5.25)

Taxonomy: Mite (family Listrophoridae).

Host: Cats; other species infest bobcats and weasels.

Geographic Distribution: Australia, southern United States, Caribbean, and Hawaii.

Location on Host: Mites clasp the hairs of cats, primarily on the tail head, tail tip, and in the perineal area.

Life Cycle: The entire life cycle is spent on the host. Infestation is by direct contact.

Laboratory Diagnosis: Laterally flattened mites can be seen clinging to cat hairs. Eggs are attached to the hairs.

   Size: Approximately 450 µm

Clinical Importance: Heavy mite infestations can affect the entire body and lead to poor condition of the hair coat. This mite is rare in North America.

PARASITE: *Leporacarus (=Listrophorus) gibbus* (Figs. 5.26 and 5.27)
         Common name: Fur mite.

Taxonomy: Mite (family Listrophoridae). This mite formerly belonged to the genus *Listrophorus*.

Host: Rabbits.

Geographic Distribution: Worldwide.

Location on Host: Throughout the fur.

Life Cycle: Transmission is by direct contact. All stages of the life cycle are found on the host.

Laboratory Diagnosis: Mites are large enough to be seen as small specks on the hairs and can be collected by combing and examining hairs with a magnifying glass or microscope.

   Size: Approximately 350–500 µm

Clinical Importance: Mites usually cause no clinical signs even though large numbers may be present.

Fig. 5.25. The body of the *Lynxacarus* mite is laterally compressed, like that of a flea and has large sternal plates that are used, along with the first two sets of legs, to encircle the hair.

Fig. 5.26. Male *Leporacarus* mites have a brown anterior shield that projects beyond the mouthparts. Males also have distinctive adanal clasping organs.

Fig. 5.27. Female *Leporacarus* from a rabbit. The female mites also show the anterior shield.

235

PARASITE: ***Chirodiscoides caviae*** (Fig. 5.28)
Common name: Fur mite.

Taxonomy: Mite (family Listrophoridae).

Host: Guinea pigs.

Geographic Distribution: Worldwide.

Location on Host: Attached to hairs.

Life Cycle: Transmission is by direct contact with an infested individual or fomite.

Laboratory Diagnosis: Mites are detected by examining hairs from the host.

Size: Approximately 350–500 μm

Clinical Importance: This mite is considered generally nonpathogenic.

PARASITE: ***Mycoptes musculinus, Myobia musculi, Radfordia* spp.** (Figs. 5.29 and 5.30)
Common name: Fur mite.

Taxonomy: Mites (families Listrophoridae and Myobidae).

Host: Mice and rats.

Geographic Distribution: Worldwide.

Location on Host: Hair coat.

Life Cycle: Transmission is by direct contact; all stages of the life cycle are found on the host.

Laboratory Diagnosis: Diagnosis is made by detecting mites on host hairs.

Size:	*Radfordia* and *Myobia*	approximately 400–450 μm
	Mycoptes	approximately 350 μm

Clinical Importance: Some infested animals tolerate large numbers of mites without clinical signs, although pruritus, erythema, hair loss, and thickened skin may occur in others. Secondary bacterial infections may develop.

Fig. 5.28. *Chirodiscoides* from a guinea pig. The first two pairs of legs are adapted for wrapping around the hair shafts of the host. Photo courtesy of Dr. David Baker, School of Veterinary Medicine, Louisiana State University, Baton Rouge, LA.

Fig. 5.29. *Mycoptes musculinus* from the hair coat of a mouse. In males, the fourth pair of legs is enlarged and directed backward. Photo courtesy of Dr. David Baker, School of Veterinary Medicine, Louisiana State University, Baton Rouge, LA.

Fig. 5.30. *Radfordia* is found at the base of the hairs. The first pair of legs is modified for feeding and project forward. *Radfordia* is similar in appearance to another rodent fur mite, *Myobia musculi*. However, *Radfordia* has two claws on the second pair of legs, while *Myobia* has only one claw.

237

PARASITE: **Avian Feather Mites** (Fig. 5.31)

Taxonomy: Mites (numerous families and species).

Host: Domestic and wild birds.

Geographic Distribution: Worldwide.

Location on Host: Species specialized for different feather environments.

Life Cycle: Most mites live on the feather surface and feed on secretions and skin and feather debris. Quill mites live in the base of the feathers and feed on host tissue or fluids.

Laboratory Diagnosis: Diagnosis is made by detection and identification of mites on feathers.

Size: Variable with species

Clinical Importance: Most feather mite infestations appear to cause little damage and are usually considered of minor clinical importance.

PARASITE: ***Ornithonyssus sylviarum, O. bursa*** (Figs. 5.32 and 5.33)
Common name: Northern fowl mite, tropical fowl mite.

Taxonomy: Mite (order Mesostigmata).

Geographic Distribution: The northern fowl mite, *O. sylviarum*, is found in temperate regions worldwide. The tropical fowl mite, *O. bursa*, is found in tropical and subtropical climates. Both species are found in the United States.

Location on Host: Mites and egg masses can be found on the skin among the feathers. In poultry, *O. sylviarum* often concentrates around the vent, causing a dark discoloration of the area.

Life Cycle: *Onithonyssus sylviarum* spends its life on the avian host, whereas individuals of *O. bursa* spend greater periods of time off the host. Wild birds can introduce the mites into poultry facilities. Under appropriate conditions, the life cycle of *O. sylviarum* can be completed in a week.

Laboratory Diagnosis: Large mites are observed on birds or in the environment.

Size: Approximately 750 μm

Clinical Importance: Scabbing and matted feathers can develop on infested birds. In severe cases, anemia, decreased production, and death may occur. Mites can act as vectors of other avian disease agents, including those causing Newcastle disease and fowl pox. Humans in contact with mites may also develop lesions.

ARTHROPODS

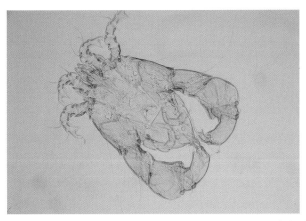

Fig. 5.31. Male *Mesalgoides* sp. mite from a wild bird. Feather mite species show great variation in morphology as a result of specialization for life in different parts of the avian feather environment.

150 μm

Fig. 5.32. *Ornithonyssus* spp. belong to the mesostigmatid order of mites. These mites have long legs in the anterior portion of the body and are more ticklike in appearance than other mites. In *Ornithonyssus* spp., the anus (*arrow*) is at the anterior end of the anal plate. The anus of *Dermanyssus* spp, a morphologically similar mite, is located in the posterior portion of the anal plate. Photo courtesy of Dr. David Baker, School of Veterinary Medicine, Louisiana State University, Baton Rouge, LA.

Fig. 5.33. Another characteristic used to differentiate *Ornithonyssus* from the similar genus *Dermanyssus* is the chelicerae (*arrow*). The chelicerae in this *Ornithonyssus* mite are shorter than the long, whiplike chelicerae of *Dermanyssus*.

PARASITE: ***Ornithonyssus bacoti*** (Figs. 5.32 and 5.33)
Common name: Tropical rat mite.

Taxonomy: Mite (order Mesostigmata).

Host: Rodents, occasionally other animals and humans.

Geographic Distribution: Worldwide.

Location on Host: Skin.

Life Cycle: Adult mites lay eggs in the environment. Mites visit the host only to feed; they spend the rest of the time in the host's bedding or nest. The life cycle can be completed in about 2 weeks.

Laboratory Diagnosis: Mites on animals or in the environment are observed.

Size: Approximately 750 μm

Clinical Importance: In large numbers, this blood-feeding mite can cause anemia, debilitation, and even death. Humans in contact with infested laboratory or pet rodents may develop lesions.

PARASITE: ***Dermanyssus gallinae*** (Fig. 5.34)
Common name: Red poultry mite.

Taxonomy: Mite (order Mesostigmata).

Host: Wild and domestic birds.

Geographic Distribution: Worldwide.

Location on Host: Mites can occur anywhere on the body.

Life Cycle: Mites visit the host at night only to take blood meals. During the day, the mites are found in crevices in the environment. The life cycle can be completed in as little as 10 days. Adults can survive in the environment for several months without feeding.

Laboratory Diagnosis: Mite infestation may be difficult to diagnose because the mites are not on the host during the day. Close examination of the environment may reveal mites under crusts of manure on perches or in nest boxes. If infestation is suspected in caged birds, the cage can be covered with a white cloth at night. In the morning, mites will be seen as small black or dark red dots clinging to the cloth.

Size: Approximately 750 μm

Clinical Importance: Heavy infestation can cause anemia and death, particularly in hatchlings. Hens may be reluctant to sit on their nests. Other animals and humans in close proximity to infested birds or their nests may also be attacked and develop lesions.

ARTHROPODS

150 μm

Fig. 5.34. *Dermanyssus gallinae* infests both domestic and wild birds. The anus of this mite is present in a more posterior position on the anal plate than in *Ornithonyssus*. *Dermanyssus* also has long, whiplike chelicerae (not visible in this figure). Differentiating the genera may be helpful in determining appropriate control measures because of differences in life cycles.

PARASITE: ***Pneumonyssoides caninum*** (Fig. 5.35)
Common name: Nasal mite.

Taxonomy: Mite (order Mesostigmata).

Host: Dogs. A similar mite, *P. simicola*, parasitizes the respiratory system of some monkey species.

Geographic Distribution: Worldwide.

Location on Host: Nasal sinuses of dogs.

Life Cycle: The life cycle of this mite is poorly understood, but transmission is thought to be by direct contact since mites are sometimes seen crawling on the nose.

Laboratory Diagnosis: Mites are observed in the nasal sinuses and passages or crawling outside the nostrils.

Size: Approximately 1 mm

Clinical Importance: Infestations are usually asymptomatic but may produce sneezing, rhinitis, sinusitis, and malaise. In captive monkeys, *Pneumonyssus* can cause significant respiratory disease.

PARASITE: ***Ophionyssus natricis*** (Figs. 5.36 and 5.37)
Common name: Snake mite.

Taxonomy: Mite (order Mesostigmata).

Geographic Distribution: Worldwide on captive snakes.

Location on Host: Mites are found on the skin or under the scales of snakes and may also infest lizards.

Life Cycle: *Ophionyssus* nymphs and adults feed and females deposit eggs in the environment after taking a blood meal. Larvae do not feed. The entire life cycle takes about 13–19 days. Infestation occurs by direct contact with an infested snake or its environment.

Laboratory Diagnosis: Identification of mites collected from snakes. Females that have taken a blood meal are dark colored. A cotton-tipped swab can be dipped in mineral oil and used to collect mites for identification.

Size: Females 0.6–1.3 mm

Clinical Importance: *Ophionyssus* infestations are common in captive snakes. Affected animals may show irritation and depression. Shedding may increase, and snakes may soak themselves more frequently in water.

Fig. 5.35. *Pneumonyssoides caninum*, the nasal mite of dogs. A related mite, *Pneumonyssus simicola*, is the lung mite of several species of African monkeys. Photo courtesy of Dr. Jeffrey F. Williams, Vanson HaloSource, Inc., Redmond, WA.

Fig. 5.36. *Ophionyssus* mites are the most common external parasite on captive snakes and may seriously affect the health of the host. Female mites lay eggs off the host, and successful control of infestation requires environmental treatment.

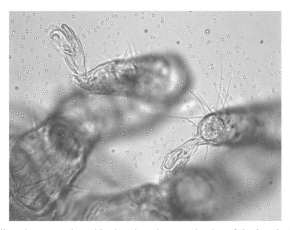

Fig. 5.37. *Ophionyssus*, like other mesostigmatid mites, has claws on the tips of the legs instead of the suckers seen in many other parasitic mites (Fig. 5.1).

243

PARASITE: **Trombiculid Mites** (Figs. 5.38–5.40)
        Common name: Chigger, harvest mite, scrub itch mite.

Taxonomy: Mites (family Trombiculidae).

Host: Wide variety of animals and humans.

Geographic Distribution: Several species parasitize a variety of hosts, including *Eutrombicula alfreddugesi*, *E. splendens* (North America), and *Neotrombicula autumnalis* (Europe).

Location on Host: Predilection sites include the face, head, and legs.

Life Cycle: Only the larval stage of chigger mites is parasitic. Eggs are laid in the environment. Larvae attach to a host and feed for 3–5 days and then complete development in the environment. Adults are predators of other arthropods.

Laboratory Diagnosis: Small, often orange or red mites are often seen in clusters on the face of the host. The presence of only larval stages is helpful in diagnosing chigger infestations.

  Size: Approximately 200–500 µm, depending on species

Clinical Importance: Mites may cause pruritus and irritation. Humans are also susceptible to infestation, with pruritic lesions frequently appearing in areas where clothing is constrictive (i.e., at the waistband of pants, top of socks, etc.).

ARTHROPODS

Fig. 5.38. Only the six-legged larvae of chiggers are parasitic, which is helpful in identification of the parasites. This *Blankaartia* sp. chigger was removed from a bird.

Fig. 5.39. Specimen of *Trombicula* sp., a cause of mammalian chigger infestation. Photo courtesy of Dr. Jeffrey F. Williams, Vanson HaloSource, Inc., Redmond, WA.

Fig. 5.40. Typical chigger lesions on the leg of a parasitologist. Chiggers may also cause pruritus and irritation on animals.

Tick Identification

Ticks are usually larger than mites, ranging in length from 3 to 12 mm, or more in the case of engorged females. Ticks are divided into two families: Ixodidae (hard ticks) and Argasidae (soft ticks). The Ixodid (hard) ticks are of greatest importance in veterinary medicine. Various hard tick species are vectors of a number of viral, bacterial, and protozoal animal and human pathogens. In addition, hard tick species cause tick paralysis and tick toxicosis.

All ticks pass from the egg through larval and nymphal stages before becoming adults and utilize one or more host animals during the developmental cycle. Eggs are always laid in the environment. Hard tick larvae are acquired by the host from the environment. All hard ticks undergo a single molt from the larval to the nymphal stage and a second molt from the nymph to the adult. These molts follow attachment and blood feeding on the host that usually lasts for several days. Tick species that remain on the host during the two molting periods are known as one-host ticks. In two-host tick species, the molt to the nymphal stage occurs on the host, but the engorged nymph leaves the host, molts in the environment, and then finds a new host. In the three-host tick life cycle, both the larva and nymph leave the host to molt, attaching to a host again after each molt. In some cases, each tick stage prefers the same host species; in others, host preference may vary with the stage of the tick. In much of North America, the most important tick species are three-host ticks. Soft tick life cycles are more variable than those of the hard ticks. Many soft tick species live in the environment and visit the host only briefly to take repeated blood meals.

All stages of ticks are large enough to be grossly visible on animals, although larvae may be only a few millimeters in length and soft ticks usually do not attach for long periods. Hard ticks are likely to be found attached in areas on the host that cannot be easily groomed, for example, the head, neck, and ears of most host species, and also the tail of horses (Fig. 5.41). Because ticks are important vectors of zoonotic diseases (Lyme disease, Rocky Mountain spotted fever, etc.), they should be removed using forceps or tweezers instead of the fingers to reduce the possibility of contact with tick body fluids containing infectious organisms. The tick should be firmly grasped directly behind the point of attachment to the skin and then pulled off. Often a small portion of skin will also be pulled away.

Hard ticks have a hard dorsal shield called the scutum. The scutum is limited to the anterior, central region of the dorsum in females, whereas in males, the scutum extends over the entire dorsal

Fig. 5.41. Ticks are most often found attached on parts of the body that are difficult for the host to groom. Unidentified ticks are attached to the ear of this dog. Photo courtesy of Dr. Jeffrey F. Williams, Vanson HaloSource, Inc., Redmond, WA.

ARTHROPODS

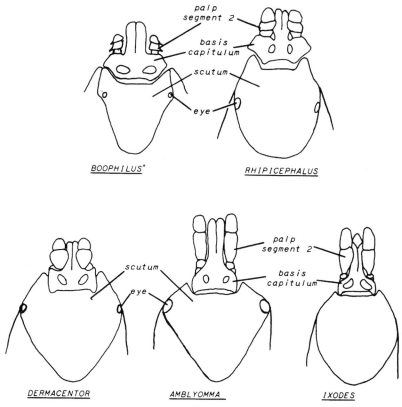

Fig. 5.42. Comparison of the basis capituli and mouthparts of females of the important Ixodid tick genera of domestic animals in North America. The scutum of the adult male hard ticks covers the entire dorsum of the parasite. *Boophilus* ticks have now been incorporated into the genus *Rhipicephalus*.

region. The mouthparts of hard ticks are evident from the dorsal surface. The Argasid (soft) ticks have a leathery integument, which often is spinose or bumpy. The mouthparts of soft ticks can be seen only from the ventral aspect of the tick.

Identification of adult hard ticks to the level of genus is not difficult in a veterinary practice. One of the most useful characteristics for identifying the genus of a hard tick is the shape of the basis capituli and mouthparts. Figure 5.42 shows these characteristics on adult females; a magnifying glass is useful for looking at the basis capituli. The pigmented markings of the scutum (referred to as "ornamentation") are another useful characteristic. Ticks with ornamentation are called "ornate"; those lacking these markings are "inornate." Additionally, in some genera, the posterior margin of the body has a series of indentations, known as festoons. Features like festoons are much more difficult to appreciate on engorged female ticks. Identification is easiest with unengorged females or males. Nymphs, like adults, have eight legs but lack the genital pore seen in adults. Using these characteristics, a dichotomous key for the genera of adult ticks (Fig. 5.43) can be followed for identification of most tick specimens in North America. Identification of six-legged larval ticks (Fig. 5.44) is more difficult and may require the assistance of an expert.

Figure 5.45 shows adult female ticks of the most common species in the United States. They also represent the most common tick genera found throughout the world. If assistance is needed with specific identification of ticks, they should be preserved and submitted to a diagnostic laboratory in 70%–80% alcohol.

Fig. 5.43. Larval tick, also called a seed tick. Tick larvae can be easily distinguished from nymphs and adults because they have only six legs. Larvae of common ticks in the United States often prefer different hosts than those of adult stages.

Fig. 5.44. Female ticks of the species most important in the United States in veterinary medicine. (*Right*) *Ixodes scapularis*, the deer tick; (*bottom*) *Dermacentor variabililis*, American dog tick; (*left*) *Amblyomma americanum*, lone star tick; (*top*) *Rhipicephalus sanguineus*, brown dog tick. More information on these species can be found on the following pages. Photo courtesy of Dr. Susan Little, Oklahoma State University, Stillwater, OK.

PICTORIAL KEY TO GENERA OF ADULT TICKS IN UNITED STATES

By Harry D Pratt

X - 30

Fig. 5.45. Key to adult tick genera found in North America. Examination of ticks with low magnification should allow identification of features used in this key. *Boophilus* ticks have now been incorporated into the genus *Rhipicephalus*. Courtesy of U.S. Public Health Service, CDC.

PARASITE: ***Amblyomma* spp.** (Figs. 5.46–5.52; see also Fig. 5.45)

Common names: Lone star tick, Gulf Coast tick, Cayenne tick, bont tick, tropical bont tick.

Taxonomy: Tick (family Ixodidae).

Host: A wide variety of domestic and wild animals serve as hosts.

Geographic Distribution: Approximately 100 species are found predominantly in tropical and subtropical areas. *Amblyomma americanum* (lone star tick) and *A. maculatum* (Gulf Coast tick) are common species in the United States. *Ambyomma cajennense* (Cayenne tick) and other species are also found on a variety of wild and domestic animals in the United States, Mexico, and Latin America. *Amblyomma hebraeum* and *A. variegatium* are important species in Africa.

Location on Host: Various, often found on domestic animals in the head and neck region.

Life Cycle: *Amblyomma* spp. are three-host ticks, meaning that each stage of the life cycle must find a new host following a molt in the environment. Larvae and nymphs feed on a wide variety of hosts; adults are often found on ruminants and other domestic animals and humans.

Laboratory Diagnosis: Long mouthparts are an important diagnostic feature of *Amblyomma*. The scutum is usually ornamented.

Clinical Importance: The long mouthparts of *Amblyomma* make attachment particularly painful and susceptible to secondary infection. Economic loss from damaged hides may occur. *Amblyomma americanum* is a vector of the bacteria causing tularemia and Q fever and several *Ehrlichia* species. Persistent infestations of *A. maculatum* can cause permanent damage to the ears of cattle known as "gotch ear." The lesions caused by *A. cajennense* are particulary painful, and it can serve as a vector of Rocky Mountain spotted fever (*Rickettsia rickettsii*). In Africa, *A. hebraeum* and *A. variegatum* transmit heartwater (*Cowdria*), tick-bite fever (*Rickettsia conori*), and Nairobi sheep disease (Nairovirus). *Amblyomma variegatum* also transmits heartwater in the Caribbean.

Fig. 5.46. Male and female *Amblyomma americanum* (lone star tick). The female (*right*) of this common U.S. tick is easily recognized by the presence of the large white spot at the posterior margin of the scutum. Males do not have conspicuous ornamentation on the scutum, although with closer inspection, some iridescent markings can be seen on the margin of the scutum and festoons.

ARTHROPODS

Fig. 5.47. Nymph of *Amblyomma americanum*. Like adults, nymphs have eight legs, but are smaller and lack a genital opening. The nymphs of *A. americanum* lack the dramatic "lone star" of adult females. Photo courtesy of James Gathany and G. Maupin, Centers for Disease Control and Prevention (Public Health Image Library).

Fig. 5.48. *Amblyomma maculatum*: (*left*) male; (*right*) female. The Gulf Coast tick is found in the southeastern United States, Mexico, and South and Central America. It feeds primarily on the head and neck of birds and mammals. Note the long mouthparts typical of this genus. Photo courtesy of Dr. Susan Little, University of Oklahoma, Stillwater, OK.

Fig. 5.49. *Amblyomma cajennense*: (*left*) male; (*right*) female. The Cayenne tick is found in Texas, Mexico, and Latin America. It parasitizes a wide variety of mammals and birds. Photo courtesy of James Gathany and Christopher Paddock, Centers for Disease Control and Prevention (Public Health Image Library).

PARASITE: *Hyalomma* **spp.** (Fig. 5.53)
Common name: Bont-legged tick, camel tick, tortoise tick.

Taxonomy: Tick (family Ixodidae).

Host: Many host species, including domestic animals. One species, *H. aegyptium*, is a parasite of tortoises.

Geographic Distribution: Asia, Europe, North Africa.

Location on Host: Various.

Life Cycle: *Hyalomma* species are usually two-host ticks, which leave the host after nymphal and adult blood meals.

Laboratory Diagnosis: Ticks of the genus *Hyalomma* have eyes and long mouthparts like those of *Amblyomma*, but lack the ornamentation usually seen on *Amblyomma* spp.

Clinical Importance: *Hyalomma* species cause tick toxicosis and serve as vectors of *Babesia*, *Theileria*, and *Rickettsia* spp.

Fig. 5.50. Larval or seed ticks, so called because of their small size. This tick has been treated with a clearing solution. Larval ticks are much smaller than adults and have only six legs. Seed ticks of some species may attach in large numbers to domestic animals or humans.

Fig. 5.51. *Ambyomma variegatum*: (*left*) male; (*right*) female. The tropical bont tick is an important vector of heartwater in cattle. This tick is also found in the Carribean.

Fig. 5.52. *Amblyomma* spp. are common in the tropics and subtropics. They are often highly ornamented with iridescent markings like these African *Amblyomma*. Some tick genera, like *Amblyomma*, have simple eyes on the margin of the scutum (*arrows*).

Fig. 5.53. *Hyalomma* spp. ticks are important disease vectors in Africa, Asia, and Australasia, although they are not found in the Western Hemisphere. They have long mouthparts, eyes, and festoons like *Amblyomma* but are not highly ornamented.

253

PARASITE: ***Ixodes* spp.** (Figs. 5.54–5.56; see also Figs. 5.45, 5.65)
Common name: Black-legged tick, deer tick, European sheep tick (castor bean tick), hedgehog tick, British dog tick, Australian and South African paralysis ticks.

Taxonomy: Tick (family Ixodidae). *Ixodes* is the largest genus of hard ticks, containing more than 200 species.

Host: Many host species, including domestic animals and humans.

Geographic Distribution: Some of the most important species in domestic animals include *I. scapularis* (black-legged or deer tick) and *I. pacificus* (western black-legged tick) in North America; *I. ricinus* (sheep or castor bean tick), *I. canisuga* (British dog tick), and *I. hexagonus* (hedgehog tick) in Europe; *I. rubicundus* (South African paralysis tick); and *I. holocyclus* (Australian paralysis tick).

Location on Host: Various.

Life Cycle: *Ixodes* species are three-host ticks.

Laboratory Diagnosis: The most helpful characteristic for identification of *Ixodes* ticks is an anal groove that runs from the posterior margin of the body to just anterior to the anus. A magnifying glass or dissecting-type microscope may be needed to appreciate this feature.

Clinical Importance: *Ixodes* spp. in North America and Europe are vectors of Lyme borreliosis and several species of *Ehrlichia*. *Ixodes ricinus* also transmits louping-ill and *Babesia* spp. in Europe. Species of this genus can also cause dermatitis and tick worry and are major causes of tick paralysis in Australia and South Africa.

ARTHROPODS

Fig. 5.54. Nymph and adult female *Ixodes scapularis*, the deer tick. This species is the primary vector of Lyme disease in the United States and is smaller than other common ticks (see Fig. 5.44 for comparison).

Fig. 5.55. The scutum of *Ixodes scapularis* is not ornamented. Photo courtesy of Agricultural Research Service, U.S. Department of Agriculture.

Fig. 5.56. The distinctive morphologic detail of the *Ixodes* ticks is the groove that runs anterior to the anus (*arrow*). In other tick genera, this groove is posterior to the anus or absent. *Ixodes* ticks also have long mouthparts.

255

PARASITE: ***Dermacentor* spp.** (Figs. 5.57–5.60; see also Fig. 5.45)

Common name: American dog tick, Rocky Mountain wood tick, winter tick, tropical horse tick.

Taxonomy: Tick (family Ixodidae).

Host: Depending on the species, a wide variety of wild and domestic hosts can be used.

Geographic Distribution: Primarily Europe, Asia, and North America. *Dermacentor variabilis* (American dog tick), *D. andersoni* (Rocky Mountain wood tick), *D. albipictus* (winter or elk or horse tick), and *D. occidentalis* (Pacific Coast tick) are found in North America and parasitize a variety of animals. *Dermacentor* (=*Anocentor*) *nitens* is a parasite of equids in Florida, the Caribbean, and Latin America. In Europe, *D. reticulatus* is an important species.

Location on Host: Various.

Life Cycle: Most *Dermacentor* spp. are three-host ticks that prefer small rodents in larval and nymphal stages and larger vertebrates in the adult stage. *Dermacentor nitens* and *D. albipictus* are one-host ticks.

Laboratory Diagnosis: *Dermacentor* spp. are usually ornamented with relatively short mouthparts and a rectangular basis capitulum.

Clinical Importance: *Dermacentor* spp. in the United States are the most common vectors of Rocky Mountain spotted fever and can also transmit anaplasmosis to cattle. *Dermacentor* (*Anocentor*) *nitens* is the vector of equine babesiosis in the United States. In Europe, *D. reticulatus* is the vector of equine and canine babesiosis. Several species of *Dermacentor* are known to cause tick paralysis.

ARTHROPODS

Fig. 5.57. *Dermacentor variabilis*: (*left*) female; (*right*) male. Like many members of this genus, *D. variabilis* (the American dog tick) is an ornamented tick. The short mouthparts, rectangular shape of the basis capituli, and presence of festoons are used in identifying the genus.

Fig. 5.58. *Dermacentor andersoni*: (*left*) male; (*right*) female; the Rocky Mountain wood tick. This tick is found in the central and western United States and Canada. Photo courtesy of James Gathany and Christopher Paddock, Centers for Disease Control and Prevention (Public Health Image Library).

Fig. 5.59. Male *Dermacentor albipictus*, the winter or moose tick. This is a brown variant of the tick, which is usually ornamented. It occurs widely in the United States and Canada and is most active in winter. Photo courtesy of Dr. Susan Little, Oklahoma State University, Stillwater, OK.

Fig. 5.60. *Dermacentor (Anocentor) nitens* engorged female (*left*) and male (*right*). Unlike most important hard ticks, this is a one-host tick species that prefers horses as host but will attach to many mammals. It is important as a vector of equine piroplasmosis in Latin America, the Caribbean, Texas, and Florida.

PARASITE: ***Rhipicephalus* spp.** (Figs. 5.61–5.66; see also Fig. 5.45)

Common name: Brown dog tick or kennel tick, brown ear tick, red-legged tick, cattle fever tick, blue tick, tropical cattle tick.

Taxonomy: Tick (family Ixodidae). Important parasites of domestic animals include *R. sanguineus* (brown dog tick), *R. appendiculatus* (brown ear tick), and *R. evertsi* (red-legged tick). Ticks previously classified in the genus *Boophilus* are now included in *Rhipicephalus*, including the former *B. microplus* (tropical cattle tick), *B. annulatus* (cattle fever tick), and *B. decoloratus* (blue tick).

Host: This genus is most important in livestock and dogs.

Geographic Distribution: *Rhipicephalus sanguineus* is found worldwide. *Rhipicephalus appendiculatus* and *R. evertsi* are found on livestock in Africa. *Rhipicephalus (Boophilus) microplus* (tropical cattle tick) is found worldwide; *R. annulatus* (cattle fever tick) is found in the Western Hemisphere and parts of Africa; *R. decoloratus* (blue tick) is an African tick.

Location on Host: Various.

Life Cycle: *Rhipicephalus sanguineus* is a three-host tick that uses a dog host for each stage of the life cycle. *Rhipicephalus appendiculatus* is also a three-host tick, while *R. evertsi* is a two-host tick and *R. microplus*, *R. annulatus*, and *R. decoloratus* are one-host ticks. After hatching from the egg in the environment, ticks locate the host, where they remain through the subsequent nymphal and adult stages. Females leave the host to lay their eggs in the environment.

Laboratory Diagnosis: *Rhipicephalus* spp. have a hexagonally shaped basis capitulum. The members of the genus that was formally called *Boophilus* have ridged palps.

Clinical Importance: *Rhipicephalus sanguineus* transmits *Babesia canis* and *Ehrlichia canis* to dogs. *Rhipicephalus* species infesting livestock, including *R. appendiculatus*, *R. evertsi*, *R. microplus*, and *R. annulatus* are the primary vectors of bovine theileriosis and babesiosis and also transmit anaplasmosis and Nairobi sheep disease to livestock.

Fig. 5.61. Engorged female *Rhipicephalus sanguineus* (brown dog tick). This species is not ornamented. In the United States, it is most common in southern states but can also be a pest in kennels in other areas since dogs are used as hosts for every stage of the life cycle. Photo courtesy of Dr. Jeffrey F. Williams, Vanson HaloSource, Inc., Redmond, WA.

Fig. 5.62. *Rhipicephalus sanguineus* male (*left*) and female (*right*). There are no markings on the scutum of this tick.

Fig. 5.63. The brown dog tick, *Rhipicephalus sanguineus*. Members of this tick genus have a basis capituli that is hexagonal in shape with flared sides (*arrow*; see also Fig. 5.42).

Fig. 5.64. *Rhipicephalus* (*Boophilus*) *microplus* female (*left*) and (*male*). This is a one-host tick of cattle that acts as the vector for bovine babesiosis.

PARASITE: *Haemaphysalis* **spp.** (Figs. 5.65, 5.67–5.68; see also Fig. 5.45)
Common name: Rabbit tick, yellow dog tick, bush tick.

Taxonomy: Tick (family Ixodidae).

Host: *Haemaphysalis* ticks parasitize a wide range of mammals and birds, depending on the species.

Geographic Distribution: Worldwide. *Haemaphysalis leporispalustris* (rabbit tick) is found in the Western Hemisphere; *H. leachi* is the yellow dog tick found in Africa and parts of Asia; and several species parasitize livestock in Europe, Africa, Asia, and Australasia.

Location on Host: Various.

Life Cycle: *Haemaphysalis* spp. are three-host ticks and leave the host after each blood meal. Larvae and nymphs typically feed on small mammals and birds, and adult ticks feed on larger mammals.

Laboratory Diagnosis: Ticks of this genus have festoons, and the second segment of the palps flares out on the lateral margin.

Clinical Importance: Large numbers of *Haemaphysalis* ticks contribute to poor condition and "tick worry." *Haemaphysalis punctata* can transmit several species of *Babesia* and anaplasmosis to livestock. *Haemaphysalis leachi* is a vector of canine babesiosis. This genus is of minor importance in North America.

Fig. 5.65. From left to right, engorged *Ixodes*, *Haemaphysalis*, and *Rhipicephalus* females. Photo courtesy of Dr. Nick Sangster and Ms. Sally Pope, Faculty of Veterinary Science, University of Sydney, Sydney, New South Wales, Australia.

ARTHROPODS

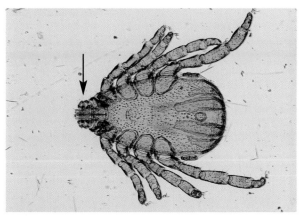

Fig. 5.66. The ridged palps of *Rhipicephaulus* (*Boophilus*) *microplus* (*arrow*) can be seen more clearly in this cleared specimen. Photo courtesy of Dr. Jeffrey F. Williams, Vanson HaloSource, Inc., Redmond, WA.

Fig. 5.67. *Haemaphysalis leporispalustris*, the rabbit tick, is found in North America and can carry the bacterial agent of tularemia, *Francisella tularensis*. Other members of this tick genus are vectors of *Babesia* and *Theileria* in Africa, Asia, and Australasia. The female tick in this photo (*right*) has host skin tissue attached to the mouthparts.

Fig. 5.68. The palps of *Haemaphysalis* ticks are wider than they are long, and in some species, the second segment of the palps flares laterally (*arrow*).

PARASITE: ***Otobius megnini*** (Figs. 5.69–5.71)
Common name: Spinose ear tick.

Taxonomy: Tick (family Argasidae).

Host: Ruminants and horses primarily, also camelids and small animals.

Geographic Distribution: North and South America, Africa, India.

Location on Host: External ear canal.

Life Cycle: Eggs hatch in the environment. Ticks enter the ear of the host and may remain for several months until the nymphal stage is completed. Nymphs leave the host after feeding and molt to the adult stage, which does not feed.

Laboratory Diagnosis: These ticks are easily diagnosed based on host location and recognition of specimens as soft ticks. *Otobius* is covered with short spines, leading to the name spinose ear tick. Hard ticks may also attach in the ears, but they have a distinctive hard, enameled appearance compared with soft ticks like *Otobius*. Also, any adult-stage ticks found in the ears will not be *Otobius*, since spinose ear ticks are parasitic only as larvae and nymphs.

Clinical Importance: Large numbers can cause severe inflammation and rupture the ear drum.

ARTHROPODS

Fig. 5.69. *Otobius*, the spinose ear tick and *Dermacentor andersoni*. This picture clearly demonstrates the difference between hard and soft ticks. The soft tick, *Otobius* (*left*), does not have the hard enamel-like surface of the Ixodid tick, *Dermacentor* (*right*). The capitulum of soft ticks is also not visible from the dorsal surface. Photo courtesy of Dr. Susan Little, Oklahoma State University, Stillwater, OK.

Fig. 5.70. Only larvae and nymphs of *Otobius*, the spinose ear tick, are parasites. They are found clustered in the ears of the host. Photo courtesy of Dr. Jeffrey F. Williams, Vanson HaloSource, Inc., Redmond, WA.

Fig. 5.71. This closer view of *Otobius* shows the spines that cover the surface of the tick. Photo courtesy of Dr. Susan Little, Oklahoma State University, Stillwater, OK.

PARASITE: ***Argas* spp.** (Fig. 5.72)
Common name: Fowl tick.

Taxonomy: Tick (family Argasidae). Important species include *Argas persicus* and *Argas reflexus*.

Host: Poultry and wild birds.

Geographic Distribution: Worldwide.

Location on Host: Various.

Life Cycle: *Argas* is a soft tick that lives in the environment, attacking birds only to feed, usually during the night. Several blood meals are taken by larval and adult ticks.

Laboratory Diagnosis: As their name suggests, soft ticks lack the hard "enameled" appearance of hard ticks. The mouthparts of soft ticks cannot be seen from the dorsal surface, which also helps to distinguish them from hard ticks. *Argas* spp. have a flattened body margin.

Clinical Importance: Heavy burdens can cause loss of production and death. *Argas* spp. act as vectors for *Borrelia anserine* and can cause fowl paralysis. They are uncommon in total-confinement poultry systems.

PARASITE: ***Ornithodoros* spp.** (Fig. 5.73)
Common name: Tampan.

Taxonomy: Tick (family Argasidae). *Ornithodoros moubata* is the African tampan; *O. hermsi* is one of the species found in the United States.

Host: Domestic livestock and humans.

Geographic Distribution: Africa, Asia, North and South America.

Location on Host: Various.

Life Cycle: These ticks are often nocturnal and are found in animal or human habitations, including dens, nests, or crevices of buildings.

Laboratory Diagnosis: In contrast to *Argas* spp. ticks, *Ornithodoros* spp. do not have a lateral sutural line and there is no distinct body margin.

Clinical Importance: Large numbers of these soft ticks can cause significant blood loss. *Ornithodoros* transmits endemic relapsing fever in humans. In the United States, *Ornithodoros* ticks are most common in the western and southwestern states.

CLASS INSECTA

Like ticks and mites, insects also belong to the phylum Arthropoda. All insects have bodies composed of three parts: the head, the thorax (which bears the legs), and the abdomen. Adult insects have six legs and some have wings. Life cycles of parasitic insects may be quite simple, in which larval stages are similar in appearance to the adults, or very complex, involving transformation from a wormlike maggot to a pupa and then to the adult. The insects of greatest veterinary importance are the lice, fleas, and flies.

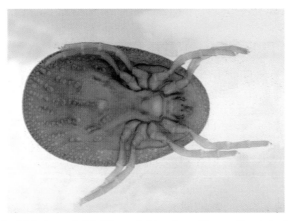

Fig. 5.72. *Argas* sp., the fowl tick, is a soft tick. The ventral location of the mouthparts is clearly seen in this organism. The surface of *Argus* is granulated. Photo courtesy of Dr. Dwight Bowman, College of Veterinary Medicine, Cornell University, Ithaca, NY.

Fig. 5.73. The surface of the soft tick *Ornithodoros* is covered with mammillae (small bumps) and there is no distinct margin to the body.

Lice (Orders Anoplura and Mallophaga)

Lice are wingless, dorsoventrally flattened insects ranging in length from about 1 to 8 mm. They are common ectoparasites of mammals and of birds and infestation may be referred to as "pediculosis." Lice are highly species specific, and the entire life cycle is completed on the host. Immature lice resemble adults but are smaller. Eggs (nits) may be observed attached individually to hair shafts and sometimes as white to yellow masses at the bases of feathers on birds. With close attention, lice can usually be seen with the unaided eye.

Lice are divided into two orders: Mallophaga (chewing or biting lice) and Anoplura (sucking lice). Birds are parasitized only by biting lice, while both biting and sucking lice are found on mammals. The biting lice feed on skin scurf and other organic material on the skin. In contrast, sucking lice feed on blood. Biting lice move rapidly, while sucking lice move more slowly and may be seen head down close to the skin surface or actually feeding. Mallophaga have blunt heads that are wider than the thorax and mandible-like mouthparts and are often a yellow color. Anoplura are generally larger than chewing lice and are gray to dusky red, depending on the quantity of blood in their intestines. The head of sucking lice is narrower than the thorax and has elongated protrusible piercing mouthparts. While species identification of lice is usually not required in veterinary practice, recognition of an organism as a biting or sucking louse may be helpful when selecting treatment.

Lice on large mammals can also be detected by examining hair coat brushings collected with a stiff-bristled brush. A magnifying lens or dissecting microscope may be useful if lice are very small. Lice may be transferred into saline, mineral or immersion oil, or into Hoyer's solution on a microscope slide with fine forceps, a swab, or a needle moistened with the same material.

PARASITE: ***Hematopinus* spp.** (Fig. 5.74)
Common name: Pig louse, short-nosed cattle louse, cattle tail louse.

Taxonomy: Insect (order Anoplura).

Host: Species important in domestic animals include *H. suis* (pigs), *H. asini* (horses), *H. eurysternus* (short-nosed sucking louse of cattle), and *H. quadripertusus* (tail louse of cattle). Sucking lice are also found on camelids (genus *Microthoracius*).

Geographic Distribution: Worldwide. *Hematopinus quadripertusus* is found primarily in the tropics and subtropics.

Location on Host: *Hematopinus* spp. are often found on the head, neck, and back of the host. *Haematopinus quadripertusus* is usually found around the tail.

Life Cycle: Transmission is by direct contact or fomites. Eggs are glued to the hairs of the host.

Laboratory Diagnosis: Members of this genus are large, about 4–5 mm in length, with the elongated heads typical of the sucking lice.

Clinical Importance: *Hematopinus* infestations can produce alopecia and pruritus, leading to self-inflicted trauma and production losses. Heavy infestations can produce anemia. *Haematopinus suis* is a common and important ectoparasite of swine; *H. eurysternus* is considered the most important cattle louse worldwide. Infestation of horses is uncommon in well-managed stables.

PARASITE: ***Linognathus* spp.** (Figs. 5.75 and 5.76; see also Fig. 5.83)
Common name: Face louse and foot louse of sheep, long-nosed cattle louse.

Taxonomy: Insect (order Anoplura).

Fig. 5.74. *Hematopinus* spp. have prominent ocular points (*arrow*) and legs of equal size. *Haematopinus suis*, shown here, is the largest louse found on domesticated animals. This dark-colored louse is usually not difficult to identify on the host. Photo courtesy of Dr. Alvin Gajadhar, Centre for Animal Parasitology, CFIA, Saskatoon, Saskatchewan, Canada.

Fig. 5.75. *Linognathus* spp. have no ocular points. Unlike *Haematopinus*, the second and third pairs of legs of these sucking lice are larger than the first pair and end in large claws. The louse shown here is *L. setosus*, the sucking louse of dogs. Members of this genus are usually 2–3 mm in length.

Fig. 5.76. Sucking louse species infesting the skin of a calf. Photo courtesy of Dr. Jeffrey F. Williams, Vanson HaloSource, Inc., Redmond, WA.

Linognathus (*continued*)

Host: *Linognathus pedalis* (ovine foot louse), *L. ovillus* (ovine face louse), *L. vituli* (long-nosed cattle louse), *L. africanus* (bovine African blue louse), *L. setosus* (dogs).

Geographic Distribution: Worldwide.

Location on Host: The face and foot lice of sheep are found primarily in those locations; other species are less restricted in distribution.

Life Cycle: Transmission is by direct contact or fomites.

Laboratory Diagnosis: Detection of lice and eggs on the host by gross observation.

Clinical Importance: As with other lice, infested animals show pruritus and dermatitis, and severe infestations can lead to production losses and anemia.

PARASITE: ***Solenopotes capillatus*** (Fig. 5.77)
Common name: Little blue cattle louse.

Taxonomy: Insect (order Anoplura).

Host: Cattle.

Geographic Distribution: Worldwide.

Location on Host: Usually found concentrated on the face, neck, shoulders, back, and tail.

Life Cycle: The entire life cycle is spent on the host with transmission by direct contact or fomites.

Laboratory Diagnosis: *Solenopotes capillatus* is similar in appearance to *Linognathus*, but *Solenopotes* has tubercles carrying spiracles that project from abdominal segments.

Clinical Importance: Large numbers of lice may cause production loss from dermatitis and anemia.

PARASITE: ***Pediculus* spp., *Phthirus pubis*** (Figs. 5.78 and 5.79)
Common name: Human head louse, body louse, crab louse.

Taxonomy: Insects (order Anoplura). *Pediculus humanus humanus* is the body louse; *Pediculus humanus capita* is the head louse; and *Phthirus pubis* is the pubic or crab louse.

Host: Humans.

Geographic Distribution: Worldwide.

Location on Host: Head lice are found in that region, while body lice live principally in clothing and visit the skin to feed. Crab lice are found in the pubic area or on other coarse body hair.

Life Cycle: Transmission of all human lice infestations is by direct contact or fomites. Head and crab lice glue their eggs to host hair, while body lice deposit their eggs in clothing.

Laboratory Diagnosis: Observation of lice and eggs.

Clinical Importance: Humans are the only hosts of these parasites. Their veterinary importance lies in the occasional detection of a human louse on a pet and resulting confusion about who gave what to whom. In these cases, the family pet has lice only because of close contact with infested humans. Human lice do not survive and reproduce on domestic animals.

ARTHROPODS

Fig. 5.77. *Solenopotes capillatus*, the little blue cattle louse, is less common than *Linognathus* spp. The projecting tubercles carrying spiracles on the abdominal segments of *Solenopotes* (*arrow*) are helpful in identification of this louse. Photo courtesy of Merial.

Fig. 5.78. *Pediculus humanus* has well-developed eyes, no ocular points, and three large pairs of legs.

Fig. 5.79. The human crab louse, *Phthirus pubis*, has a distinctive crab-shaped body.

PARASITE: **Sucking Lice of Laboratory Animals** (Figs. 5.80 and 5.81)

Taxonomy: Insect (order Anoplura).

Host: Rodents, rabbits.

Geographic Distribution: Worldwide.

Location on Host: Predilection sites variable, depending on species.

Life Cycle: As with other lice, transmission is by direct contact with an infested animal or fomites.

Laboratory Diagnosis: Detection of eggs and lice on hair and morphologic identification of lice.

Clinical Importance: Large numbers of lice may cause loss of condition and possibly anemia.

PARASITE: *Bovicola* **spp.** (Figs. 5.82–5.87)
Common name: Biting louse.

Taxonomy: Insect (order Mallophaga).

Host: *Bovicola bovis* (cattle), *B. equi* (horses), *B. ovis* (sheep), *B. caprae* (goats), *B. breviceps* (camelids).

Geographic Distribution: Worldwide.

Location on Host: In general, preferred sites include the neck, shoulder, and back, but lice can spread throughout the body.

Life Cycle: Like the sucking lice, all stages of biting lice are found on the host, and transmission is by direct contact with an infested animal or fomites.

Laboratory Diagnosis: Infested animals should be observed, although *Bovicola* spp. are only a few millimeters in length and may be difficult to see. Hair coat brushings can also be examined with a magnifying glass.

Clinical Importance: These common external parasites cause pruritus and dermatitis and are associated with production losses and secondary infections in heavy infestations.

Fig. 5.80. Sucking lice (*Polyplax*) species from a rat. Typical of sucking lice, the head is narrower than the thorax in this specimen.

Fig. 5.81. *Polyplax* egg glued to a rat hair. The presence of lice eggs ("nits") on the hairs is helpful in diagnosis of infestation.

Fig. 5.82. Like other biting lice, the head of *Bovicola* spp. is broader than the thorax. Pictured here is the bovine parasite *Bovicola bovis*. Photo courtesy of Dr. Robert Ridley, College of Veterinary Medicine, Kansas State University, Manhattan, KS.

271

Fig. 5.83. Biting lice of domestic animals are usually smaller than sucking lice. *Bovicola bovis* (*arrow*) is pictured here with one of the bovine sucking lice, *Linognathus*. Photo courtesy of Dr. Robert Ridley, College of Veterinary Medicine, Kansas State University, Manhattan, KS.

Fig. 5.84. *Bovicola ovis* is a small white or tan louse that can be very difficult to detect on a heavily fleeced sheep. Photo courtesy of Dr. Jeffrey F. Williams, Vanson HaloSource, Inc., Redmond, WA.

Fig. 5.85. Section of bovine skin with louse eggs (nits) attached to the hairs. Photo courtesy of Dr. Jeffrey F. Williams, Vanson HaloSource, Inc., Redmond, WA.

Fig. 5.86. Biting lice (*Bovicola equi*) in the hairs of a horse.

Fig. 5.87. Lesions on the shoulder and neck of a horse with a heavy burden of biting lice. Photo courtesy of Dr. Jeffrey F. Williams, Vanson HaloSource, Inc., Redmond, WA.

PARASITE: *Trichodectes canis* (Figs. 5.88–5.90)

Taxonomy: Insect (order Mallophaga).

Host: Dogs and other canids. Cats have their own species of biting louse, *Felicola subrostratus*.

Geographic Distribution: Worldwide. Another species of biting louse, *Heterodoxus spinigera*, may also be found on dogs in tropical and subtropical areas.

Location on Host: Predilection sites for *T. canis* are the head, neck, and tail, but lice will be found throughout the hair coat in heavy infestations.

Life Cycle: Transmission is by direct contact or fomites. Louse eggs are glued to host hairs.

Laboratory Diagnosis: Recovery and identification of lice. *Felicola* is the only louse infesting cats, although infestations on cats may be difficult to diagnose because of the effective grooming habits of the host. Dogs can be infested with the biting lice *Trichodectes* and *Heterodoxus*, as well as the sucking louse, *Linognathus setosus*.

Clinical Importance: Large infestations of lice cause pruritus and poor hair condition. *Trichodectes* is the most common dog louse seen in the United States and can act as an intermediate host for the tapeworm *Dipylidium caninum*.

Fig. 5.88. *Trichodectes canis* is the canine biting louse.

Fig. 5.89. The head of *Felicola subrostratus*, the feline biting louse, is notched at the tip.

Fig. 5.90. White louse eggs (nits) can be seen attached to the hairs of this infested kitten. Photo courtesy of Dr. Jeffrey F. Williams, Vanson HaloSource, Inc., Redmond, WA.

PARASITE: **Avian Lice** (Figs. 5.91–5.93)

Taxonomy: Insects (order Mallophaga).

Host: Lice are common external parasites of birds, and multiple louse species may be found occupying different niches on the same host species. All avian lice are biting lice.

Geographic Distribution: Worldwide.

Location on Host: Lice can be found on all areas of birds, with different species showing specific predilection sites.

Life Cycle: Similar to other lice; the entire life cycle is spent on the host, and transmission is by direct contact or fomites.

Laboratory Diagnosis: Detection of lice and eggs on the host with morphologic identification of lice.

Clinical Importance: Heavy infestations may cause loss of condition. Sick or malnourished birds often carry large numbers of lice.

Fig. 5.91. There are more than 700 species of avian lice, all of which are biting lice. They show a variety of body shapes. Shown here is *Menopon gallinae*, the shaft louse of chickens.

Fig. 5.92. *Lipeurus caponis*, the wing louse of poultry.

Fig. 5.93. *Columbicula columbae*, the slender pigeon louse, on the flight feathers of a pigeon. Photo courtesy of Dr. Jeffrey F. Williams, Vanson HaloSource, Inc., Redmond, WA.

PARASITE: ***Gliricola porcelli*** (Fig. 5.94)
Common name: Slender guinea pig louse.

Taxonomy: Insect (order Mallophaga).

Host: *Gliricola porcelli* is the most common louse of guinea pigs. Two other species of biting lice, *Gyropus ovalis* and *Trimenopon jenningsi*, are also found on guinea pigs.

Geographic Distribution: Worldwide.

Location on Host: *Gliricola porcelli* prefers the fine hair around the back legs and anus, whereas *Gyropus ovalis* is found around the head and face.

Life Cycle: Transmission is by direct contact.

Laboratory Diagnosis: Detection and identification of lice and eggs. *Gyropus ovalis* is a broader louse than *Gliricola* and has a wide head. Eggs of *Gyropus ovalis* can be found most easily around the back of the ears. *Trimenopon jenningsi* is a dark brown louse that is less common than the other two species.

Clinical Importance: Light infestations are usually asymptomatic. Heavier infestations may be associated with hair loss, unthriftiness, and pruritus, especially at the back of the ears. Louse infestation may not be evident until the death of the host, when lice move up to the hair tips as the body temperature declines.

Fig. 5.94. *Gliricola porcelli*, one of three species of biting louse infecting guinea pigs.

Fleas (Order Siphonaptera)

Fleas are laterally compressed, wingless insects, typically medium to dark brown in color. Unlike many insects, they do not demonstrate clear delineations between body regions (head, thorax, and abdomen). The sucking mouthparts are usually seen protruding from the ventral aspect of the head. The three pairs of legs originate on the thorax. The enlarged third pair of legs facilitates the incredible jumping potential of these insects. In veterinary medicine, fleas are most often encountered on dogs and cats; however, they also live on a variety of other animals, including birds. Fleas are more likely than lice to move onto a different host species if the preferred host is unavailable, although they may leave after obtaining a blood meal. The adult flea is the only parasitic stage of the life cycle. The egg, larva, and pupa are found in the environment.

Fleas can be seen with the naked eye. They are most easily collected from the host by using a quick-acting insecticide and then removing individual fleas from the hair coat or combing them out with a flea comb. On birds, fleas may be attached to the unfeathered portions of the host and can be removed with forceps. Fleas should be placed in 70% ethanol for fixation and storage. They may be cleared in 5% potassium hydroxide or mounted in Hoyer's solution to allow visualization of reproductive structures used in identification. The presence of combs on the cheek (genal comb) or at the back of the first thoracic segment (pronotal comb), the shape of the head, and host preference are important characteristics used in identification. Figure 5.95 is a key for identification of some common species in North America. In many cases, a specialist is required for specific identification. When submitting fleas for identification, it is best to submit as many individuals as possible to ensure that both sexes are represented and that structures damaged on one individual are still intact on another.

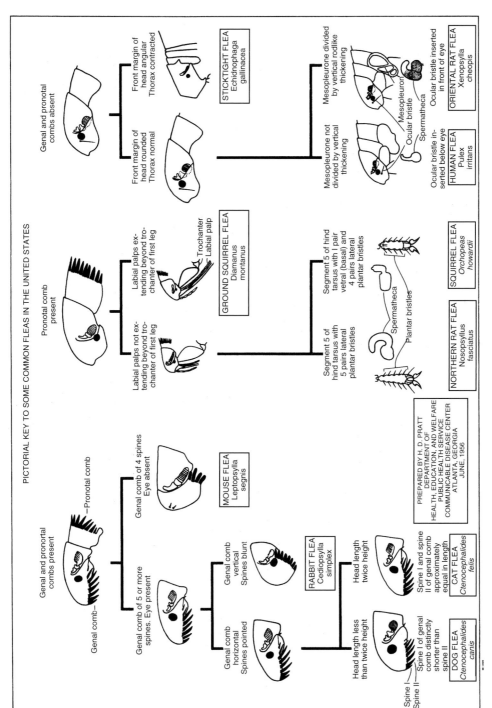

Fig. 5.95. Key to common flea species in the United States. Courtesy of U.S. Public Health Service, CDC.

PARASITE: *Ctenocephalides felis felis* (Figs. 5.96–5.99)
Common name: Cat flea.

Taxonomy: Insect (order Siphonaptera). A similar species, *Ctenocephalides canis*, also occurs but is less common than *C. felis felis* on both dogs and cats.

Host: Cats, dogs, ferrets. Occasionally, populations may adapt to living on confined animals, such as goats or calves in a barn.

Geographic Distribution: Worldwide. *Ctenocephalides* is the most common flea of dogs and cats.

Location on Host: Fleas can be found throughout the hair coat, but predilection sites include the tailhead, neck, and flanks.

Life Cycle: Adult cat fleas seldom leave the host. Females deposit eggs that fall off the host and hatch in the environment. Flea larvae feed on organic debris and adult flea feces and pupate in the environment. Adults are stimulated to emerge from the pupa by vibration and mechanical compression. Under optimum conditions, the life cycle can be completed in about 2 weeks.

Laboratory Diagnosis: Cat fleas have both pronotal and genal combs.

Size:		
	Adult female	approximately 2.5 mm in length
	Adult male	approximately 1 mm in length
	Larva	approximately 5 mm in length

Clinical Importance: Low levels of flea infestation may be mildly pruritic. Large flea populations can produce severe pruritus, alopecia, and anemia. Animals that develop flea-bite hypersensitivity may suffer severe dermatologic disease even when flea numbers are very low.

Fig. 5.96. Female *Ctenocephalides felis felis*. The cat flea is the most common flea found on both dogs and cats. It is difficult to differentiate from the less common *Ctenocephalides canis*. Characteristics helpful in identifying this genus are the genal and pronotal combs. Photo courtesy of Dr. Byron Blagburn, College of Veterinary Medicine, Auburn University, Auburn, AL.

ARTHROPODS

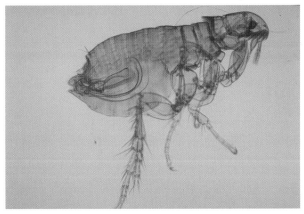

Fig. 5.97. Male *Ctenocephalides felis felis*. Male cat fleas are smaller than females. Photo courtesy of Dr. Byron Blagburn, College of Veterinary Medicine, Auburn University, Auburn, AL.

Fig. 5.98. *Ctenocephalides* spp. eggs are about 0.5 mm long (*arrow*). Larvae and pupae (covered with sand grains) of the cat flea are also shown in this figure. The surface of the pupa is sticky and becomes camouflaged with environmental debris. Photo courtesy of Dr. Byron Blagburn, College of Veterinary Medicine, Auburn University, Auburn, AL.

Fig. 5.99. Pet owners may find larvae of the cat flea, *C. felis felis*, in their homes and present them for identification. Mature larvae are about 5 mm long. The two "anal stuts" projecting from the posterior end of the body (*arrow*) are distinctive. Photo courtesy of Dr. Byron Blagburn, College of Veterinary Medicine, Auburn University, Auburn, AL.

PARASITE: *Pulex irritans* (Fig. 5.100)
Common name: Human flea.

Taxonomy: Insect (order Siphonaptera). *Pulex simulans* is a closely related species found on dogs and cats in the New World.

Host: Humans, pigs, dogs, cats.

Geographic Distribution: Worldwide.

Location on Host: General distribution on the host.

Life Cycle: Like *C. felis felis*, only adults are found on the host; other stages are present in the environment.

Laboratory Diagnosis: Identification of adult fleas. *Pulex irritans* has no genal or pronotal combs and possesses an ocular bristle below the eye.

Clinical Importance: Worldwide, *P. irritans* is found more often on swine than on humans or cats and dogs. Heavy flea infestations can produce intense irritation and pruritus. *Pulex irritans* is uncommon in North America, although it has been recorded from most states in the United States. *Pulex* spp. can serve as a vector of *Yersinia pestis*, the bubonic plague bacillus, and *Rickettsia typhi*, the agent of murine typhus.

PARASITE: **Fleas of Rodents and Rabbits** (Figs. 5.101 and 5.102)

Taxonomy: Insects (order Siphonaptera).

Host: A variety of species parasitize rodents and rabbits, including *Xenopsylla cheopis* (oriental rat flea), an important vector of bubonic plague. *Xenopsylla cheopis* will also readily feed on dogs, cats, humans, and other animals when normal rodent hosts are unavailable.

Geographic Distribution: Worldwide.

Location on Host: General distribution on the host. *Spilopsyllus cuniculi*, a flea of rabbits, attaches to the skin in the ears for long periods of time in a manner similar to *Echidnophaga gallinacea*, the sticktight flea of birds (see below).

Life Cycle: Similar to other fleas. Some species of rodent flea only visit the host to feed, unlike the common cat flea, which is resident on the host as an adult.

Laboratory Diagnosis: Rodent and rabbit fleas are identified based on morphologic characteristics.

Clinical Importance: *Xenopsylla cheopis* and some other rodent fleas are vectors of bubonic plague, caused by *Yersinia pestis*, and murine typhus, caused by *Rickettsia typhi*. Because the bacteria interfere with normal flea feeding, fleas rapidly move from host to host, spreading infection. Other rodent fleas can transmit tapeworms, trypanosomes, and myxomatosis to rabbits.

Fig. 5.100. The human flea, *Pulex irritans*, is less common on people in industrialized countries. It may also be found on companion animals and pigs. The absence of genal and pronotal combs and location of the ocular bristle are helpful in identification.

Fig. 5.101. *Xenopsylla cheopsis*, the oriental rat flea. Fleas belonging to several genera are found on rodents and rabbits. Photo courtesy of Dr. Byron Blagburn, College of Veterinary Medicine, Auburn University, Auburn AL.

Fig. 5.102. *Cediopsylla simplex*, a rabbit flea. Photo courtesy of Dr. David Baker, School of Veterinary Medicine, Louisiana State University, Baton Rouge, LA.

PARASITE: ***Echidnophaga gallinacea, Ceratophyllus* spp.** (Fig. 5.103)
Common name: Sticktight flea, European chicken flea.

Taxonomy: Insects (order Siphonaptera).

Host: *Echidnophaga gallinacea*, the sticktight flea, is found on poultry, wild birds, and occasionally on dogs, cats, and other animals. *Ceratophyllus* spp. are parasites of wild and domestic birds, especially chickens.

Geographic Distribution: Worldwide. *Echidnophaga* is found primarily in tropical and subtropical regions of the New World.

Location on Host: The sticktight flea is usually found on nonfeathered skin on the head, comb, and wattles of poultry.

Life Cycle: The life cycle of poultry fleas is similar to other fleas, but female *Echidnophaga* attach permanently to the head of the host. Eggs are deposited either onto the ground or into the sore created at the attachment site.

Laboratory Diagnosis: Identification of adult fleas. Female *Echidnophaga* can be identified by their location and attachment. This species also lacks genal and pronotal combs and has a sharply angled head. *Ceratophyllus* has a pronotal comb.

Size: Female *Echidnophaga*   approximately 2 mm in length
          Ceratophyllus   approximately 4 mm in length

Clinical Importance: Sticktight fleas may cause severe irritation by their attachment to birds and other hosts. Heavy infestations can produce anemia. In wild birds, attachment near the eyes may lead to blindness and death. Heavy infestations of *Ceratophyllus* have been associated with anemia, restlessness, and decreased production.

ARTHROPODS

Fig. 5.103. *Echidnophaga gallinacea*, the sticktight flea, has no combs and a sharply angled head.

Flies (Order Diptera)

Flies belong to the order Diptera, and some species are parasites in the adult or larval stage. Parasitic adult flies are usually blood feeders. Larval flies parasitizing animals are referred to as either "bots" ("grubs" and "warbles" are synonymous terms) or "maggots." Bots are obligate parasites found in specific internal locations in the host. Mature bot larvae are barrel shaped and may have rows of spines on the body. Maggots are fly larvae associated with "fly strike," or "fly blow." In most cases, they are opportunistic parasites. Adult flies attracted to wounds or hair stained with feces or blood lay their eggs on the animal, and larvae feed on debris and necrotic tissue. Maggots are more elongated than bots and are narrower at the anterior than at the posterior end. They are usually present on the surface of the body in conjunction with wounds or hair soiled with feces, urine, blood, or other organic material. A specialist can identify the genus of a bot or maggot by examining the pattern of the spiracular plates surrounding the breathing holes (spiracles) on the posterior end of the larva.

PARASITE: ***Cuterebra* spp.** (Figs. 5.104–5.106)
Common name: Rodent bot fly.

Taxonomy: Insect (order Diptera).

Host: Rodents and rabbits are the principal hosts. Dogs, cats, and rarely humans may also be infected.

Geographic Distribution: Western Hemisphere.

Location on Host: Larvae are found in subcutaneous cysts in various locations. In dogs and cats, they are seen most often on the head and neck.

Life Cycle: Adult flies lay eggs around rodent holes or trails. Larvae crawl onto animals and enter through facial orifices. Following migration to subcutaneous sites, the *Cuterebra* larva forms a visible nodule with an external breathing hole. After completing development, the larva leaves the host through the breathing hole and pupates on the ground.

Laboratory Diagnosis: *Cuterebra* larvae can usually be identified by location on the host. Specific identification is performed by examination of larval spiracular plates.

Clinical Importance: The presence of one or two bots in both the normal rodent hosts or dogs and cats is usually not associated with clinical problems, although secondary bacterial infections may develop. In dogs and cats, abnormal migration to the nervous system or other tissues occasionally occurs and produces disease.

ARTHROPODS

Fig. 5.104. *Cuterebra* larvae are about 2.5 cm in length and dark colored when fully developed. Photo courtesy of Dr. Philip Scholl, Agricultural Research Service, U.S. Department of Agriculture, University of Nebraska, Lincoln, NE.

Fig. 5.105. Veterinary practitioners occasionally remove young *Cuterebra* larvae from animals and, because of their small size and white color, may have difficulty recognizing them as *Cuterebra*. Starting at the left, this figure shows larvae at 6, 8, 10, and 13 days after infestation of the host. Photo courtesy of Dr. Philip Scholl, Agricultural Research Service, U.S. Department of Agriculture, University of Nebraska, Lincoln, NE.

Fig. 5.106. This lesion caused by *Cuterebra* in a cat has become secondarily infected. The posterior end of the bot with its brown spiracular plates is visible (*arrow*). Photo courtesy of Dr. Jeffrey F. Williams, Vanson HaloSource, Inc., Redmond, WA.

PARASITE: ***Gastrophilus* spp.** (Figs. 5.107–5.109)
Common name: Stomach bot.

Taxonomy: Insect (order Diptera). Species include *G. intestinalis*, *G. nasalis*, and *G. haemorrhoidalis*.

Host: Horses and other equids.

Geographic Distribution: Worldwide.

Location on Host: Equine stomach.

Life Cycle: Adult flies deposit eggs on the legs or face of horses. After hatching, larvae enter through the mouth and spend a period of development on the tongue and gums before moving to the stomach. After a period of 8–11 months in the stomach, bots pass out in the feces and pupate on the ground.

Laboratory Diagnosis: Bots are usually identified by presence in the stomach at necropsy, but they may also be seen in the feces at different stages of development following treatment of the host with macrolide anthelmintics. They can be recognized as bots by their barrel shape and rows of spines.

Clinical Importance: Horses appear to tolerate small to moderate burdens of bots. Large numbers may cause gastric ulceration. In rare instances, humans in close contact with horses are infested and develop a transient dermatitis usually occurring on the face.

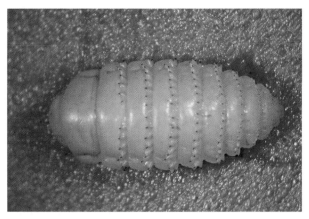

Fig. 5.107. Equine stomach bot, *Gastrophilus*. Species can be distinguished based on patterns of spines on the body, but species identification is unnecessary for control and treatment of the parasite. Photo courtesy of Dr. Philip Scholl, Agricultural Research Service, U.S. Department of Agriculture, University of Nebraska, Lincoln, NE.

Fig. 5.108. Second-instar *Gastrophilus* larvae. Following treatment with macrolide anthelmintics or other effective drugs, young *Gastrophilus* larvae may also be present in manure. Although the less mature larvae lack the barrel shape of mature bots, they still show the distinctive rows of spines around each segment. Photo courtesy of Dr. Philip Scholl, Agricultural Research Service, U.S. Department of Agriculture, University of Nebraska, Lincoln, NE.

Fig. 5.109. The eggs of *Gastrophilus intestinalis*, the most common equine bot species, can be seen attached to the hairs of the forelegs. Photo courtesy of Dr. Jeffrey F. Williams, Vanson HaloSource, Inc., Redmond, WA.

PARASITE: ***Hypoderma bovis, H. lineatum*** (Figs. 5.110–5.112)
Common name: Cattle grub, ox warble.

Taxonomy: Insect (order Diptera).

Host: Cattle are the normal hosts; horses and goats are occasionally infested. Other species of *Hypoderma* parasitize deer and reindeer, and *Przhevalskiana silenus* is a similar parasite of goats in the Mediterranean region.

Geographic Distribution: North America, Europe, Asia.

Location on Host: Visible nodules with an external opening appear on the backs of infested animals.

Life Cycle: Adult flies deposit eggs on cattle. After hatching, larvae penetrate through the skin and migrate to sites either along the esophagus or in the tissue surrounding the spinal cord. After a period of development lasting several months, the larvae migrate to the host's back and form subcutaneous nodules with a breathing hole. After several more months of development, larvae emerge and pupate on the ground and adult flies are formed.

Laboratory Diagnosis: Diagnosis can usually be made based on parasite location in the host and history.

Clinical Importance: Damage from *Hypoderma* comes from several sources. Adult fly activity associated with oviposition worries cattle and may interfere with grazing; migrating larvae cause necrotic tracks in muscle tissue and the hide is damaged for leather production. In addition, if larvae die while along the esophagus or spinal cord, serious inflammatory reactions can lead to bloat or paralysis.

ARTHROPODS

Fig. 5.110. Early third-instar cattle grub, *Hypoderma lineatum*. Grubs or warbles can be distinguished from fly maggots by their barrel-shaped bodies and typical location in the host. Photo courtesy of Dr. Philip Scholl, Agricultural Research Service, U.S. Department of Agriculture, University of Nebraska, Lincoln, NE.

Fig. 5.111. *Hypoderma* sp. grub emerging from its subcutaneous location on the back of the bovine host. Photo courtesy of Dr. Philip Scholl, Agricultural Research Service, U.S. Department of Agriculture, University of Nebraska, Lincoln, NE, and Dr. Jerry Weintraub, Agriculture Canada, Lethbridge, Alberta, Canada.

Fig. 5.112. The hairy body of adult warble (bot) flies makes them look more like bees than flies. The presence of adult warble flies, like this *Hypoderma bovis*, is distressing to potential hosts, which will actively try to avoid the flies. Photo courtesy of Dr. Philip Scholl, Agricultural Research Service, U.S. Department of Agriculture, University of Nebraska, Lincoln, NE, and Dr. Jerry Weintraub, Agriculture Canada, Lethbridge, Alberta, Canada.

PARASITE: ***Oestrus ovis, Rhinoestrus* spp.** (Fig. 5.113)
          Common name: Nasal bot.

Taxonomy: Insects (order Diptera).

Host: *Oestrus ovis* larvae are found in sheep and goats. *Rhinoestrus* larvae are found in horses. Other species parasitize deer and camels (e.g., *Cephalopina titillator*).

Geographic Distribution: *Oestrus ovis* is found worldwide. *Rhinoestrus* infestation occurs in Africa, Europe, and Asia.

Location on Host: Nasal passages and sinuses.

Life Cycle: Adult female flies deposit larvae in or near the nasal passages. Larvae develop in nasal passages and sinuses. When development is complete, they fall out of the nose and pupate on the ground.

Laboratory Diagnosis: Nasal bots are not usually presented for identification because of their location, but they are sometimes found by owners in water troughs or on the ground after they exit the host. Specific identification is made by examination of the spiracular plates.

Clinical Importance: Although infested animals show increased levels of nasal discharge, small or moderate numbers of bots are usually well tolerated. Sheep will attempt to avoid ovipositing female flies by keeping their muzzles near the ground or under available shelter (buildings, cars, one another, etc.). Bots occasionally wander to abnormal sites, where they may cause serious disease.

PARASITE: ***Dermatobia hominis*** (Fig. 5.114)
          Common name: Human bot fly.

Taxonomy: Insect (order Diptera).

Host: Cattle, humans, dogs, other domestic and wild animals.

Geographic Distribution: Central and South America.

Location on Host: Various subcutaneous sites.

Life Cycle: Adult female *Dermatobia* glue clusters of eggs to various muscid flies and mosquitoes. When these organisms visit a host, the *Dermatobia* larvae are deposited and enter the subcutaneous tissue, where each larva develops in a nodule with a hole in the skin through which respiration occurs. Larvae leave the host to pupate.

Laboratory Diagnosis: Identification of larvae is based on shape and pattern of the spiracles.

Clinical Importance: This species is best known as a human parasite, although it is primarily a pest of cattle.

PARASITE: **Louse Flies, Including *Melophagus ovinus*** (Figs. 5.115 and 5.116)

Common name: Sheep ked, louse fly.

Taxonomy: Insects (order Diptera).

Fig. 5.113. Ovine nasal bot, *Oestrus ovis*. These bots are occasionally seen by producers when they leave the small ruminant host to pupate or following treatment. Photo courtesy of Dr. Philip Scholl, Agricultural Research Service, U.S. Department of Agriculture, University of Nebraska, Lincoln, NE.

Fig. 5.114. *Dermatobia hominis* bots are often seen in the second-instar larval stage. At this stage, they have a distinctive narrow, spineless posterior end that becomes less prominent as they continue development. Photo courtesy of Dr. Philip Scholl, Agricultural Research Service, U.S. Department of Agriculture, University of Nebraska, Lincoln, NE.

Fig. 5.115. Adult and pupal stages of the sheep ked, *Melophagus*. Although sometimes mistaken for ticks, these organisms are insects with six legs and three main body parts. Ked excrement, which resembles flea feces, can also be found on the host and is helpful in diagnosis. Photo courtesy of Dr. Jeffrey F. Williams, Vanson HaloSource, Inc., Redmond, WA.

Louse Flies, Including *Melophagus ovinus* (*continued*)

Host: Sheep and goats are parasitized by *M. ovinus*, the sheep ked. Louse flies may be found on a variety of animals. Examples include *Hippobosca variegata* on horses, cattle, and camels; *Lipoptena* spp. on deer; *Hippobosca longipennis* on dogs; and *Pseudolynchia* spp. on birds.

Distribution: Worldwide, although in North America, only the sheep ked and the pigeon fly (*Pseudolynchia*) are found on domestic animals.

Location on Host: Various.

Life Cycle: In some species, winged adult flies are temporary parasites while feeding; in others, they lose their wings after finding a host and become permanent parasites. The sheep ked, *Melophagus*, has no functional wings and is transmitted only by direct contact of hosts. Adult female sheep keds deposit larvae that pupate immediately on the skin of the host.

Laboratory Diagnosis: Identification is based on adult flies. Hippoboscid flies generally have a rather flat, leathery appearance compared with other flies. Ked feces, which resemble flea feces, may be found on the host.

Clinical Importance: Sheep keds can cause significant damage to the skin, making it unsuitable for leather production, and can also reduce the value of the sheep fleece. Biting activity of flies causes pain and irritation.

PARASITE: **Fly Strike or Blow Flies** (Figs. 5.117 and 5.118)

Taxonomy: Insects (order Diptera). Many of the maggots causing fly strike belong to the families Calliphoridae (blow flies) and Sarcophagidae (flesh flies).

Host: Various, not host specific.

Geographic Distribution: Worldwide.

Location on Host: Various, wherever there is blood or other body secretion that attracts female flies.

Life Cycle: Larvae of most of the flies in this group are not obligatory parasites. Adults are attracted by the odors of decaying organic material and deposit their eggs on carrion. Wounds or skin on animals soiled with blood or feces may also attract the flies. Larvae feed primarily on necrotic material, and when development is completed, they leave the host and pupate in the environment.

Laboratory Diagnosis: Recognition of maggots on animals is sufficient for diagnosis of fly strike. Specific identification of fly larvae requires examination of larval spiracles.

Clinical Importance: "Fly blown" animals can be seriously affected by fly larvae. The presence of large numbers of maggots may produce tissue destruction, toxemia, and even death.

ARTHROPODS

Fig. 5.116. Typical hippoboscid louse flies showing the flattened appearance of the body with relatively large legs and wings. Photo courtesy of Dr. Alvin Gajadhar, Centre for Animal Parasitology, CFIA, Saskatoon, Saskatchewan, Canada.

Fig. 5.117. A case of ovine "fly strike" or "fly blow" in which an animal has become infested with fly maggots. In most cases, these flies are not true parasites and would be equally attracted to carrion. Sheep are particularly susceptible to fly strike in warm weather if wool is persistently wet or becomes soiled with blood or feces. Photo courtesy of Dr. Dwight Bowman, College of Veterinary Medicine, Cornell University, Ithaca, NY.

Fig. 5.118. *Lucilia* spp. is one of the genera of blow flies that cause facultative myiasis (fly strike). Blow flies are typically metallic blue, green, or bronze in color. *Lucilia* spp. infestations of sheep are a source of significant economic loss to the Australian sheep industry. Photo courtesy of Dr. Nick Sangster and Ms. Sally Pope, Faculty of Veterinary Science, University of Sydney, Sydney, New South Wales, Australia.

PARASITE: ***Cochliomyia hominivorax, Chrysomya bezziana*** (Figs. 5.119 and 5.120)
Common name: Screwworm.

Taxonomy: Insects (order Diptera). Screwworms belong to the blow fly family (Calliphoridae). Several species of sarcophagid flies are also obligatory parasites but are of less importance.

Host: Wild and domestic animals, humans.

Geographic Distribution: *Cochliomyia hominivorax*, the New World screwworm, is found in South America. The Old World screwworm, *Chrysomya bezziana*, occurs in Africa, India, and Southeast Asia.

Location on Host: Various, often on body openings or the edges of wounds.

Life Cycle: Adult female flies deposit eggs on the host. Larvae feed invasively on living tissue. Following completion of development, larvae fall to the ground and pupate. Adults emerge and mate. The entire life cycle can be completed in as little as 24 days.

Laboratory Diagnosis: Examination of larval spiracles is important for larval identification. The larvae also have two posterior tracheal trunks, which look like dark lines extending anteriorly from the posterior end. Although screwworm has been eradicated from the United States, reintroduction is possible. If screwworm infestation is suspected, larvae should be collected in 70% alcohol and submitted to federal or state veterinarians for identification.

Clinical Importance: Screwworm infestation is a serious disease that can rapidly lead to the death of the host. The parasite was eradicated from the United States in the 1960s through a sterile-male release program. This program has now been successful in removing the fly from Mexico and Central America, with only occasional outbreaks still reported.

PARASITE: **Biting Flies** (Figs. 5.121–5.128)
Common name: Horse fly, deer fly, mosquito, black fly, sand fly, tsetse fly, horn fly, stable fly, midge, and so on.

Taxonomy: Insects (order Diptera). Biting flies belong to many families within the order.

Host: Domestic and wild animals and humans.

Geographic Distribution: Worldwide.

Location on Host: Various, although many biting flies have predilection sites.

Life Cycle: Like other Diptera, biting flies lay eggs that hatch into larvae. Pupation follows a period of larval development, followed by the emergence of adult flies. In some biting fly species, like the mosquito, only the females are blood feeders. In other species, adults of both sexes feed on blood.

Laboratory Diagnosis: Although detailed descriptions of biting flies are not within the scope of this book, some generalizations can be made that allow basic identification (see figures).

Clinical Importance: Biting flies have enormous importance in veterinary medicine because of their role as disease vectors. Mosquitoes alone transmit important protozoan, helminth, and viral diseases of animals and humans. In addition, the activity of biting flies causes irritation, and their bites can lead to allergic dermatitis and, in some cases of massive fly attacks, even toxemia and death.

ARTHROPODS

Fig. 5.119. Screwworm infestation on the ear of a calf. If untreated, these infestations are often fatal. Photo courtesy of Dr. Donald B. Thomas, U.S. Department of Agriculture Subtropical Agriculture Research Laboratory, Weslaco, TX.

Fig. 5.120. Screwworm maggots. If screwworm infestation is suspected in the United States, larvae should be submitted in 70% alcohol to state or federal veterinarians.

Fig. 5.121. Tabanid flies. These large biting flies with big eyes are familiar worldwide. Horse flies may reach 2.5 cm in length. Deer flies, *Chrysops*, also belong to this group. Deer flies are smaller and have distinct bands on their wings; horse flies have unmarked or diffusely marked wings. This figure shows a large *Tabanus* sp. horse fly. Photo courtesy of Dr. Jeffrey F. Williams, Vanson HaloSource, Inc., Redmond, WA.

Fig. 5.122. Horse fly from the genus *Haematopota*, which is uncommon in North America. Photo courtesy of Dr. Alvin Gajadhar, Centre for Animal Parasitology, CFIA, Saskatoon, Saskatchewan, Canada.

Fig. 5.123. Most people in the world need little description of mosquitoes since they are common in so many regions. Mosquitoes belong to a number of genera, and their larvae develop in water. These delicate flies with long legs have mouth-parts that are at least twice as long as the head. Photo from Agricultural Research Service, U.S. Department of Agriculture.

Fig. 5.124. *Culicoides* (midges or no-see-ums) are very small biting flies (rarely larger than 2 mm) with patterned wings. Species are found worldwide. Photo from Agricultural Research Service, U.S. Department of Agriculture.

Fig. 5.125. *Stomoxys calcitrans*, the common stable fly. These flies are very similar in appearance to the house fly, *Musca domestica*, but when at rest in the environment, their mouthparts project from the head at a right angle, which can be seen without magnification. Photo courtesy of Merial.

Fig. 5.126. Horn flies, *Haematobia irritans*, are a major pest of cattle in North America and other parts of the world. Horn flies can be identified by their behavior. They cluster on the dorsum of the host, heads pointing toward the ground. If disturbed, they fly a short distance into the air and rapidly settle on the host again. Photo courtesy of Dr. Jeffrey F. Williams, Vanson HaloSource, Inc., Redmond, WA.

Fig. 5.127. *Glossina*, the tsetse fly, is the vector of trypanosomiasis in domestic animals and humans in Africa. Species of this fly reach up to 14 mm in length. Like stable flies, the mouthparts of the fly project forward from the head, but the wings of tsetse flies lie across the back like scissors. Photo courtesy of Dr. Andrew Peregrine, Ontario Veterinary College, University of Guelph, Guelph, Ontario, Canada.

Other Insects

PARASITE: ***Cimex* spp.** (Fig. 5.129)
Common name: Bedbug.

Taxonomy: Insect (order Hemiptera).

Host: Humans and domestic animals. Other members of the genus parasitize birds and bats.

Geographic Distribution: Worldwide.

Location on Host: Bedbugs do not have specific predilection sites on the host.

Life Cycle: Bedbugs visit the host only at night to feed and spend daylight hours in cracks and crevices in human or animal environments. Eggs are laid in the environment.

Laboratory Diagnosis: Identification of dorsoventrally flattened insects. Adults are 5–7 mm in length. In human infestations, bedbug feces may be seen in the bed.

Clinical Importance: Bedbugs are most important as human parasites, but they will also attack domestic animals. In the United States, bedbugs have recently become more common human parasites as the use of broad-spectrum pesticides for other insect pests has declined.

Fig. 5.128. *Simulium*, the black fly or buffalo gnat, has worldwide distribution. These small flies have a humpbacked appearance. Eggs are laid in rapidly flowing water. In large numbers, black flies cause irritation, dermatitis, and even fatal toxemia or exsanguination. Photo courtesy of Dr. Jeffrey F. Williams, Vanson HaloSource, Inc., Redmond, WA.

Fig. 5.129. Adult bedbug, *Cimex* sp., from a motel in Florida, USA.

CHAPTER 6

Parasites of Fish

Stephen A. Smith

Fish can serve as definitive, intermediate, or paratenic (transport) hosts in the life cycle of many species of protozoan, metazoan, and crustacean parasites. Most of these parasites can be readily identified grossly or microscopically, and as with mammalian parasites, the correct identification and an understanding of their life cycle are important in the prevention or management of an outbreak of disease due to parasites.

Protozoan parasites probably cause more disease in both ornamental and cultured fish than any other group of parasites. An example of a common protozoan disease in fish is white spot disease, or "ich," caused by *Ichthyophthirius multifiliis* in freshwater fish or by *Cryptocaryon irritans* in marine species. Other protozoan parasites that commonly occur on fish include *Tetrahymena* spp., *Trichodina* spp., *Trichophyra* spp., *Amyloodinium* spp., *Ichthyobodo* spp., and *Henneguya* spp.

Metazoan parasites can be found as larval or adult forms in almost every tissue of fish. Most can be grossly identified as monogeneans, digenetic trematodes, nematodes, cestodes, acanthocephalans, or crustaceans, but specific identification generally involves special staining techniques or clearing of specimens.

Examples of common fish helminths include monogeneans on the gills and skin; larval digenetic trematodes (metacercariae) in the eyes, skin, musculature, and abdominal cavity; larval cestodes and nematodes in the visceral organs and abdominal cavity; and an assortment of adult trematodes, nematodes, cestodes, and acanthocephalans in the lumen of the gastrointestinal tract. In addition, a number of arthropod parasites and leeches can be found occurring on or attached to the skin and fins of fish.

TECHNIQUES FOR RECOVERY OF ECTOPARASITES

A variety of nonlethal techniques that include skin, fin, and gill biopsies have been developed for the diagnosis of the common external parasites of fish. Most of these biopsy techniques can be performed on live fish without the use of anesthesia, although light sedation often simplifies the procedure and makes it less stressful for the fish.

Skin Biopsy (Mucus Smear)

The skin is the primary target organ for many of the external fish parasites. Therefore, a biopsy of the skin (Fig. 6.1) is one of the most useful and common samples for diagnosing ectoparasitic problems. This biopsy is performed by gently scraping a small area on the surface of the fish with a scalpel blade or the edge of a microscope coverslip in a cranial to caudal direction. Care should

FISH

Fig. 6.1. Collection of mucus sample via a skin biopsy from the side of a fish for external-parasite examination.

Fig. 6.2. Collection of a fin biopsy by clipping a small portion of the distal tip of the pectoral fin.

be taken to use only a minimal amount of pressure to obtain this superficial scraping, since damage to the skin may result in secondary bacterial and fungal infections or osmoregulatory imbalance in the fish.

The mucus from the skin scraping should be transferred immediately to a drop of aquarium, tank, or pond water (either fresh or salt water, depending on the species of fish, but *not* city tap water or distilled water) on a glass microscope slide and a coverslip carefully applied. This wet mount should then be examined under the compound microscope for the presence of free-swimming, attached, or encysted protozoan or metazoan parasites.

Fin Biopsy (Fin Snip)

A fin biopsy (Fig. 6.2) is obtained by snipping a small piece of tissue from the peripheral edge of one of the fins. This procedure is more traumatic to the fish than a skin biopsy, since a physical

Fig. 6.3. Collection of a gill biopsy by lifting the operculum (gill chamber cover) and removing a few distal filaments (lamellae) of the gill.

wound is produced. The fin snip should be transferred immediately to a drop of aquarium, tank, or pond water on a glass microscope slide, spread to its full extent, and a coverslip carefully applied. This wet mount should then be examined under the compound microscope for the presence of protozoan or metazoan parasites.

Gill Biopsy (Gill Snip)

A gill biopsy (Fig. 6.3) is obtained by inserting the tip of a pair of fine scissors into the branchial cavity behind the operculum (gill cover) and cutting off the distal ends of several of the primary gill lamellae attached to the gill arch. Since only the tips of the primary lamellae are removed, minimal bleeding should occur. The gill tissue should be transferred immediately to a drop of aquarium, tank, or pond water on a glass microscope slide; the individual lamellae separated; and a coverslip carefully applied. This wet mount should then be examined under the compound microscope for the presence of protozoan or metazoan parasites.

RECOVERY OF ENDOPARASITES

Examination of fish feces for the presence of internal parasites is accomplished with the same techniques as those used for mammals and birds. A fresh fecal sample is collected with a pipette either from the bottom of the aquarium or as it hangs from the vent of the fish. If an appropriate sample cannot be acquired from the environment or if examination of a specific individual is desired, the application of gentle pressure on the sides of a netted fish often produces the desired sample. The fecal specimen is then processed by standard flotation, sedimentation, or direct smear techniques and evaluated for the presence of parasite eggs and larvae. Though specific parasite identification is generally impossible, fecal examination does provide useful information about the types of parasites (nematodes, trematodes, cestodes, acanthocephalans) that may be present in a fish.

FISH

PARASITES OF FISH

PARASITE: *Ichthyophthirius multifiliis* (Figs. 6.4 and 6.5)
Common name: "Ich" or freshwater white spot disease.

Taxonomy: Protozoa (ciliate).

Geographic Distribution: Freshwater fish worldwide.

Location in Host: Within the surface epithelial layer of the skin, fins, and gills.

Life Cycle: This parasite has a direct life cycle, with free-swimming, ciliated tomites (theronts) in the water invading the skin, fins, and gills of fish. The tomites penetrate into the epithelial tissues and form large, feeding trophozoites (trophonts) that eventually excyst from the host and enter the water, where each develops into a cyst. The cyst stage then undergoes multiple divisions, producing numerous infective tomites that are released to the environment to infect other fishes.

Laboratory Diagnosis: This large, holotrich ciliate has a characteristic C-shaped macronucleus and is detected in wet mounts of skin biopsies and gill and fin snips.

	Size:	Trophozoite in tissue	up to 1 mm in diameter
		Tomite in water	25–50 × 15–22 μm

Clinical Importance: The parasite causes small, raised, white lesions on skin, fins, and gill tissue. Penetration into and excystation out of the epithelial tissue by the parasite causes loss of integrity of external tissues and results in disruption of normal homeostatic osmoregulatory processes.

PARASITE: *Cryptocaryon irritans* (Fig. 6.6)

Common name: Marine white spot disease.

Taxonomy: Protozoa (ciliate).

Geographic Distribution: Marine and brackish water fishes worldwide.

Location in Host: Within the surface epithelial layer of the skin, fins, and gills.

Life Cycle: The life cycle is similar to that of freshwater *Icthyopththirius multifiliis*: free-swimming, ciliated tomites in the water invade the skin, fins, and gills, penetrate into the epithelial tissues, and form large, feeding trophozoites that eventually excyst from the host into the water and develop into cysts. The cyst stage then undergoes multiple divisions, producing numerous infective tomites that are released to the environment to infect other fishes.

Laboratory Diagnosis: This holotrich ciliate, which does *not* have a C-shaped nucleus like *I. multifiliis*, is detected in wet mounts of skin biopsies and gill and fin snips.

	Size:	Trophozoite in tissues	up to 1 mm in diameter
		Tomite in water	25–50 × 15–22 μm

Clinical Importance: *Cryptocaryon irritans* causes small, raised, white lesions on the skin, fins, and gill tissue. Penetration into and excystation out of host epithelial tissue by the parasite causes loss of integrity of external tissues and results in disruption of normal homeostatic osmoregulatory processes.

Fig. 6.4. *Ichthyophthirius multifiliis* trophozoite. This ciliate, which produces small, raised, white lesions on the skin, fins, and gills of fish, is commonly called "ich" or "white spot disease." This freshwater parasite varies in size, ranging from 100 to 1000 μm, depending on the stage of maturation, available nutrition, and host species.

Fig. 6.5. Encysted trophozoite of *Ichthyophthirius multifiliis* embedded in the epithelial tissues of a gill filament of a goldfish (*Carassius auratus*).

Fig. 6.6. *Cryptocaryon irritans* trophozoite. This ciliated parasite, which has a similar life cycle to *Ichthyophthirius multifiliis*, occurs in marine fish species.

PARASITE: *Tetrahymena* **spp.** (Fig. 6.7)

Taxonomy: Protozoa (ciliate). Species include *T. corlissi* and *T. pyriformis*.

Geographic Distribution: Freshwater fish worldwide.

Location in Host: Trophozoites are generally found on surface epithelial layers of the skin and fins but may occasionally be found in deeper skin tissues, muscle, and abdominal organs.

Life Cycle: This parasite forms reproductive cysts in the freshwater environment in which two to eight infective tomites are produced.

Laboratory Diagnosis: Small, cylindrical- to pyriform-shaped ciliates can be found in wet mounts of skin biopsies.

    Size: Trophozoite   55 × 30 µm

Clinical Importance: This facultative parasite can become histophagous and invade the skin, muscle, and internal organs causing osmoregulatory problems and body system dysfunction.

PARASITE: *Uronema* **spp., including** *U. marinum* (Fig. 6.8)

Taxonomy: Protozoa (ciliate).

Geographic Distribution: Marine and brackish water fishes worldwide.

Location in Host: Surface epithelial layers of skin and fins of marine fish, but may also invade deeper skin tissues, muscle, and abdominal organs.

Life Cycle: This parasite (similar to freshwater *Tetrahymena* spp.) forms reproductive cysts in the marine environment in which several infective tomites are produced.

Laboratory Diagnosis: Small, cylindrical- to pyriform-shaped ciliates can be found in wet mounts of skin biopsies.

    Size: Trophozoite   50 × 30 µm

Clinical Importance: This facultative, histophagous parasite (similar to freshwater *Tetrahymena* spp.) can invade the skin, muscle, and internal organs, causing osmoregulatory problems and body system dysfunction.

PARASITE: *Epistylis* **spp.** (Fig. 6.9)

Taxonomy: Protozoa (ciliate). Species include *E. colisarum* and *E. lwoffi*.

Geographic Distribution: Freshwater fish worldwide.

Location in Host: Attached to surface epithelial layers of the skin and fins.

Life Cycle: This sessile, peritrichous ciliate divides by binary fission along the longitudinal axis, producing two daughter cells.

Laboratory Diagnosis: This colonial parasite is detected in wet mounts of the skin and is identified by its conical or elongated cylindrical body, branched noncontractile stalk, and epistomal disk for attachment.

    Size: 150–300 × 40–60 µm

Clinical Importance: The epistomal disk used for attachment to the host causes a localized skin lesion and mechanical disruption of the normal osmoregulatory process of the skin. Generally, fish develop skin lesions only in heavy infestations.

Fig. 6.7. Trophozoites of *Tetrahymena* spp. in a skin biopsy of a hybrid striped bass (*Morone saxatilis* × *M. chrysops*). This small ciliate also infects many species of ornamental aquarium fish.

Fig. 6.8. Tissue section showing numerous trophozoites of *Uronema* spp. invading the deeper tissues of a summer flounder (*Paralichthys dentatus*) species. This marine organism causes pathology similar to that of *Tetrahymena* spp. of freshwater species of fish.

Fig. 6.9. *Epistylis* sp. is a colonial ciliate that has a conical or elongated cylindrical body, a noncontractile stalk, and an epistomal disk for attachment to the host. The parasite generally causes only localized skin lesions.

PARASITE: *Trichodina* **spp.** (Fig. 6.10)

Taxonomy: Protozoa (ciliate). Related genera include *Trichodinella* spp., *Hemitrichodina* spp., *Dipartiella* spp., *Paratrichodina* spp., and *Tripartiella* spp.

Geographic Distribution: Freshwater, brackish, and marine fish worldwide.

Location in Host: Generally on the external surface of the skin, fins, and gills, though a few species are parasitic in the urinary tract of fish.

Life Cycle: This peritrichous ciliate divides by binary fission, producing two daughter cells.

Laboratory Diagnosis: This flattened, circular, ciliated protozoan is detected in wet mounts of skin biopsies and gill and fin snips and is identified by its prominent internal denticular (toothlike) ring and its ventrally located concave adhesive disk.

   Size: Variable, 150–300 × 40–60 μm

Clinical Importance: These organisms are usually ectocommensal but can become ectoparasitic when environmental and host conditions are suitable. This mobile scrub-brush-like parasite may cause localized to generalized skin lesions and disruption of the normal respiratory process of the gill and osmoregulatory processes of the skin. Generally, the parasite is only a problem in heavy infestations of the skin and gill.

PARASITE: *Trichophyra* **spp.** (Fig. 6.11)

Taxonomy: Protozoa (ciliate).

Geographic Distribution: Freshwater fish worldwide.

Location in Host: Attached to epithelial surfaces of the skin, fins, and gills.

Life Cycle: This parasite reproduces by endogenous budding.

Laboratory Diagnosis: The parasite can be observed in wet mounts of skin biopsies and gill snips and is diagnosed by its numerous suctorial tentacles.

   Size: 30–50 μm

Clinical Importance: This small, sedentary parasite is generally only a problem in heavy infestations, where this pincushion-like ciliate attaches to the skin, fin, and gill tissues and causes irritation and localized lesions that disrupt normal respiratory and osmoregulatory processes of the fish.

PARASITE: *Amyloodinium ocellatum* (Fig. 6.12).
          Common name: Velvet disease or rust disease.

Taxonomy: Protozoa (flagellate). Other genera include *Oodinium* spp. and *Piscinoodinium* spp.

Geographic Distribution: Freshwater, marine, and brackish fish worldwide.

Location in Host: Attached to epithelial tissues of the skin, fins, and gills.

Life Cycle: The trophozoite attaches to the host via an attachment disk with filiform projections that penetrate into the epithelial tissue of the host. The trophozoite detaches from the host and forms an encysted tomont that divides and produces up to 256 free-swimming, infective dinospores that are released into the water.

FISH

Fig. 6.10. *Trichodina* sp. from a skin biopsy of a tropical freshwater Oscar (*Astronotus ocellatus*). These flattened ciliates have a prominent circular, denticular ring (*arrow*), upon which specific identification is based.

Fig. 6.11. *Trichophyra* sp. on a gill biopsy of a channel catfish (*Ictalurus punctatus*). This freshwater ciliate parasite has a "pincushion" appearance (*arrow*) and is often found on the skin and gills of pond-reared fish.

Fig. 6.12. *Amyloodinium ocellatum* on the gill tissue of a striped bass (*Morone saxatilis*). This organism is the cause of "velvet" or "rust" in ornamental marine species of fish. *Oodinium* sp. is a similar parasite in freshwater fish.

FISH

313

Amyloodinium ocellatum (*continued*)

Laboratory Diagnosis: Large, cylindrical dinoflagellates may be seen in wet mounts of gill snips where the organism is attached to the lamellae of the gill tissue.

Size:	Trophozoite attached to tissues	up to 150–200 μm in length
	Dinospores in water	12–15 μm in diameter

Clinical Importance: This ectoparasite primarily causes irritation of the gill, resulting in hyperplasia of the epithelial tissues and fusion of gill lamellae. Outbreaks may be fatal in heavily infected fish, especially in fish that are weakened or stressed by other conditions.

PARASITE: *Ichthyobodo (=Costia) necator* (Fig. 6.13)

Taxonomy: Protozoa (flagellate).

Geographic Distribution: Freshwater fish worldwide.

Location in Host: Attached to epithelial tissues of the skin, fins, and gills.

Life Cycle: The attached feeding stage alternates with a free-swimming nonfeeding stage and reproduces by simple transverse division.

Laboratory Diagnosis: This very small flagellate with two unequal flagella extending from its posteriolateral groove is detected in wet mounts of skin biopsies and gill snips. The parasite is diagnosed by its small size and characteristic rapid erratic movements through the water.

Size:	Trophozoite	10–20 × 5–10 μm

Clinical Importance: This often-overlooked parasite is extremely pathogenic in young fish and older fish with lowered resistance. *Icthyobodo* causes irritation of the skin and gill tissue, resulting in hyperplasia of the epithelial tissues and fusion of gill lamellae.

PARASITE: *Myxobolus* spp., including *M. cerebralis* (Fig. 6.14)

Taxonomy: Protozoa (Myxosporea). Numerous genera and species including *Ceratomyxa* spp., *Kudoa* spp., *Sphaeromyxa* spp., *Myxidium* spp., and *Henneguya* spp.

Geographic Distribution: Freshwater, brackish, and marine fish worldwide.

Location in Host: Generally the epithelial tissues of the gills, skin, or intestine, but may also invade the muscle, cartilage, and other internal organs.

Life Cycle: The myxospore stage of this parasite develops in an annelid or polychaete worm to produce an actinospore stage that either penetrates or is eaten by the definitive fish host. The sporoplasm stage then develops and produces a polysporic cyst in the target tissue of the fish.

Laboratory Diagnosis: Variable-sized cysts found within wet mounts of various tissues contain spores with ellipsoidal, rounded, or spindle-shaped smooth valves.

Size:	Spore	7–10 μm in diameter

Clinical Importance: Infection of salmonids with *M. cerebralis* may cause loss of melanophore control in the skin resulting in black-colored tails in very young fish, or skeletal deformities due to cartilage destruction in older fish. This protozoan is a significant pathogen of wild and cultured trout populations. Other myxosporidian species may cause white cysts within the skin, gill, or muscle tissue.

Fig. 6.13. *Ichthyobodo necator*, attached to the skin (*arrow*), is an extremely pathogenic flagellate parasite of freshwater fish that is often overlooked due to its small size.

Fig. 6.14. Spores of *Myxobolus* sp. (a myxosporidian) in cartilaginous tissues of a rainbow trout (*Oncorhynchus mykiss*). Note the two polar capsules within the spore.

FISH

PARASITE: *Henneguya* **spp., including** *H. ictaluri* (Fig. 6.15)

Taxonomy: Protozoa (Myxosporea). Numerous genera and species; see *Myxobolus* spp.

Geographic Distribution: Freshwater, brackish, and marine fish worldwide.

Location in Host: Generally the epithelial tissues of the gills and skin, but may also invade muscle and internal organs.

Life Cycle: The myxospore stage of this parasite develops in an annelid or polychaete worm to produce an actinospore stage that either penetrates or is eaten by the definitive fish host. The sporoplasm stage then develops and produces a polysporic cyst in the target tissue of the fish.

Laboratory Diagnosis: Variable-sized cysts found within wet mounts of gill or other tissues containing spores with ellipsoidal, rounded, or spindle-shaped smooth valves, with or without caudal appendages.

Size: Spore $19 \times 4.5\,\mu m$, with two caudal appendages of $45\,\mu m$ each

Clinical Importance: *Henneguya ictaluri* causes a hyperplastic reaction in the epithelial cells of the gills, causing severe branchitis with respiratory compromise, and is a significant pathogen of the commercial catfish industry.

PARASITE: **Monogeneans** (Fig. 6.16)

Taxonomy: Monogenea (Monopistocotylea). Including the genera *Gyrodactylus* spp., *Dactylogyrus* spp., and *Neobenedenia* spp.

Geographic Distribution: Freshwater, brackish, and marine fish worldwide.

Location in Host: Attached to external surface of the skin, fins, and gills.

Life Cycle: Monogeneans complete their viviparous or ovoviviparous life cycle on one host. Larvae are morphologically similar to adults.

Laboratory Diagnosis: These small- to medium-sized flatworms have a posterior attachment organ, or opisthaptor, that may have hooks, anchors, clamps, or suckers. Monogeneans can be detected in wet mounts of gill snips or skin biopsies.

Size: Up to 5mm in length

Clinical Importance: These parasitic flatworms cause local damage at the site of attachment and also through their feeding activity on the external surfaces of the fish.

PARASITE: **Larval flukes** (Fig. 6.17)

Taxonomy: Trematode (Digenea).

Geographic Distribution: Freshwater, brackish, and marine fish worldwide.

Location in Host: Encysted metacercaria can be found in various tissues of the fish, including the skin, gills, muscle, eyes, brain, and visceral organs.

Fig. 6.15. Giemsa-stained spores of *Henneguya* sp. (a myxosporidian) from a ruptured cyst in the gill filament of a fresh-water channel catfish (*Ictalurus punctatus*). Note the two anterior polar capsules within the spore and forked caudal appendages.

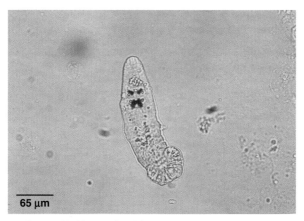

Fig. 6.16. Adult monogenean from a skin biopsy of a rainbow trout (*Oncorhynchus mykiss*). These external parasites have hooks, anchors, clamps, or suckers for attachment to the skin, fins, and gills.

Fig. 6.17. Encysted metacercariae of two different species of digenetic trematodes in the muscle of a bluegill (*Lepomis macrochirus*). The smaller organism (B) is commonly called "black spot disease" (*Neascus* sp.), and the larger, paler one (Y) is commonly called a "yellow grub" (*Clinostomum* sp.). Both are larval stages that will not complete metamorphosis until ingested by a carnivorous definitive host.

Larval flukes (*continued*)

Life Cycle: Digenetic trematodes require at least one intermediate host, commonly a snail or other mollusk, to complete their life cycle. Eggs are deposited in the water by the definitive host (mammal, bird, or fish), which hatch, and release free-swimming miracidia that enter a first intermediate snail host. The developing parasites emerge into the water from the snail as free-swimming cercariae that penetrate the tissues of a second intermediate host, commonly a fish. The parasites then become encysted metacercariae and do not develop further until ingested by the appropriate carnivorous host (e.g., fish-eating bird, fish, or mammal) where the parasite becomes a mature adult.

Laboratory Diagnosis: Larval trematodes are generally visible grossly within the fish tissue.

Size: Metacercaria Variable, up to several millimeters

Clinical Importance: These parasites are often unsightly in tissues, but generally are of minimal significance unless large numbers of metacercariae interfere with organ function.

PARASITE: *Argulus* **sp.** (Fig. 6.18)
Common name: Fish louse.

Taxonomy: Arthropod (Crustacea, Branchiura).

Geographic Distribution: Freshwater, brackish, and marine fish worldwide.

Location in Host: Generally on the external surfaces of the skin and fins.

Life Cycle: Eggs, which are laid in water, release free-swimming copepod larvae that attach to suitable fish hosts and metamorphose several times before reaching the adult stage.

Laboratory Diagnosis: These grossly visible dorsoventrally flattened, oval parasites have two prominent sucking disks, two dark-colored eyespots, and a centrally located piercing stylet.

Size: 3–5 mm

Clinical Importance: This crustacean causes damage by piercing the external tissues of the host and ingesting cellular fluids, and often causing a severe localized reaction at the site of stylet penetration. These parasitic arthropods may be important vectors in the transmission of certain viral, bacterial, and protozoan fish diseases.

PARASITE: *Lepeophtheirus* **spp.,** *Caligus* **spp.** (Fig. 6.19)
Common name: Sea louse.

Taxonomy: Arthropod (Crustacea, Copepoda).

Geographic Distribution: Marine fish worldwide.

Location in Host: Generally on the external surfaces of the skin and fins.

Life Cycle: Attached female lice release eggs into the water where the eggs hatch releasing free-swimming nauplii larvae. The copepod metamorphoses through multiple free-swimming and then attached larval stages (copepodid and chalimus) to become parasitic adults feeding on the mucus, skin, and blood of the fish.

FISH

Fig. 6.18. *Argulus* sp. from a goldfish (*Carassius auratus*), commonly known as a "fish louse." This ectoparasitic crustacean can be found on the skin and fins of freshwater fish. Other species can be found on brackish and marine species of fish.

Fig. 6.19. *Lepeophtheirus salmonis*. Sea lice on the skin of an Atlantic salmon (*Salmo salar*). This copepod has several free-swimming stages known as nauplii that molt into an infectious copepodid stage. Once on the fish, the copepodid molts into parasitic chalimus stages (C-I through C-IV), then a pre-adult stage (pA) before becoming a reproductive adult (A = female adult). Photo courtesy of Dr. Larry Hammell, Atlantic Veterinary College, University of Prince Edward Island, Charlottetown, PEI, Canada.

Laboratory Diagnosis: These grossly visible parasites have a large cephalothorax that acts like a suction organ for holding the louse on the fish. Females, which are larger than males, often have two long egg sacs trailing from their body.

Size: 5–8 mm

Clinical Importance: This crustacean causes physical, enzymatic, and inflammatory damage at the site of attachment and feeding resulting in hemorrhagic ulcerative skin lesions. These parasitic arthropods may also be important vectors for certain viral fish diseases.

FISH

PARASITE: ***Ergasilus* spp.** (Fig. 6.20)
        Common name: Gill louse.

Taxonomy: Arthropod (Crustacea, Copepoda).

Geographic Distribution: Freshwater, brackish, and marine fish worldwide.

Location in Host: Most commonly found attached to the gills, rarely the skin and fins.

Life Cycle: Females release eggs into the water that hatch and release free-swimming larvae. The copepod metamorphoses through numerous free-swimming stages to become either free-living males or attached parasitic females feeding on the mucus and skin of the fish.

Laboratory Diagnosis: These parasites have a large modified prehensile antennal segment for grasping gill filaments of the fish. Gravid females commonly have two egg sacs trailing from their body.

    Size: 4–6 mm

Clinical Importance: This crustacean causes traumatic crushing damage at the site of attachment to the gill filaments of the host resulting in focal devitalized gill tissue.

PARASITE: ***Lernaea* spp.** (Fig. 6.21)
        Common name: Anchor worm.

Taxonomy: Arthropod (Crustacea, Copepoda).

Geographic Distribution: Freshwater fish worldwide.

Location in Host: Most commonly found attached to the skin and fins.

Life Cycle: Females release eggs into the water that hatch and release free-swimming larvae. The copepod metamorphoses through several free-swimming stages with mating occurring during the last copepodid stage. After mating, the female attaches to the skin of the fish and transforms into an unsegmented wormlike parasite. The anterior end becomes modified into an anchor-like holdfast organ buried in the skin, while the posterior end hangs free in the water.

Laboratory Diagnosis: These parasites have a large anchor-like anterior end and a long unsegmented body. Females commonly have two egg sacs trailing from their body.

    Size: 4–6 mm

Clinical Importance: This crustacean produces a localized, hyperplastic inflammatory reaction at the site where the parasite is embedded in the tissue.

PARASITE: **Leeches** (Fig. 6.22)

Taxonomy: Phylum Annelida (subclass Hirudinea).

Geographic Distribution: Freshwater, brackish, and marine fish worldwide.

Location in Host: Attached to external tissues of the skin, fins, and gills.

Life Cycle: Leeches are hermaphroditic and reproduce by reciprocal fertilization.

FISH

Fig. 6.20. *Ergasilus* spp. Adult female copepod parasites removed from the oral cavity of a freshwater striped bass (*Morone saxatilis*) where they were firmly attached to the gill filaments. Each parasite has a cephlathorax with modified grasping appendages, a central abdomen, and two elongated egg sacs.

Fig. 6.21. *Lernaea* spp. This parasitic copepod, commonly known as an anchor worm, has several free-swimming larval stages before becoming infective to the host. After mating, the male generally dies, while the female burrows into the flesh of the fish. The anterior end of the parasite develops into an anchor-like adaptation that becomes embedded in the tissues of the fish, while the posterior end becomes modified into an unsegmented, wormlike body with two egg sacs that hang from the fish's body. Photo courtesy of Dr. Roy P. E. Yanong, Tropical Aquaculture Laboratory, University of Florida, Ruskin, FL.

Fig. 6.22. Leeches of an unidentified species attached to the skin of a cultured hybrid striped bass (*Morone saxatilis* × *M. chrysops*). These parasites can cause anemia in fish, as well as act as vectors of hemoparasites and other pathogens.

FISH

321

Leeches (*continued*)

Laboratory Diagnosis: These grossly visible flat to cylindrical wormlike parasites have a varying number of body divisions and generally both anterior and posterior suckers.

Size: Variable, up to several centimeters in length

Clinical Importance: Besides the physical damage caused by attachment and bloodsucking activities, leeches are vectors for a variety of fish pathogens, including viruses, bacteria, and hemoparasites.

PARASITE: **Thorny-headed worm** (Fig. 6.23)

Taxonomy: Phylum Acanthocephala.

Geographic Distribution: Freshwater, brackish, and marine fish worldwide.

Location in Host: Lumen of the posterior intestinal tract.

Life Cycle: These parasites have an indirect life cycle, with usually a crustacean intermediate host.

Laboratory Diagnosis: Eggs are observed on standard fecal flotation or direct smear.

Size: 50–65 × 30–40 μm

Clinical Importance: These parasites generally do not cause any clinical signs in fish. Rarely, a severe infestation will result in perforation of the intestinal tract, with subsequent peritonitis.

PARASITE: **Nematode Parasites** (Fig. 6.24)

Taxonomy: Nematode.

Geographic Distribution: Freshwater, brackish, and marine fish worldwide.

Location in Host: Lumen of the intestinal tract.

Life Cycle: Both direct and indirect life cycles have been reported.

Laboratory Diagnosis: A variety of nematode-type eggs may be observed on standard fecal flotation or direct smear.

Size: Variable

Clinical Importance: Adult nematodes generally do not cause significant clinical signs in fish. A severe infestation sometimes will result in mechanical blockage of the intestinal tract and/or chronic weight loss.

FISH

Fig. 6.23. Egg of an acanthocephalan parasite from a black crappie (*Pomoxis negromaculatus*).

Fig. 6.24. Unidentified nematode egg from a largemouth bass (*Micropterus salmoides*).

Bibliography

Atkinson, C. T., Thomas, N. J., and Hunter, D. B. 2008. Parasitic Disease of Wild Birds. Wiley-Blackwell, Ames, IA.

Baker, D. G. 2007. Flynn's Parasites of Laboratory Animals, 2nd ed. Blackwell Publishing, Ames, IA.

Ballweber, L. R. 2006. Diagnostic methods for parasitic infections in livestock. Vet. Clin. North Am. 22:695–706.

Barnard, S. M., and Upton, S. J. 1996. A Veterinary Guide to the Parasites of Reptiles: Protozoa. Krieger Publishing Co., Malabar, FL.

Bowman, D. D. 2009. Georgis' Parasitology for Veterinarians, 9th ed. Saunders, St. Louis, MO.

Bowman, D. D., Hendrix, C. M., Lindsay, D. S., and Barr, S. C. 2002. Feline Clinical Parasitology. Iowa State University Press, Ames, IA.

Clyde, V. L., and Patton, S. 1996. Diagnosis, treatment and control of common parasites in companion and avian birds. Semin. Avian Exot. Pet Med. 5:75–84.

Coles, G. C., Bauer, C., Borgsteede, F. H. M., Geerts, S., Klei, T. R., Taylor, M. A., and Waller, P. J. 1992. World Association for the Advancement of Veterinary Parasitology (W.A.A.V.P.) methods for the detection of anthelmintic resistance in nematodes of veterinary importance. Vet. Parasitol. 44:35–44.

Coles, G. C., Jackson, F., Pomroy, W. E., Prichard, R. K., von Samson-Himmelstjerna, G., Silvestre, A., Taylor, M. A., and Vercruysse, J. 2006. The detection of anthelmintic resistance in nematodes of veterinary importance. Vet. Parasitol. 136:167–185.

Egwang, T. G., and Slocombe, J. O. D. 1982. Evaluation of the Cornell-Wisconsin centrifugation flotation technique for recovering trichostrongylid eggs from bovine feces. 1982, Can. J. Comp. Med. 46:133–137.

Foreyt, W. J. 1997. Veterinary Parasitology Reference Manual. Iowa State University Press, Ames, IA.

Fowler, M. E. 2010. Medicine and Surgery of Camelids, 3rd ed. Wiley-Blackwell, Ames, IA.

Garcia, L. S. 2006. Diagnostic Medical Parasitology, 5th ed. ASM Press, Washington, DC.

Georgi, J. R., and Georgi, M. E. 1992. Canine Clinical Parasitology. Lea & Febiger, Philadelphia.

Greiner, E. C., and Ritchie, B. W. 1994. Parasites. In Avian Medicine: Principles and Application, ed. B. W. Ritchie, G. J. Harrison, and L. R. Harrison, 1007–1029. Wingers Publishing Co., Lake Worth, FL.

Hendricks, C. M. 2002. Laboratory Procedures for Veterinary Technicians, 4th ed. Mosby, St. Louis, MO.

Hoffman, G. L. 1999. Parasites of North American Freshwater Fishes. Cornell University Press, Ithaca, NY.

Jacobs, D. E. 1986. A Colour Atlas of Equine Parasites. Gower Medical Publishing, London.

Jacobson, E. R. 2007. Infectious Diseases and Pathology of Reptiles. CRC Press, Boca Raton, FL.

Kassai, T. 1999. Veterinary Helminthology. Butterworth-Heinemann Publishing, Oxford.

Kaufmann, J. 1996. Parasitic Infections of Domestic Animals. Birkhäuser Verlag, Boston.

Kennedy, M. J., Mackinnon, J. D., and Higgs, G. W. 1998. Veterinary Parasitology: Laboratory Procedures. Alberta Agriculture. Food and Rural Development Publishing Branch, Edmonton.

Kettle, D. S. 1995. Medical and Veterinary Entomology, 2nd ed. CAB International, Wallingford, UK.

Klingenberg, R. J. 2007. Understanding Reptile Parasites. Advanced Vivarium Systems, Irvine, CA.

Levine, N. D. 1980. Nematode Parasites of Domestic Animals and Man, 2nd ed. Burgess Publishing, Minneapolis, MN.

Lom, J., and Dykova, I. 1992. Protozoan Parasites of Fishes. Developments in Aquaculture and Fisheries Science 26. Elsevier, Amsterdam.

Ministry of Agriculture, Fisheries and Food. 1986. Manual of Veterinary Parasitological Laboratory Techniques. Reference Book 418. Her Majesty's Stationery Office, London.

Mullen, G., and Durden, L. 2009. Medical and Veterinary Entomology, 2nd ed. Academic Press, New York.

Neimester, R., Logan, A. L., Gerber, B., Egleton, J. H., and Kleger, B. 1987. Hemo-De as a substitute for ethyl acetate in formalin-ethyl acetate concentration technique. J. Clin. Microbiol. 25:425–426.

Owen, D. G. 1992. Parasites of Laboratory Animals. Royal Society of Medicine Services, London.

Roberts, R. J. 2001. The parasitology of teleosts. In Fish Pathology, 3rd ed. ed. R. J. Roberts, 254–296. W. B. Saunders, Philadelphia.

Smith, S. A. 1996. Parasites of birds of prey: their diagnosis and treatment. Semin. Avian Exot. Pet Med. 5:97–105.

Smith, S. A. 2002. Non-lethal clinical techniques used in the diagnosis of fish diseases. J. Am. Vet. Med. Assoc. 220:1203–1206.

Smith, S. A., and Noga, E. J. 1992. General parasitology of fish. In Fish Medicine, ed. M. K. Stoskopf, 131–148. W. B. Saunders, Philadelphia.

Smith, S. A., and Roberts, H. E. 2009. Chapter 8: parasites of fishes. In Fundamentals of Ornamental Fish Health, ed. H. E. Roberts, 102–112. Wiley-Blackwell, Hoboken, NJ.

Soulsby, E. J. L. 1965. Textbook of Veterinary Clinical Parasitology. F. A. Davis Co., Philadelphia.

Soulsby, E. J. L. 1982. Helminths, Arthropods, and Protozoa of Domesticated Animals, 7th ed. Williams & Wilkins, Baltimore, MD.

Taira, N., Ando, Y., and Williams, J. C. 2003. A Color Atlas of Clinical Helminthology of Domestic Animals. Elsevier Science, Amsterdam.

Taylor, M. A., Coop, R. L., and Wall, R. L. 2007. Veterinary Parasitology, 3rd ed. Blackwell, Ames, IA.

Telford, S. R. Jr. 2009. Haemoparasites of the Reptilia. CRC Press, Boca Raton, FL.

Thienpont, D., Rochette, F., and Vanparijs, O. F. J. 1979. Diagnosing Helminthiasis through Coprological Examination. Janssen Research Foundation, Beerse, Belgium.

U.S. Department of Agriculture. 1976. Ticks of Veterinary Importance. Agriculture Handbook 485. U.S. Government Printing Office, Washington, DC.

Valkiūnas, G. 2005. Avian Malaria Parasites and other Haemosporidia. CRC Press, Boca Raton, FL.

Wall, R., and Shearer, D. 2001. Veterinary Ectoparasites: Biology, Pathology and Control. Blackwell Science, London.

Weiss, D. J., and Wardrop, K. J. 2010. Schalm's Veterinary Hematology, 6th ed. Wiley-Blackwell, Ames, IA.

Williams, R. E., Hall, R. D., Broce, A. B., and Scholl, P. J. 1985. Livestock Entomology. John Wiley & Sons, New York.

Wison, S. C., and Carpenter, J. W. 1996. Endoparasitic disease of reptiles. Semin. Avian Exot. Pet Med. 5:64–74.

Woo, P. T. K. 2006. Protozoan and metazoan infections. In Fish Diseases and Disorders: Volume 1, ed. P. T. K. Woo, 816. CABI Publishing, Oxfordshire, UK.

INDEX